THE ORIGIN OF THE ZODIAC

by the same author

ASTROLOGY IN EVERYDAY LIFE
MAGIC AND DIVINATION
THE UNCLOUDED EYE
YOUR CHARACTER IN THE ZODIAC

Jupiter leaving Aries for Taurus
(*Painting by Baldassare Peruzzi in the Farnesina Palace, Rome*)

THE ORIGIN OF
THE ZODIAC

RUPERT GLEADOW

Jonathan Cape Thirty Bedford Square London

FIRST PUBLISHED 1968
© 1968 BY RUPERT GLEADOW

JONATHAN CAPE LTD, 30 BEDFORD SQUARE, LONDON, WC1

SBN 224 61399 5

PRINTED IN GREAT BRITAIN BY
EBENEZER BAYLIS AND SON, LTD,
THE TRINITY PRESS, WORCESTER, AND LONDON

Contents

Contents

List of Illustrations

List of Tables

Acknowledgments

The author would like to make the following acknowledgments:
to Mr Cyril Fagan for help during absence from home;
to his wife Helen Gleadow for plates 4, 17, 21, and 23;
to the Alinari Organization for permission to reproduce the
    frontispiece;
to the Edwards Egyptological Library of University College,
    London, for Plates 15, 16, 18, 19 and 20
to the Trustees of the Science Museum, Dr H. R. Calvert, and
    Mr H. A. Saunders, for the use of the globe mentioned on
    page 200;
to Mr G. F. Kunz and J. B. Lippincott Co., Philadelphia, for Plate 2;
to the Warburg Institute and Professor B. L. van der Waerden for
    Plate 10;
to the Trustees of the British Museum for the remaining plates.

Ἐκ Διὸς ἀρχώμεσθα

From Zeus begin we, never unmentioned we
Of mortal race may leave Him; everywhere the ways
Are full of Zeus, and all the market-places of men
And all the seas are full, and all the roads and harbours.
Him do we need at every time and in every place,
For we are of His lineage; and He kindly grants
Favouring signs to men, stirring the people to toil,
Reminding them that they must earn their livelihood.
He also tells when soil is best for beeves and cattle
And when the hour is right to trench the rising plants
And sow the seed; for He Himself in heaven placed
The constellations, and He planned what signs are best
For men from year to year, to tell His just decrees,
That every task may fill duly its proper hour
And all things may be brought to pass in decent order,
To Him both first and last do men and creatures pray.
All hail, Great Father, wonder and primal boon to men,
Thou are the earliest race. Ye too, ye Muses, ye
Honey-sweet voices; grant, and aid my invoking prayer,
To sing of the stars in all my heaven-sequent song.

Aratos, Phainomena, 1–18.

TO MY WIFE HELEN

1. *The Zodiac As We Know It*

ZODIAC is a word that is commonly known but few would be prepared to say just what the zodiac is. The ancient Greek word *zodiakos* meant (a circle) 'of animals', or perhaps even 'of little pictures of animals', but why, where, and when the animals were chosen is an intriguing question which this book hopes to answer. Meanwhile the identity of the twelve signs can best be remembered with the aid of the traditional rhyme:

> The Ram, the Bull, the Heavenly Twins,
> And next the Crab the Lion shines,
>   The Virgin and the Scales,
> The Scorpion, Archer, and Sea-Goat,
> The Man that bears the Watering-Pot,
>   The Fish with glittering tails.

Everyone has heard that constellations bearing these twelve names do exist in the sky, and may also realize that every person on earth is supposed to be 'born under' one of them. The sign under which one is born can be quite readily ascertained if the hour of birth is known. As the idea of being 'born under' a sign is often repugnant to scientists, it is necessary to differentiate between the science of astronomy and the practice of astrology. Astronomy is concerned with measuring the constitution and movements of the heavenly bodies, and astronomers are usually supposed to be determined to believe that celestial bodies have no traceable influence on human life. Astrology, on the other hand, is the supposed science and art of interpreting the influence of the heavenly bodies on mankind. Usually astrology is thought by astronomers to be a delusion, but obviously it is not possible to recount the history of a subject while affecting towards it an attitude of superior disbelief. It will be necessary therefore to assume that the claims of both astronomy and astrology deserve to be taken equally seriously.

The zodiac is a circle of twelve constellations, each of exactly thirty degrees extent, lying along the path of the sun, and by means of which the positions of the sun, moon and planets can be measured. It has often been said that it originated in Babylon, and this, though not entirely true, is not implausible, for no other ancient civilization believed so implicitly in the doctrine 'As above, so below'. To a Babylonian or Assyrian it seemed quite rational to suppose that events on earth followed or resembled those in heaven, since the same divine powers were in charge of both. It is not known why Jupiter, as a planet, became the 'natural significator' of wealth, success, prosperity and expansion, while Saturn represented poverty and restriction, rather than the other way round. Possibly Saturn's association with law and righteousness is due to the astronomical fact that his path appears to conform most strictly to that of the sun; but this does not explain why Venus became 'the planet of love and friendship', or why Mars became connected with violence, maleness, athletics, and war.

The study of the stars differs from most other methods of predicting the future in appearing to be more objective. The stars provide data which are the same for every observer. This is not the case in practices in which the observer himself provides the data he is to interpret. Men have not normally distinguished between methods using subjective data, such as clairvoyance, and those requiring objective data, such as the study of handwriting or the stars. In some cases it might be thought difficult to make such a distinction: in psychometry or object-reading, the diviner holds an object such as a pen or watch which has been commonly used by the person on whose behalf the consultation is being made; and in augury, the birds and their behaviour are equally visible to everyone in the neighbourhood. The intention, however, is in all cases much the same, to discover something unknown in order to act on the information made available.

The zodiac, however, which was often used for trying to find the answer to such problems, and was largely instrumental in the development of astronomical science, is a circle drawn through that part of the sky which includes the track of the sun, moon, and planets. Since the earth, as it rotates round the sun, is tipped at an angle of 23° 27″ to the horizontal, the alternating phenomena of summer and winter are produced, and half of the zodiac lies to the north of the (celestial) equator and half to the south. The sun's path through the zodiac is called the ecliptic, which means the line on which eclipses may occur, and does not alter at all from year to year. The ecliptic is thus the most constant of all celestial phenomena. But a circle has no natural beginning, and man therefore had to ordain a beginning from which celestial phenomena could be measured. Nowadays this seems to be most readily provided by the equator, which is a great circle in the sky lying directly over the earth's equator. Another great circle is imagined as lying at right angles to the first and passing through the north and south poles. The north and south poles of the sky are, naturally, those points on the celestial sphere which are immediately over the terrestrial poles. Measurements made along the equator are spoken of as made in 'right ascension', and those towards the poles as made in 'declination'.

In earlier times, when most celestial measurements were designed to give the position of the sun, moon, or a planet, it was more convenient to measure from the path these bodies actually follow. This had the advantage that high numbers were not required; measurements along the solar path were given in signs of the zodiac, and measurements at right angles to this were said to be in 'latitude'. But how did the zodiac come to have 360 degrees, and to be divided into twelve signs?

The idea of dividing all circles into 360 degrees originated independently in Babylon, Egypt, and China, as an obvious approximation to the length of the year, which brings the sky back to the same point after 365·2422 days. Similarly, the division of the year into twelve is due to the fact that this is a more convenient number than can be obtained from an inconstant variation between twelve, thirteen, and fourteen months, as used to happen in countries where the calendar was wholly determined by the moon. All months are, however, originally moon-periods, as their name tells us. And in Islamic countries the month still begins, as it used to in ancient Greece and many other lands, with the first appearance of the new crescent of the moon after sunset.

The zodiac originated, then, as a time-measuring device, without any notion of people being 'born under' different signs. So there is no need to reject the zodiac as a superstition, which originally it certainly was not. Where and how it was first used is the main subject of this book, together with the related questions of why the signs were twelve in number, and where and how they received the names which they still bear.

The importance of the number twelve in the study of the stars is not due merely to the fact that it is almost the number of new moons in a year. A lunar year comprises 354 days, so that it is eleven days short of a full solar year, and on the 355th day begins the thirteenth lunar month. Apart from this the number 12 is useful in itself because it is the lowest number having two pairs of factors: 3×4, or 2×6. It is small enough for a classification into twelve to be carried easily in one's head, which is not the case with the lunar numbers 27 and 28; a classification into 28 possible types is obviously more troublesome to remember than a division into only twelve. This element of convenience explains the frequent choice of twelve as a symbolic or 'magic' number, as in the twelve apostles, the twelve stones of the high priest's breastplate, the twelve days of Christmas, similar lists in other folk-songs, and the thirteen of the witches' coven (representing the sun and the twelve months or signs).

'Mere superstition' is never any explanation of anything, at least among fairly backward peoples; for when there is no practical reason for a belief, there is no reason for it ever to have grown up at all. Only a relatively sophisticated culture like our own would believe in superstitions of no known origin or purpose, such as that black cats should be 'lucky', though nobody knows why. Today, many people think it superstitious to believe that a person is influenced by the sign under which he or she was born. Others take the effect to be perfectly real and factual, probably because it is not in any way a guess or a matter of choice, but a firm datum obtained by calculation.

For centuries it has been customary in the West—though not in India—to begin the zodiac from the vernal equinox. This is the point where the sun appears to cross the equator from south to north at the spring equinox of the northern hemisphere; and the event occurs annually on March 20th, 21st, or 22nd. It is, however, fairly obvious, and also known from ancient records, that in earlier times men, even at a high state of civilization, were frequently unable to locate these dates exactly, or those of the other equinoxes and solstices, by observing the sky with the instruments available at the time.

There is an even more crucial difficulty: the equinox never occurs in exactly the same spot two years in succession, but its place slowly rotates round the sky, taking about 25,800 years to complete the circuit. This phenomenon is called the Precession of the Equinoxes, and in consequence of it the beginning of the (tropical) zodiac, which is generally known as the First Point of Aries, also moves slowly backwards round the sky at the same rate, amounting to 50 seconds of arc—that is to say, of space, not of time—annually. If it were normally measured from the so-called First Point of Aries, the zodiac would be a moving one, just as the equinoxes and solstices, which are so often marked in diaries, are moving points, recording astronomical events which never occur in exactly the same spot on the sun's path for two years in succession.

It is obvious that early astronomers, working with only the most primitive instruments, if any, would not have chosen to measure their zodiac from an invisible moving point which they were unable to observe. Yet this is precisely what the First Point of Aries is. It has never been anything other than an invisible point; that it also moved was not at first taken for granted, but was discovered to be a fact by Hipparchus about 120 B.C. It seems therefore fairly certain that the original zodiac, in terms of which astrology was doubtless invented, was measured from points which were both visible and fixed, namely the Fixed Stars.

Hence we now have two zodiacs, the tropical or moving zodiac, which is measured from the tropics, and the fixed or sidereal zodiac, which is measured from the fixed stars, but moves forward, when related to the calendar, by one day every 72 years. The difference between the two zodiacs is known by the Indian name of 'ayanamsha', and is gradually increasing at the rate mentioned above, fifty seconds a year; it was thought to amount to 24 degrees exactly in April 1947, so that the year when there was no difference at all must have been A.D. 220. About that date, and for a century or two on either side, astrologers cannot have known which zodiac they were using.

The word 'sidereal', by which the zodiac of constellations is distinguished, merely means 'of the stars'; the word 'tropical', which applies to the other version of the zodiac, means that it is measured from the four turning-points of the sun, which are called the tropics. Two of these are not strictly turning-points at all, but only marking-points, being the places where the apparent sun crosses the equator northbound (in March) or southbound (in September). The other two, the Tropics of Cancer and Capricorn, are circles drawn on the sky to mark the positions where the sun reaches its greatest distance from the equator, or on the earth to mark the latitude where this happens directly overhead. These points are called solstices, because the sun appears to stand still, in the sense that it changes from northward to southward motion, or vice versa.

It is often supposed that the constellations received their names on account of fancied resemblances. This is not very plausible in view of the fact that most constellations do not resemble anything at all. There are only two or three whose shape does explain their name, Gemini and Scorpio, and in part Leo. Gemini is so called because it contains two fairly bright stars of approximately the same magnitude, and Scorpio does have, in countries where it is not obscured by street lighting, a tail like that of a scorpion. Leo's shape reminds one of a couchant beast, which explains why it was known to the Babylonians as The Great Dog. Orion in Egypt was always a human figure, but surely the name of the Virgin (which means nothing more remarkable than a young girl) makes it plain that the name was not derived from any fortuitous resemblance.

Remembering that the people who invented these names were quite untouched by the modern predilection for materialism, one ought not to be surprised at finding no material resemblance to virgins, men bearing water-pots, and so forth. The zodiac was not created in an endeavour to establish in heaven signs for supposedly superstitious purposes, but was simply an early attempt to create a calendar based on observation. When the moon was full in the Virgin it told the Babylonians that they could soon expect to see the young corn standing up fresh and virginal in the furrows. This was far more use to them than having months called after historical characters like Julius and Augustus, or mere numbers like the Latin *septem*, *octo*, *novem* and *decem*. Months named after gods, heroes, or numbers would not have been specially useful or memorable; they were much more likely to be named after the events of that season of the year.

Before we can say for certain that the zodiac contains elements of observation, we must try to discover where the observations were expected to be made, whether in the sky or on the earth.

It is obvious that the zodiac would have been much more useful to early civilizations as a calendar incorporating allusions to climatic conditions than as a scheme designed to facilitate fortune-telling. Besides, what is 'fortune-telling'? We know that men practised it centuries ago, but what methods did they use, and what is the connection between that and the belief in being 'born under' one of the twelve signs?

The study of the future is a perfectly normal human practice, and has been almost universal on earth. Only the current fashion for materialism has decreed that prediction of the future must be impossible. This belief, though compulsory in some countries and plausible in others, has not been able to render non-existent the actual faculties which men and women have used. The faculty to perceive what is happening elsewhere in time and space is one which, to some extent, we all possess, though in a sophisticated country few care to develop it, while most prefer to be thought to believe what every one else believes. It is argued that a man cannot 'know' the future because it has not yet happened. This may appear to be good logic, yet the trend of the future is often regrettably plain. It is sometimes quite easy to foresee the future, without needing to call on any special faculties.

Intuition is not by any means just a mysterious and unexplained certitude. It was defined by Jung as 'perception by way of the unconscious, or perception of unconscious contents'. So the act of trying to set one's intuition to work could result, in some circumstances, in what might be called a piece of fortune-telling. There would be nothing abnormal or mysterious about this; we ought not to feel obliged to deny or devaluate such capacities in ourselves, when we know that they have always existed and been widely used among people at very different stages of culture, as for instance the Roman augurs, the Chinese students of the 'I Ching', and the Tibetan State Oracle before it was suppressed by the Chinese conquerors. There is no need to suppose that the use of any such faculties must necessarily be dishonest, insincere, or even incorrect. Admittedly 'controls' cannot be established in order to make the data the same for every observer; but before condemning divination one ought at least to try to practise it for oneself, in order to discover how the faculty works, and what states of mind inhibit it. The present writer has found the Tarot much more reliable than either geomancy or astromancy, but has not experimented much with other methods. This, however, does not imply anything against the other methods, since one's inability to use them may always be for some personal and individual reason.

There is thus a good reason why prediction should be possible, in general, regardless of the method used; it is that the inner self, or unconscious, or 'spirit', has often already decided what result it intends to produce, or what event to provoke, as the conclusion of a current line of thought or action. It will not have told the conscious mind, so the person himself will not consciously know, but in trying to discover this event one is not trying to discover something which 'does not exist', but on the contrary something which has already been definitely decided, though not by the conscious mind. So foretelling the future, when it is thus attempted, is not impossible at all. It only differs from other and more occasional forms of foreknowledge in that it is not involuntary, but is done deliberately, and, if successful, is just another form of telepathy, and is no more impossible or extraordinary than that.

So any person who maintains that it is always and necessarily impossible to know the future cannot be held to know what he is talking about unless he is prepared to say what methods he himself has used to try to know it, and what limitations or difficulties the practitioner must expect to encounter in trying to do so.

Predicting the future is thus merely a question of having learnt how to set one's intuition to work, and to recognize what types of question one is unlikely to be able to answer; for instance, some methods are useless with questions of time or dates. After all, the study of the unconscious is now a completely respectable academic subject, and there is no obvious reason why some awareness of expected events should not be included in the unconscious, provided we restrict ourselves to the future of persons present in the room. There is an adequate reason why questions of general interest, such as what horse will win tomorrow's race, should in most cases remain unanswered, being outside the foreknowledge of the unconscious, because usually there is no close or direct link between the querent and the quesited, that is to say, between the asker of the question and the answer, or the persons to whom the event is actually going to happen.

This, however, is only mentioned incidentally as an explanation of the widespread practice of prediction; for obviously nothing could be more superstitious than to rule that all the successes prediction has ever scored must be attributed to 'pure chance', ignoring the influence of the unconscious.

How the zodiac became involved with the belief in predicting the future is uncertain. The automatic classification of people by the period during which they were born was perhaps not the original method. Plato, in the *Phaedrus*, speaks of the 'soul', or as we should nowadays say, the 'unconscious', choosing to follow one of the twelve gods. And naturally these gods were not mere idols made of wood and stone—or mud, as Christians have often supposed, being perhaps misled by the apocryphal story of Bel and the Dragon—but were quite genuine patterns which actually worked in the collective mind. Besides, the choice of which god to follow would not be made by the conscious mind; if it were, many women would choose before the age of twenty to devote themselves to Aphrodite as the goddess of love, and then later would want to make a choice more in accord with their real nature, when they found that life as a temple prostitute was not their ideal. The 'choice', as Plato called it, was not really a conscious one, but merely the recognition of what kind of spirit was trying to express itself through one's inner being; for instance, if one has a natural inclination for poetry, music, or divination, then one's ruling power is plainly Apollo.

So perhaps originally, when it was still thought that the 'soul' exercised a choice in order to discover its real nature, the classification may have been according to the way people chose to occupy their time, all huntsmen being 'ruled' by Diana, and 'the servants of Poseidon' being merely another way of saying 'sailors'. But later, when this purely religious attitude to the problem of choice began to fade or to appear too difficult, men began to think of the rulers of the zodiac no longer as spiritual powers, but as the physical bodies of the

23

'planet sacred to Hermes' and the rest, and later still as mere planets.

The twelve signs were justifiably called in Greek a zodiac, since they are all animals except one inanimate object, The Scales, naturally sacred to Hephaistos the smith, and three and a half human signs, namely the Twins, the Virgin, the Waterman, and the former half of the Archer.

Not being a physical body, the zodiac has no gravitational pull: hence the alarm and discomfort felt by scientists at the idea of people believing in it, and their strong desire to disprove any 'mysterious influence of the stars'. Yet the influence interpreted by astrologers in calculating horoscopes is quite simply gravitational attraction, for in every horoscope the longitudes of the planets are calculated from the centre of the earth and not from the place of observation. This, of course, was not the practice two thousand years ago; but if the difference it makes, called parallax, were allowed for, and the planets' light used instead of their weight, the moon's position when it is near the horizon could be over a degree out, and in that case horoscopes for its return to its natal place would be two hours wrong, which would alter them completely.

Not many astrologers would now attribute to the zodiac a physical influence in the form of radiation from the fixed stars. If such an influence existed, the zodiac should not be divided into twelve segments of thirty degrees each, but should respond principally to the location of the Milky Way and of stars of the first two magnitudes, which it does not. A simpler solution would be to compare the zodiac to the earth's magnetic field, in consonance with the theory of relativity. Even so, no explanation arises for a division into twelve rather than any other number; and the signs would have to be measured from the sun's perigee and apogee, or else from the four natural turning-points of the tropical year (the equinoxes and solstices), for which there is no extant evidence.

A third possible explanation of how there could be a correspondence between events in the zodiac and events on earth might be 'synchronicity'. By this word, coined by C. G. Jung, is meant that every event—in so far as it is produced not by one urgently overriding force, but by various approximately equal but not quite constant or calculable forces—is characteristic of the moment at which it occurs and of the interacting forces then in play.

If this principle be sound, then to some extent divination should be possible, provided that the diviner could quite suppress the influence of his own personal expectation and preference — which he would certainly find difficult. This would explain reported cases of diviners foretelling events with which they had no apparent connection. And similarly the birth of a child to independent life would be characteristic of the moment, and thus a horoscope could have a degree of meaning without obliging us to believe in any 'mysterious influence of the stars'.

The focus of this notion is that patterns of thinking do exist, and not only in our conscious minds, but most of all in instinct. Common examples are the untaught skill of birds in building nests, or in migration, or the group-mind of a termitary. These patterns are called archetypes, and Jung has shown that they do not need to be communicated in language, but occur spontaneously, without communication or instruction, consciously or unconsciously, in widely separated individuals. So the group-mind of the human race is real, and does work in certain patterns, of which the zodiac could be one.

What of the origin of this particular archetype? Some archetypes, such as Sun-god and Earth-mother, grow out of the inescapable analogies of natural phenomena; another example is the association of the colour red with blood, war, vitality, and the planet Mars, which becomes very red when in perigee. Others, such as the Christian cross and the Muslim crescent, have been invented at a particular period and may not influence all humanity. These started as mere signs or emblems of a community, but became so charged with meaning that they rapidly rose to the rank of psychological symbols, and finally, to those who accept them, inevitable patterns. An archetype is an apparently inevitable mental pattern common to large groups of people; it may be described as a natural metaphor, like the Balance of Justice, which to us now is an inevitable notion, but was not so to palaeolithic man.

There is nothing patently inevitable about the signs of the zodiac; we could easily imagine them in another order. And if their names are arbitrary, as they seem to be, where is the inevitability which must characterize a universal idea?

In the psychological realm we all know the enormous importance of first impressions. A bird, when it emerges from the shell, adopts as its parent the first living creature it sees, and this impression is ineffaceable, as Konrad Lorenz and others have demonstrated.

An idea, in fact, tends to work in the terms in which it was conceived, or perhaps rather, in whatever terms best express the original idea. Monsieur Guillotin was horrified by the political use to which his invention was put, but in effect it remained what it always was, a humane killer. The Christian Churches were all founded to propagate the teaching of Christ, and though they have often done the opposite they are still thought of as organizations to that end. Islam still wears the shape of its desert origin, and Communism the shape of the protest it now no longer needs to make. So possibly the zodiac may still work in its ancient shape despite the ignorance and defiance of astrologers.

2. *The Rediscovery of the Ancient Zodiac*

BEFORE the equinox could be reliably located men would not have chosen to measure the zodiac from such a point. Two thousand years ago there may have been half a dozen men on earth who could locate the equinox, but there is no reason to think there was anyone at all in 1000 B.C. Those astrologers today who maintain that the zodiac is incredibly ancient, and that it has always been measured from the equinox, are evidently up against a difficult problem.

Nowadays an astrologer has only to look up in his ephemeris to see where the equinox falls; the problem has been solved for him by the ephemeris-maker, so that he forgets that it ever was a problem. Twenty centuries ago, however, the position of the equinox was so unimportant that it was largely ignored, as we can see from the following quotation from Manilius: 'So one degree in tropical signs is to be distinguished, which moves the world and alters the seasons ... Some place this power in the eighth degree, others prefer the tenth, and there has even been a writer who has allotted to the first degree the alteration and shortening of the days.' (Book III *ad fin.*) Manilius, who is still a well-known writer on astrology, will not have been the only person to think that it did not greatly matter if one was a bit vague about where the true equinox fell. For quite evidently, as can be confirmed by quotations from the Michigan Astrological Papyrus, from Pliny (*Nat. Hist.* XVIII, 59), from Columella (IX, 14), from the *Apotelesmatica of Pseudo-Manetho*, from Achilles Tatius, and elsewhere, the sign Aries was not normally in those days taken to begin from the spring equinox.

This, however, is a relatively recent rediscovery, and the credit for it belongs to an Irishman named Cyril Fagan, who first published his findings in 1947. His reasoning collided head-on with the habits and beliefs of astrologers, who for some fifteen hundred years had been quite happily using a zodiac measured from the equinox.

When the light of this rediscovery began to shine in at the windows of occidental astrologers, naturally their first temptation was to pull down the blinds. For the revelation raised several awkward questions. Was the current zodiac now to be abandoned, though it had worked to everyone's apparent satisfaction for 2,000 years? Did the original version of the zodiac work better, or indeed did it work at all? Much difficulty was caused by asking which zodiac should be called fixed, and which should be labelled movable. And, worst of all, were all horoscopes now to be altered?

It is now evident that all horoscopes ought to be altered, because the oldest version of the zodiac was without doubt that measured from the fixed stars. And the stars from which it was measured are known: they were Aldebaran, or the Bull's Eye, in 15° of Taurus; Antares, or the Scorpion's Heart, exactly opposite in 15° of Scorpio; Regulus, the Lion's Heart, in 5° of Leo; and Spica, the Ear of Corn, in 29° of Virgo. But since European astrologers have for centuries been using the movable zodiac, owing to precession the Bull's Eye has moved forwards outside the constellation of the Bull and is now said to be in 8° of the Twins; and similarly the Scorpion's Heart is now said to be not in the Scorpion at all, but in Sagittarius, and the Lion's Heart is in the Virgin. In fact, till recently the original form of the zodiac was quite unknown in the occident, or rather, though the constellations were not unknown, they were not used.

But the alteration caused no small jolt, partly because followers of the sidereal version of the zodiac were able to show that their system worked at least as well as the other, and partly because their measuring-point lay no fewer than 24° away (in 1947) from the First Point of Aries. This meant that four-fifths of the entire population were no longer born under the sign to which they had been accustomed, but under the preceding constellation. Four-fifths of all Leonians were indignant at being pushed backwards into Cancer, four-fifths of all Cancerians complained that they could not possibly be under Gemini, the Geminians proved that they could not be under Taurus, and so on until the entire circle was in an uproar.

Everyone took for granted that the constellations must have the same influence as the signs of the same name — which was indefensible and self-contradictory — and on this basis proved the sidereal zodiac impossible, and thus excused themselves, in their own eyes, from examining the evidence. One lady even held a meeting for the express purpose of getting the sidereal zodiac condemned by the popular vote of an audience which had never studied it, but only heard a debate on the subject. At this meeting certain statistics were not allowed to be read out, for fear they might prove the case, and the chairman rather thoughtlessly remarked at the end: 'We need more statistics!' Such was the chaos in the world of astrology.

Although there is no need to suppose that the zodiac has any physical influence, sidereal astrologers were probably gratified by the discovery of a quite outstandingly large ultra-violet nebula one degree east of Spica, that is to say, on the measuring-point of the sidereal zodiac.*

The latest developments, though they have no relevance to the history or meaning of the zodiac, have been rather unexpected, at any rate by those who set a high value on promiscuous disbelief. For if astrology does not work at all, there can be no question of one astrological method being any better or worse than any other; on that supposition all methods must be equally worthless. One system of prediction might for a time have a run of luck, but no system, however apparently irrational, could be any worse than any other.

But since the rediscovery of the original version of the zodiac, and in spite of all the resistance of tradition and inertia, it appears that more and more students of astrology are becoming converted to its use, and the tropical version is being gradually abandoned, except by those professional astrologers who have been committed to the other for too long to risk change. The reason for this alteration of view appears to be not mere theoretical argument, but the empirical results of work done. Nevertheless, any comparative evidence, however convincing, must be, on the above assumption, illusory.

In the last thirty years astrologers have realized the value of supporting their belief with statistics. Up to the present the best figures produced have been those of Donald A. Bradley in a very thorough publication called *Profession and Birthdate*.† Working on the published birthdates of 2,492 American clergymen, Mr Bradley found for the sun's position between 79° and 109° of tropical longitude a probability ratio of −4·54, which is rated at odds of well over

* *Sky and Telescope Magazine*, U.S.A., May 1959.
† Llewellyn Publications, California.

100,000 to 1 against the result being merely accidental. This was supported by odds of nearly 1,000 to 1 for the frequency of Mercury in Aries, and about 30 to 1 for Mars or Venus in Aries and Leo respectively. Further, Mr Bradley's figures consistently favoured the sidereal zodiac against the tropical, which of course they ought not to do if the zodiac is entirely meaningless.

On the other side, in the nineteen forties an American astronomer named Hynek decided to disprove some part of astrology, and chose for this purpose the aphorism that the aspects of Mercury indicate the intelligence of the person born. His results succeeded in disproving this, to the annoyance of the more dogmatic astrologers; but the more empirical declared that they had long since discovered for themselves the falsity of this traditional aphorism, as of various others in the textbooks. In fact had Dr Hynek consulted them they could have saved him trouble!

The difficulty always is to obtain sufficient birth-data, especially if the hour is wanted; and the hour is always said to be the most important factor. One cannot easily look up the dates of birth of a thousand divorced couples to compare with those of a thousand happily married couples; and yet such a comparison ought to be illuminating.

An even more curious development is the latest 'synetic' zodiac. The measurement of the circle from Spica in 29° Virgo may have been traditional, but it left open the question of whether that point was exact or only approximate. It is hard to imagine any empirical test which would decide the matter.

Yet a solution was found, and published over the signature of Garth Allen in *American Astrology Magazine* for May 1957. The method employed was based on disasters causing much loss of life. The Krakatoa eruption on August 27th, 1883, cost over 30,000 lives, and that of Mont Pélée in Martinique, on May 8th, 1902, took even more. It has long been traditional to cast horoscopes for the sun's passage across the equator and through the tropics of Capricorn and Cancer — the equinoxes and solstices. It was now thought that, if the sidereal version of the zodiac were superior, there should be significance in horoscopes drawn for the entry of the Sun and Moon into the constellations. Mr Allen computed the Moon's entry into Capricorn preceding both these disasters, and found them suggestive but inexact. They suggested that Saturn should be exactly on the horizon, so he recalculated the charts for that moment, and in both of them the moon turned out to be in the same minute of longitude, merely 29° 54′ Sagittarius sidereal. This, he thought, might mean that the celestial longitude which he was calling 29° 54′ Sagittarius ought to be called 0° 0′ Capricorn.

He then made similar calculations for many of the worst disasters in American history—the 20 worst train wrecks, 126 worst mine disasters, explosions, fires in public buildings, and so forth. In 14 of the 126 mine disasters Saturn was within 100 minutes of an angular cusp, and the odds against this happening by chance he computed at nearly 100,000 to 1. The alteration in the Moon's longitude did not, as one might expect, sometimes strengthen and sometimes weaken the indications of disaster; a correction of −6′ consistently strengthened and a correction of +6′ consistently weakened the indications. Finally, by using the Sun as well as the Moon, a correction of −6′ 5″ was arrived at. In consequence every horoscope may now be marked not only SZ or TZ, according as the sidereal or tropical zodiac is being used, but 'Sy Z' for 'synetic'.

The entries of the Moon into the tropical signs were so patently useless that in fact they were never used; and to anyone accustomed to the vagueness of predictions from 'solar entries' into the signs of that zodiac in the last hundred years it must seem very surprising that so precise a correction as −6′ 5″ should seem possible, and even more that it should be accepted. Why are astrologers not taking the path of least resistance? Because, of course, to them astrology is not a superstition where method does not matter, but a serious branch of study, what in Latin is called *disciplina* and in current usage a science.

When we attempt to trace the history of the zodiac, we shall find that the sidereal version is the older. The younger version was adopted, more or less by mistake, through the enormous prestige of Claudius Ptolemy, who wrote apparently favouring it between A.D. 120 and 150. From the astronomical point of view this method of measurement, as used today, is the most convenient now that we have well-equipped observatories; but for an early civilization with neither tradition nor equipment it was out of the question. And if, as we have seen, an idea will continue to work in the racial mind in the terms in which it was first devised, then for astrological purposes the original mental pattern of the sidereal zodiac may evoke in that mind a greater response than the newer tropical pattern.

In either case it is worth quoting Ptolemy's reason for adopting the tropical zodiac: 'The zodiac, being a circle, has no natural beginning, so the sign of the Ram, which begins from the Vernal Equinox, is taken as the beginning of the twelve; and, as if the zodiac were a living being, they make it begin with the excessive moisture of spring, and make the other seasons follow, because all creatures in their first youth have an excess of moisture and, like the spring, are still delicate and growing.' (*Tetrabiblos* I, 10.)

Nothing could be less scientific than these words of the great scientist! For they state quite clearly that Cancer owes its influence to the fact of following the summer solstice. Then what happens in the southern hemisphere, where Cancer follows the winter solstice? Logically, the influence of Cancer must be replaced by that of Capricorn. But Ptolemy, of course, had never heard of the southern hemisphere, and so indefensible is his argument that modern astrologers have tacitly let it drop, even when they use his zodiac.

People are sometimes surprised that the great astronomers Hipparchus and Ptolemy should have concerned themselves with astrology. But are they likely to have respected the prejudices of our age rather than their own? To them it was a hypothesis worth exploring, like so many others.

In the same way we are obliged to accept the zodiac as a geocentric phenomenon. It has been claimed that, since the discovery that the earth is not the centre of the solar system, the sun and not the earth should be the centre of the horoscope. But we live on the earth, not on the sun, and accordingly the horoscope shows the directions of influences converging on the earth.

In tracing the history of the zodiac we are obliged, for brevity's sake, to speak as if the constellations and signs exerted an influence; but, as we have seen, this influence, if it exists, may come from the racial mind and not from cosmic rays or gravitational pull. It may, in fact, be a projection of thought, a piece of racial imagination, and yet a valid projection if the racial mind does work in that way.

This will seem improbable to the extraverted person who likes to think nothing so real as historical facts and kickable objects. But meaning is not a function of either historical fact or physical sensation. The power of an idea is independent of both past history and physical substance. Since the power of a collective idea can be tremendous in politics, perhaps it may also be in other ways.

Meanwhile, the obscure part of the trail is its beginning in the past. So let us begin at the end and work backwards, exploring history, tradition, and the implications for human imagination of the expected correspondences of sky and earth.

3. *What Astrology Is and Does*

WHEN a person having no knowledge of astrology first comes across the subject, very probably one of the earliest questions he may want to ask will be: 'How scientific is it?' or 'How reliable is it?' The answer is that, if by 'scientific' you mean 'regularly using consistently factual data interpreted according to known and consistent principles', it is completely scientific. When a person declares that at his birth the sun was in so many degrees, minutes, and seconds of some given sign, and also states the year and place of his birth, this enables anyone to calculate that his Ascendant (which means the degree of the zodiac rising on the eastern horizon) was in however many degrees and minutes of whatever sign it actually was. Reliable, however, astrology is not—not because predictions sometimes fail, but because different students may make diametrically opposite predictions. In science this never happens, though scientists make predictions every day; and a learned study which, however consistently it follows its principles, yet leaves room for different students to come to opposite conclusions, cannot fairly be called reliable.

It was in the generation after Aristotle that astrology took the Greek world by storm. Many astonishing predictions were made, and in the stories these predictions usually came true, for there is rarely any point in telling a story about a prediction which failed—though we shall cite one in a future chapter.

It is not obvious why it should ever have appeared likely that character or events might be foretold by noting what planets or constellations were rising at the birth of a baby. But nevertheless it remains true that the horoscopic datum, and therefore the horoscope itself, is a scientific fact from which no one will ever escape so long as he lives. Foretelling the future, for instance, from the fact that on a certain day both the Moon and Venus were seen from Babylon inside a single halo, was a common practice in Babylonian civilization; but why men began to imagine that the chart of the heavens for the moment of birth represented a kind of indelible stamp made on the 'native', as the person born is called, is a mystery to which nobody has yet suggested any solution. Yet since the analysis of character and the prediction of events, by astrology, have played a considerable part in several ancient civilizations, and still continue in our own time, it may be of interest to describe how they were done and for that matter still are done.

By derivation the word 'horoscope' means 'a consideration of the hour', and is quite correctly applied, since considerations drawn from a mere knowledge of the month of birth are not sufficient and do not constitute a horoscope.

The sun, on whose heat and light our lives depend, is naturally the most important body in any horoscope. It is said to represent the desires of the heart and to be the most essential element of character. The two other most important elements of the horoscope are the Moon and the Ascendant. The Moon is taken to represent one's manner and general style of behaviour; but the Ascendant, which has sometimes been thought to represent the body, derives its influence exclusively from the sign of the zodiac rising on the eastern horizon, modified by any planets which may be rising also. Thus if a man has the Sun conjoined to the restrictive influence of Saturn, but the Moon affected by the expansive influence of Jupiter, he will be habitually and chronically depressed, but his friends will not realize this because he will try to compensate for it by a cheerful or jovial manner. But conversely, if his Sun is in conjunction with Jupiter and his Moon afflicted by Saturn, he will be a born optimist but in manner and clothes rather careless and dirty.

But apart from the Sun, Moon and Ascendant every planet has its own character. Jupiter represents cheerfulness, expansion, optimism and prosperity, but Saturn the opposite—restriction, pessimism and poverty. Venus is the planet of love and friendship, and she and Jupiter are called benefics because the events they cause are the sort men like; Mars and Saturn, on the other hand, are called malefics, because the events attributed to them are most frequently harmful. Mars is not always and unmitigatedly evil, for, although he is the planet of violence, he also 'rules' (i.e. corresponds to) sport, all forms of muscular exertion, and masculinity. Venus, of course, is always regarded as feminine, and no doubt it was on account of astrology that the planet came to have this character. Mercury, the little

35

planet of children which never runs more than 28° from the Sun its father, has no sex, but 'rules' trade and commerce, ambiguity, reading and writing, and thievery—perhaps because small children, though they often have a vivid sense of 'me' and 'mine', inevitably only develop later a sense of 'you' and 'yours'.

After Uranus had been discovered, at the end of the eighteenth century, it was decided by astrologers, or 'discovered' as they would say, that this was a very dangerous planet, having rulership over electricity and inventions, dramatic events, and the unexpected generally. Similarly Neptune, discovered in 1840, signifies renunciations and many other forms of catastrophe, nervous agitation, and all morbid forms of excitement. Though Uranus can occasionally act as a benefic, enabling people to take advantage of opportunities against which most sensible neighbours would warn them, the influence of Neptune is almost uniformly disastrous, particularly in combination with Mars, for that corresponds to unwise acts performed in a fit of violent agitation. Pluto, however, discovered in 1930, is not so bad; this is frequently the influence under which young people first leave home.

The distances apart of the planets determine whether they have any influence on each other. For instance, if Mars and Jupiter are 60, 90, 120, or 180 degrees apart, they are thought to exert a combined influence weaker but similar to that which they would exert if they were in conjunction. The margin of error allowed for 'aspects' has usually averaged, in Europe, eight degrees. And until recently occidental astrologers used to think that 'aspects' measuring approximately one-third ('trine') or one-sixth ('sextile') of the zodiac were 'good', but those which divided the circle by two ('opposition') or four ('square') were 'bad'. At one stage any misfortune, such as a broken arm, could be attributed to a 'bad' aspect of any planet, even Jupiter or Venus, and the fact that the aspect was 'bad' was held to outweigh completely the fact that the planet was 'good'. In India, on the other hand, all planets in signs 120 degrees apart are considered to be 'in trine', though their actual distance apart may vary from 91° to 149°.

Events are predicted by various techniques. Nowadays it is frequently the custom in the West to set up a chart for the moment when the Sun or Moon reaches either the exact minute and second of longitude that it held at birth, or the opposite point. The 'solar return' thus calculated describes the events of the ensuing year, and the 'lunar return' (or demi-lunar) those of the ensuing month or fortnight. These charts need to be calculated with considerable accuracy, for it makes all the difference between a dramatic disaster and an extravagant triumph, whether the planet on the ascendant be Uranus or Jupiter or Saturn; or maybe no planet at all is there.

Another technique which used to be very popular for foretelling the future was the 'day for a year' method. By this the horoscope was 'progressed' so that, for example, the planets for the thirtieth day after birth made mutual aspects, and also aspects to the horoscope of birth, from which the events of the thirtieth year of life could be foretold. There was also a somewhat similar system called 'primary directions', in which a measure of, usually, one degree was taken to be equivalent to one year. An intermittent argument went on, however, as to whether the motion corresponding to one year should be exactly one degree or the average daily motion of the Sun, namely 59′ 8″, or even the amount of motion actually accomplished by the Sun on the corresponding date in the native's youth. It is easy to see that if Venus, the planet of love and friendship, comes to an aspect of Mars, the 'natural significator' of masculinity, the native, if a female, would be expected to have a love-affair or get married; but if the Sun came to a 'bad' aspect of Uranus, the planet of the unexpected, then an unforeseen distraction or disappointment would be more likely.

In casting a horoscope the first thing necessary is a circle to represent the heavens. Some centuries ago it was quite common to evade the difficulty of drawing a circle by drawing a traditional square form divided into twelve compartments, but nowadays convenient 'books of blank maps' can easily be obtained from specialist booksellers. In every horoscope cast in the northern hemisphere, south is at the top and north at the bottom; east, representing that which is coming into being, is on the left, and west on the right. The whole space of the horoscope is almost always divided into twelve segments, which are called 'houses', and are drawn on the diagram as if they were all equal. But careful inspection of the figures written against the 'cusps' which divide them will usually reveal that they vary widely from the 30° which would make them all equal. A few horoscopes may be drawn according to the 'equal house' systems, either counting from the Ascendant or from the Midheaven, but most horoscopes have very unequal houses. The figures are given in various published tables, except for the equal house systems, which do not require any. The commonest system is that called after the well-known seventeenth-century astrologer Placidus. It became popular because it was adopted by the principal English publisher of astrological literature, but cannot possibly be right because in the Arctic Circle it frequently fails to work. In the sixteenth century the most popular system in Europe was probably that called after Regiomontanus, but it fell out of use, not because it was wrong but because tables according to the rival system of Placidus were more easily available. The only theoretically impregnable system is that of Campanus (that is to say, Giovanni Campanella, who died about 1297). This divides the celestial sphere in what one would think was the most reasonable and scientific way, by means of the three great circles which all intersect one another at right angles—namely, the horizon, the meridian, and the prime vertical; but even in the latitude of England its results are so surprising that sooner than accept such unequal houses many astrologers still use other systems.

Over two thousand years ago, when astrology was still at its beginnings, there were only eight houses, and this is probably the reason why the eighth house is called the House of Death; at one time it was the last. More recently there have been twelve houses, and it may be of interest to give a list of the departments of life to which they correspond:

First: personality generally.
Second: money and finance.
Third: brothers and sisters, short journeys.
Fourth: one parent, usually the father, the last period of life.
Fifth: children, pleasure, theatres, gambling.
Sixth: health and servants, the armed forces.
Seventh: marriage and open enemies.
Eighth: death and other people's money.
Ninth: religion and long journeys.
Tenth: profession and standing in the world, one parent.
Eleventh: friends, also children again.
Twelfth: secret enemies, hospitals.

The first thing in a horoscope that an astrologer needs to know is what sort of a chart it is, for besides being that of a man, a dog, a limited company, or a government, it may be a solar or lunar return applying to any of these. When he has been told this essential information, the astrologer looks first to see which planets are nearest to the meridian and horizon, for these are the most vital sensitive points; and it is noteworthy that persons born at midnight have more ambition than those born at noon. It is as though those born at noon do not feel that they have to make any special effort to remain at the top, having been born there, whereas those born at midnight, being almost equally strongly under the influence of the Sun, want admiration and feel that they deserve it, but never seem to have enough of it, because the earth gets in their way.

One clearly practical use for a horoscope is in ascertaining whether or not two people will get on well together. Naturally it is not possible to foresee whether they will actually meet; but if they meet and marry it is quite easy to tell even without knowing the precise hour of birth of either, whether there will be serious disagreement. This technique is referred to by Jung in his book *The Interpretation of Nature and the Psyche*. All that is necessary is to consider the planets in each horoscope as making whatever aspects they do make to those of the other. If the Sun in one chart falls on the Moon of the other, then the relationship will be harmonious. If, on the other hand, Saturn or Mars of the one falls on Neptune of the other, sooner or later there will be disruption. In such a case divorce would not be for mere infidelity, but because the couple decide that they simply cannot bear to live together. There are on record marriages which have ended in crimes of violence, but the surprising thing is that these unfortunate cases can always be forecast, not only by an exceptionally gifted astrologer, but by any person able to read the chart.

Here, then, as an example of a horoscope, is that of the emperor Augustus. It has been calculated not in the sidereal zodiac, as used today, even less in the Tropical Zodiac used in the Middle Ages, but in the Hellenistic Zodiac, which Theogenes or any other astrologer would probably have used at the time. As can be seen, the Sun was close to the rising point, and the Moon in Capricorn. The date usually given for the emperor's birth is September 23rd, 63 B.C.; but since we know from his coins that he had the Moon in Capricorn, and are also told that he had an excellent horoscope, there is no question of his having been born when the Moon was in Aquarius, or the Sun disastrously 'afflicted'; and since both these things were the case on September 23rd, Augustus was obviously born on the 22nd, when the Moon was very well aspected and in the right sign.

Indian astrology differs from occidental astrology in various ways, principally in that it divides the life of every person into several periods of which the West knows nothing. These periods come under the dominion not only of the seven planets known to the ancients, but also of Rahu and Ketu. These are not planets at all, but simply the points where the Moon, which never gets more than about 8° away from the ecliptic, actually crosses it. In position they are always exactly opposite one another, and their motion amounts to 3′ retrograde per day.

Another point occasionally marked on horoscopes is the so-called 'part of fortune'. This is not a planet but an imaginary point found by adding to the Ascendant the distance from the Sun to the Moon. Naturally it has no influence of its own, but its aspects are thought to give some idea of the native's destiny or of some characteristics of it. By using the planets instead of the Moon there is a whole series of other 'parts' or points which can be calculated in a similar manner. They have evocative names like 'the pomegranate' and 'the lightning-flash', but are little regarded and not often encountered.

4. *Medieval Magic and Psychology*

In the last twenty centuries the sign of the Virgin has aged about thirty years. She used to be a pretty girl of fifteen, and now she is represented as a hard and selfish 'old maid'. How has this come about?

One might expect that so long as the signs of the zodiac are unaltered their characters would remain the same century after century. Astrologers would certainly think so. But on what, in fact, is their character based? Partly on symbolism, but partly also on observation. The sociological value of the writings of astrologers is the picture they give us of the mental attitudes of their epoch, the social structure, the professions, and so forth.[1] All this is observed. But other elements in the character of each sign are provided by the symbol and its attributions, to which astrologers feel that observation should somehow be made to fit.

Since Claudius Ptolemy decided to regularize the distribution of signs between the four 'elements' (fire, earth, air and water) and the three 'qualities', it has been necessary to think of Virgo as the mutable sign of Earth; and since Earth was considered a cold, practical element, Virgo had to be represented as cold and practical.

The three 'qualities' were derived from Ptolemy's system of measuring the zodiac from the solstices and equinoxes. The most important and effective signs were those which followed on the cardinal points, and were called Cardinal; they were said to act of themselves. Next came the Fixed signs, which were stable rather than active, and finally the Mutable or Common signs, which depended on the action of others. The Virgin is one of these.

Further, the ruling planet of Virgo is Mercury, the messenger of the gods, whose realm of activity covers writing, thinking, commerce, theft and communication; so the Virgin had no choice but to be intellectual and the perfect secretary, whose gift is for dealing with subtleties and little things.

Such are the *a priori* characteristics to which the sign of the Virgin has been expected to conform, regardless of observation. They comprise a large part of the following typical description of Virgo, to be found in Vivian Robson's *Student's Textbook of Astrology*, printed in 1922. The words entirely in capitals are suggested by the symbol of the VIRGIN, and those with a capital letter are derived from the attributions of Mercury, Earth, or the Mutable Quality, but those in italics suggest *Leo* rather than Virgo.

> Cool, Practical, Discriminating, *very Critical, often destructively so*, Impassive, Faddy Over Little Things, very Inquisitive, MODEST, RETIRING, faithful, Intellectual, *strong opinions*, fond of Art, Literature, Science, and Mathematics, fond of collecting, Good Memory and Reasoning Power, not very original, slow to anger and forgiveness, QUIET, Persuasive, Very Good At Detail Work, fond of Gardening, Reading, COOKING AND NEEDLEWORK, etc.; often servile to *rich and distinguished people, fond of telling people their faults*, worry over Little Things but *brave in emergency, insist on respect*, often rather OLD-MAIDISH.

This description differs quite remarkably from the descriptions of fifteen or twenty centuries earlier. Although, from the symbol and its ruler Mercury we have to be told that the Virgonian is quiet and persuasive, at the same time she insists on being respected, is brave but snobbish, indulges frequently in destructive criticism, and is fond of telling people their faults. This may be the typical old maid of fifty, or it may be the self-centred and bossy Lion, but it is far indeed from the pretty maid of fifteen who was the original symbol.

The pretty maid was an angel—she had wings. She represented Astraea, the goddess or heavenly power of Justice, who dwelt on earth in the Golden Age. No wonder that her natives were described as the most helpful and charming in the zodiac! But Ptolemy, when he made Virgo a sign of Earth, could not help but cut off her wings; so now we are presented with this cold, selfish, viperish old maid!

There is, however, a factor of continuity in this surprising change. It is not wholly to be accounted for by a change in social manners (much for the worse, apparently), nor yet by animadversions upon the altered interpretation of the symbol and the possibly defective observational powers of astrologers. For the sign of the Virgin, as tropically measured in 1947, covered the last 24 degrees of the constellation Leo, and only the first 6 degrees of the constellation Virgo. And the Lion, if we read the old astrologers, is a great one for making himself respected, is 'brave in emergency' but not otherwise, is hard and overbearing, destructively critical, and not above telling people their faults.

So we cannot leap to the conclusion that the characters of the zodiac are nonsense. From that one area of the sky which is now called Virgo and two thousand years ago was labelled Leo, astrologers have observed that the people born are cold, overbearing, selfish, critical, and brave in emergency. Two thousand years ago they tacked this observation on to the symbol of the fearless and dominating Lion; more recently they have changed the interpretation of the Virgin in order to make her fit that character. The fact that they have done so suggests that their observations were perhaps not wholly without foundation. The archetype of the zodiac may have been working twenty centuries ago.

For Virgo is not the only sign to have changed its character; the rulership of Mars over Scorpio is another attribution which has become with the passing centuries more problematic. Scorpio, we have been told in recent textbooks, is deep, profound, secretive, fond of mysterious things, penetrating, obscure, and hard to understand. It seems to follow from this that it has not been understood. For anything more in contradiction to the forthright character of Mars would be hard to find. This seems to be a case where the experience of astrologers has moved gradually farther and farther away from the traditional ruling planet, until in the end it is only lip-service to claim Mars as ruler of Scorpio.

The situation was not the same in the seventeenth century, if we can take on trust that human character was really so unpleasant as the astrologers of those days represented it. For their descriptions of the signs were more outspokenly offensive, and form a possibly useful social comparison to our own.

William Lilly in 1647 gives Scorpio the following description: 'A corpulent, strong, able body, somewhat a broad or square face; a dusky, muddy complexion, and sad dark hair, much and crisping; a hairy body, somewhat bow-legged, short necked; a squat well-trussed fellow.'

The character to go with this is that of Mars when 'well dignified' : 'In feats of war and courage invincible, scorning that any should exceed him; subject to no reason, bold, confident, immovable, contentious, challenging all honour to themselves; valiant, lovers of war and things pertaining thereto, hazarding himself in all perils, unwilling to obey or submit to anybody; a boaster of his own acts; one that slights all things in comparison of victory, and yet of prudent behaviour in his own affairs.' When 'ill dignified' he is 'a prattler, without modesty or honesty, a lover of slaughter and quarrels', and many other things besides.

In the early nineteenth century this becomes (Zadkiel 1835) : 'A well-set form of middle stature, rather corpulent; swarthy complexion, black curling hair, broad and plain face. The temper is very unsociable and rash; they are generally revengeful, ungrateful, quarrelsome and wicked; yet of good genius and ready apprehension, excelling in mystery, etc.'

'Mystery' means of course mysterious studies like astrology and occultism. The bad character of Scorpio has for centuries been legendary, in fact Lilly in his translation of Bonatti's aphorisms[2] goes so far as to call its natives 𝕿𝖗𝖆𝖎𝖙𝖔𝖗𝖘 . But the supposed wickedness of this sign was due in part to the accident that one of the few genuinely suggestive resemblances to be seen in the sky is to the tail of a poisonous insect, and in part to the fact that by Ptolemy's scheme of rulerships it was allotted to a malefic planet, namely Mars. Aquarius, which modern astrologers have idealized on account of the incoming 'Aquarian Age', was given a perfectly odious character by Vettius Valens, simply because it was ruled by Saturn.

But the description of character was only one use to which the zodiac was put. A knowledge of it was required for predicting the future, and also for the practice of magic, and therefore during the dark ecclesiastical ages, when only the Church kept alive the flame of learning, the question often arose whether astrology was permissible and orthodox, or whether it ought not rather to be condemned. There are several reasons why one might expect it to be condemned, although belief in it was very general.[3]

For between astrology and magic there could be no very clear distinction so long as men believed that the verification of predictions could be contrived by obliging demons. Besides, astrology could be a public nuisance. Tertullian (about A.D. 155–222) reports with glee that astrologers had been officially expelled from Rome because they were so much consulted by persons wishing to know how long the emperor would live, and whether he could or would be murdered.

By churchmen astrology was rarely regarded as impossible, but quite frequently as dangerous; for if the future could be predicted, were men still responsible for their actions? Might they not begin to pretend that sin had been forced upon them by the stars? The most common attitude to this danger was that of Abelard and Hugh of St Victor, who lived in the eleventh century. They distinguished *naturalia* from *contingentia*, and admitted that prediction was possible of such 'natural' things as sickness, fertility, and the weather, but not of such things as were dependent on God's providence or man's free will. The opponents of astrology liked to claim that it taught determinism, but this was not always a quite honest accusation.

The solution of the problem is quite easy once you know it, but took centuries to discover. Yet an observant astrologer, in the course of ten or twenty years, must easily find among his acquaintances several persons who at different times suffer the same aspect, for example the transit of Uranus over the Sun by conjunction or opposition. Observing them, he expects to notice that, while the aspect is in force, each recipient of it will undergo an experience of the type described in his textbooks as 'Uranian'; but he cannot tell in advance upon what level any given native will take the aspect. Some resent and fight the change in their circumstances, most are made unhappy by having to adapt themselves, a few by taking the tide at flood gain worldly advantage, but others increase their understanding, make spiritual progress, and suffer little or nothing. The influence will arrive in any case, but the free will consists in deciding to use it well or badly, cheerfully or sadly.

It was hard to make this distinction in medieval times, because it was often thought that if anything was predictable by astrology, then everything must be predictable. There seems no reason for this sweeping assumption; it is the usual over-simplification of seeking a one-factor solution, just as some people nowadays talk as if everything could be explained by economics. In Augustine's time people would try to catch the astrologer out by presenting the horoscope of an animal for delineation, and Augustine, though he had abandoned astrology, says that the best astrologers could not be taken in this trap. Modern astrologers, on the other hand, admit that the same horoscope can apply to a man, a dog, and a limited company, if they come into being at the same place and moment.

Augustine, however, was cured of his belief in astrology by learning that a slave and a rich friend had been born at the same moment in two houses not a mile apart—'whence I concluded for certain', says he, 'that true predictions made by consulting the stars were not due to skill but to luck, and false ones not to lack of skill but to lack of luck'.[4] This is a typical piece of that static thinking which regards the horoscope as a story complete in every detail, like a novel whose end is determined before you begin to read, rather than a chart of currents and winds to be used for navigation.

St John Chrysostom, who was born in Antioch in 347 and became Patriarch of Constantinople, argues that it is not the function of astronomy to learn from the stars who are being born, but merely to predict from the hour of birth what is going to happen, which, says Thorndike, 'seems a quite fallacious distinction upon his part'. Although Thorndike agrees in this with St Augustine, all modern astrologers would be against him, and accept Chrysostom's distinction. Chrysostom is trying to argue against astrology, but such was the spirit of his age that he could not help accepting it in part. He criticizes the Magi for their coming to Bethlehem, since as astrologers they ought to have known that their visit would cause trouble, and also for calling Jesus 'King of the Jews', whereas later Christ told Pilate that His Kingdom was not of this world. That, however, is a trap into which fell also the early Christians and even the Churches from time to time.

Not infrequently in medieval times there was discussion whether the planets were living beings—'animals', as it is sometimes translated. If so, they might be capable of sin, as was supposed by Bildad the Shuhite in the Book of Job.[5] Plato was the father of all those who allowed the planets to have souls, and Bernard Sylvester called them gods without being accused of heresy.

The horoscope of Christ was another dangerous topic, since no one wanted to be accused of making God subject to the controlling influence of the heavenly bodies He had created. Roger Bacon wrote to the Pope that in the opinions of astrologers God had willed the nativity of His Son to be in harmony with the constellations, in so far as Jesus partook of human nature.

St Hildegard of Bingen, about 1140, suggested that Christ perhaps chose astrologically favourable moments for the performance of His miracles, although she also claimed that the revelations of the stars concerned the past only, and not the future. Since Our Lord Himself had said, 'There shall be signs in the sun, and in the moon, and in the stars',[6] and since His birth had been announced by a star, it was natural enough for Christians to believe in astrology. But Thorndike suggests that the story of the star and the three Magi was only inserted into the Gospel to conciliate the very wide belief in astrology in the second century. For it will have seemed only natural to the readers of that time that the birth of the sublimest of all beings should be announced with portents by the sublimest of all sciences.

There is only one record of an astrologer being burnt at the stake, and that was Cecco d'Ascoli in 1327. He had broken a ban imposed upon him by the Inquisitor of Bologna, forbidding him to teach and condemning two of his books; hence he counted as a relapsed heretic. The real reason for his death may well have been personal enmity, since his writings that have come down to us are no more offensive than those of such orthodox thinkers as Albert the Great and Cardinal d'Ailly. He does not advocate, though he suggests the possibility of, conjuring demons out of the sky by incantation.

When medieval characters disapproved of astrology, they almost always did so on the ground that it was possible but wicked. Very unusually Hippolytus, in his so-called *Refutation of All Heresies* (about A.D. 200), maintained that it was irrational and impracticable. This obliged him, of course, to contend that magic likewise was an impossible imposture. His attitude sounds more modern, but why assume that the magician and astrologer are conscious frauds, rather than self-deceived? Hippolytus, like all refuters of heresies, was an uncharitable character.

The difficulty is the common one of trying to have an opinion upon a subject where one is not an expert. What should one say about an unlikely science such as astrology? If one has a real sense of security, and a faith unweakened by any dogmatic obligation to believe or disbelieve without evidence, then one finds it superfluous to have rigid views about the special subjects of others. Yet such security is rare. Hence the need to believe, or disbelieve, in order to feel certain about a picture of the world which is fundamentally weak and invalid because based on dogma rather than understanding.

Ungrounded disbelief is only the reverse of groundless belief, and both are equally superstitious. Faith is not blind; faith is knowledge of what one can do. Those who have faith do not need to go about believing and disbelieving in things for the pleasure of it. And hence there is no occasion to think that one need either believe or disbelieve in astrology. If one is an expert on the subject, one knows what can be done with it; if not, one has only one's own experience on which to erect a supposition, and one knows that that experience is inadequate. The attitude of such a man as Hippolytus, who claims to have proved that it cannot work and rules all evidence unnecessary, is peculiarly unintelligent—though not of course unparalleled in modern times.

Despite the disapproval of Hippolytus and Augustine, and the isolated case of Cecco d'Ascoli, the profession of astrologer does not seem to have been a dangerous one in medieval Europe. Many eminent thinkers accepted astrology in varying degrees, and many astrologers had wealthy patrons and grew rich.

In France the earliest wealthy astrologer known to us is Caecilius Argicius Arborius, who lived at Dax in Aquitaine in the third century A.D., and was the grandfather of the well-known Latin poet Ausonius.[7] His astrology, however, resembles that of the Greco-Roman world, and scholars have concluded that it came to him via Marseilles, and not from the Druids, although we are told by Roman writers that they were experts in divination and discussed the motions of the heavens. A Latin play called *Querolus*, satirizing astrologers, was acted in Aquitaine in the fifth century.

From this time on there were many successful astrologers in France and Italy. Louis XIII employed Morin de Villefranche, and Pope Paul III employed Gauricus, who obligingly proved that Luther would go to Hell because he was born under that much-abused sign Scorpio. This was particularly easy since Luther, like many other people, had several planets in that sign. Not improbably, however,

Gauricus faked not only the hour but also the year, since Cardan and Junctinus and Melanchthon are all agreed against him.

We do not know the name of any astrologer accredited to an English king, but Henry VII's portrait is found in a manuscript of Guido Bonatti's enormous astrological textbook, which had been specially copied for him. Bonatti had a now-forgotten method of judging what he called 'revolutions', meaning in this case the Sun's entry into the cardinal signs. This consisted in determining which planet was to be 'lord of the year', according to rather complicated rules; no planet, for instance, could be lord of the year if it was retrograde or too close to the Sun. He also illustrates the rather useful propensity of astrologers for copying older textbooks without adapting them, when he says that Mars in Taurus in a 'revolution', if oriental, signifies peace both in the parts of Babylon and in the West, but if occidental, epidemics; if retrograde, diseases among children, but if direct, hatred from women—on the authority of Albumasar.

Bonatti's career was long and successful, and his greatest achievement was the defence of Forlì in 1282. At this time he was a prominent and wealthy citizen, well over sixty, and his patron was the town's military commander, Guido da Montefeltro.

Bonatti was very precise in selecting hours for the start of Montefeltro's aggressions. On the chosen day he would mount the tower of San Mercuriale—well-omened name!—and give three signals on a bell, first for the moment to arm, then to mount, and finally to set out.

So successful were these expeditions that after a time Pope Martin IV dispatched an army in order to subjugate Forlì. Montefeltro then consulted Bonatti, who must have spoken to him somewhat as follows: 'I cannot promise you victory in the field, for the signs are contradictory; and besides, I have the horoscope of the enemy commander, which I obtained from a colleague, and for him there are signs of victory and feasting. You, however, are not due to suffer anything unpleasant. We must give all the influences a chance to work—it is no use hoping that some of them will fail—so I suggest that you withdraw your army from the town, and give the women instructions to feast the enemy lavishly; any little rape or seduction will be easily forgiven when we return, for once the enemy troops are drunk we shall rush in and massacre them!'

Montefeltro agreed, the massacre went off as planned, and everyone was delighted, including the women, and especially Bonatti, who was wounded while carrying medicines to the injured; for, since he had predicted this, his reputation now stood higher than ever. The only unsatisfied person was the Pope, who, as soon as convenient, sent a larger army. This time Forlì submitted in earnest, and Montefeltro moved to a district where his military talents would stand a better chance. No doubt Bonatti had advised him that resistance was useless at the moment; and Montefeltro thus becomes one of the clearest examples of the astrological use of free will. He lost his city in either case, but he chose to do so without bloodshed. Later he made his peace with the Pope, and died in the Franciscan Order. Bonatti may possibly have done the same, for quite a number of Franciscans had written on astrology and astrological medicine.

Nor was such study entirely dogmatism and guesswork; it did attempt to relate the human body to the forces of the universe in which we live, and out of this the desire to experiment developed.

A common and easy form of experiment was the strictly astrological one of a 'decumbiture', or horoscope set for the moment of a patient taking to his bed. If in such a case Saturn or Mars was found on the meridian or horizon, the patient would be expected to die, but if Jupiter or Venus, then he would recover quickly; and the Moon's sign, or the sign rising, should indicate that part of the body where the trouble was chiefly located. In general, Aries as the first sign was taken to rule the head, and so on through the zodiac until the last sign, Pisces, ruled the feet (see Plate 2). But this was evidently a little too simple; for Virgo, which rules the bowels, a much commoner site of infection than the feet, rises at sunrise in September, and from then on until the following March cannot rise at all during the hours of daylight. So a scheme was elaborated whereby the head was not always ruled by Aries, but each planet could signify any part of the body, depending on how far it was from its own sign. And a planet in its own sign—that is to say in a sign which it ruled, in its exaltation, or in its triplicity, 'term', or 'face'—was always thought to be well-disposed, even if by nature it was one of the malefics.

It was also expected, of course, that any person having the Sun or the malefic planets in Aries would be especially liable to headaches, and so on all round the circle.

At this date the zodiac was simply a tradition whose origin, although unknown, was presumed to be divine. The uses to which it was put were still being elaborated, and there are many extant pictures in which the signs were associated with the seasons; but in Europe they were almost all based on the equinox as starting-point.

One of the first medieval thinkers to appreciate the value of experiment was Albert the Great, a famous churchman who gave much study to astrology and magic, and died two years before Bonatti's triumph at Forlì. He was one of the first to publish lists of observed details on which generalizations might be based, although his observations were neither planned nor systematic. Unlike Augustine and Gregory the Great, he accepted astrology, and solved the problem of free will very easily. 'There is in man a double spring of action, namely nature and the will; and nature for its part is ruled by the stars, while the will is free; but unless it resists it is swept along by nature and becomes mechanical.'[8] This appears to be very true; but for 'will' one might equally well write 'higher self' or 'incarnating entity'.

There was of course a distinct slump in astronomical knowledge in the Middle Ages, but in spite of this astrology never died out, though it sometimes became, through ignorance, as futile as the modern Sunday newspapers with their division of the calendar and the whole population into only twelve types. The Venerable Bede, for example, did nothing unusual when he compiled a list of rules for divination from thunder according to the direction and time of day at which it was heard; many such are known from Constantinople.

Another substitute for horoscopical calculation was the attempt to predict a child's character from the letters of its name, the day of the week on which it was born ('Monday's child is fair of face', and so forth), or, slightly more astronomical, from the day of the moon's age. One fourteenth-century moon-book claims to have been written by Adam from his own experience! The other most popular suppositious author was the prophet Daniel.

But these moon-books can only have been designed for the unlearned. In the time of Charlemagne's successor, Louis the Pious, every great lord had his own astrologer, and William the Conqueror's chaplain was devoted to star-gazing; hence, perhaps, the representation of Halley's Comet in the Bayeux Tapestry. England in the twelfth century had two well-known astrologers, Daniel of Morley and Roger of Hereford; yet in the reign of Henry I considerable consternation was felt when the Archbishop of York died unshriven with a textbook of astrology under his pillow! Since he was already unpopular, the coffin was stoned and the people wished to refuse him Christian burial. The book was the well-known work by Firmicus Maternus, written in Sicily in the fourth century.

By this time the revival of learning, through translations from the Arabic, was going strong. It began perhaps as early as the tenth century, and one of the most famous of Arab astrologers was Albumasar, who died in 886, after spending many years as official astrologer to the Caliph of Baghdad. His book on 'revolutions' was republished in 1905.

Alcandrus, who is quoted by the Emperor Frederick II's magician Michael Scot, gave a list of the 28 'Mansions of the Moon', but since he tells us to discover under which mansion a man is born by a numerological calculation of his name and his mother's, his astronomical knowledge was apparently inconsiderable.

The same remark would apply to some of the methods of the medieval Greek alchemists,[9] which profess to declare whether a sick man will recover, or a runaway slave be found, by turning his name into a number, adding the number of days since the Sun entered Gemini (which was regarded as the beginning of summer), then dividing by 7 or 9 and judging by the house of the horoscope in which the remainder fell.

About the same time John of Salisbury rebukes Thomas à Becket for persistently consulting all kinds of fortune-tellers, even after he became Archbishop of Canterbury.[10] And, as an attempt to satirize astrology, and fortune-telling in general, a 'hermaphrodite's horoscope' was invented in Latin verse, which may be translated as follows:

'Tis said my parents, while my mother carried me,
    Inquired of heaven what the child would be.
Mars said: 'A girl'; Phoebus: 'A boy'; but 'Neither's right!'
    Cried Juno: hence I was hermaphrodite.
They asked my death. 'Hanging,' said Mars; 'With steel run
    through,'

Said Juno; Phoebus: 'Drowning.' All came true.
A tree o'erhangs a stream; I climb; but from its sheath
    By chance my sword slips; on to it I fall.
Caught by the foot, my head the wave beneath,
    The poor hermaphrodite is pierc'd, hanged, drown'd and all![11]

The eleventh century is the time when we first find diagrams of the astrological man, a human figure with the signs of the zodiac applied to the different parts of the body. One of the earliest bears this legend: 'According to the ravings of the philosophers the twelve signs are thus denoted.'

The distinction between astronomy and astrology begins to be perceptible in the writings of Isidore of Seville about A.D. 630, but was first formulated about the time of Hugh of St Victor, who died in 1141. Hugh distinguished *mathematica*, the science of abstract quantity, from *matesis* (without an H), which meant astrology. In the next century Albert the Great made the distinction dependent upon the length of the E in *mathesis*.

The incapacity of medieval astrologers to use their zodiac accurately is very plain in two books attributed to Hermes Trismegistos. In the *De Revolutionibus Nativitatum*, of unknown date but printed at Basle in 1559, the Father of Wisdom is made to recommend that the sun's motion be taken 'with the instrument mentioned in the Almagest (which the Greeks call The Great Construction)', and that the return of the sun and planets to their places should be calculated by their mean motions, not their actual motions, the length of the solar year being taken as $365\frac{1}{4}$ days less one-hundredth part of a day. This book is the ancestor of the modern custom of calculating annual horoscopes both for individuals and for political prediction, but it assumes the impossibility of computing the exact time of the equinox, besides suggesting that Hermes lived later than Ptolemy. The same difficulty occurs in another book attributed to him.

The interpretation of the signs of the zodiac in terms of mythology and analogy was usual and, as today, very few writers speculated on the origin of the names. One who did was Helpericus, a ninth-century monk who wrote on the ecclesiastical calendar. Some of the names he finds quite simple: Aquarius and Pisces are explained by the rainy season, Leo by the heat, and Libra by the equinox; in Cancer the sun begins to walk backwards. The Scorpion's sting and the Archer's arrow are both compared to the sting of hail-showers, and Capricorn is the lower turning-point of the sun because kids graze uphill, 'as everyone knows'. The Ram, however, was either named because the sun breaks up the frozen earth as a ram attacks with its horns, or else because rams, having slept on their left side all the winter, now start to sleep on their right. In the month of Taurus oxen work to prepare the ripening of the corn, but the explanation of Gemini is an incoherent allusion to Castor and Pollux. Virgo, finally, is so called because the earth is exhausted and no longer bears any fruit—the transition from the pretty girl to the old maid is on the way.

Both in India and in the Greco-Roman world there was a doctrine of a Great Year, at the end of which the planets, and consequently the world, would return to the state of the beginning. Astrologers rather naturally imagined that at creation all the planets stood in the first degree of Aries, and could not help concluding that when this universal conjunction should be repeated there would come an apocatastasis, or restoration of all things; and this, no doubt, is one origin of the doctrine of the millennium and the return of the Golden Age—the other being a misapplication to the physical plane of the doctrine that the soul's ultimate destiny is perfect adaptation and union with God. If the conjunction of all the planets occurred in any other part of the zodiac, the restoration of all things was not expected; in the Middle Ages it was thought that such a conjunction in Capricorn would produce another Deluge, and in Cancer would result in destruction of the world by fire.[12]

The idea is an archetypal one—not just a Freudian longing to return to the peaceful existence of the womb—because it is ultimately unavoidable: the only logical ultimate aim is perfect adaptation on all levels, which means not just the heat-death of entropy, but union with the Creative Force. Hence we find the doctrine of the millennium cropping up everywhere, in the Revelation of St John, in Shelley ('The world's great age begins anew'), in Virgil, in Yeats, in More's *Utopia* and Marx's Socialist state, because the astronomical possibility of a universal conjunction chimes in with the universal yearning for perfection in the human heart.

The length of the Great Year was a matter of speculation, and in India became too long to be interesting, but this was because it could not then be accurately calculated. To discover when all the planets will be conjoined in the first degree of Aries would take an electronic computer, now that three more planets are known. The period of the Great Year, however, could fairly be taken as a little under 26,000 years, since this is the period of the Precession of the Equinoxes.

When the zodiac was first invented, precession was not imagined, and the sun was thought to cross the equator in the constellation Aries always at the same point. In fact the point of crossing moves westward at a speed of about 50·2 seconds of arc per year. Hence it takes about two thousand years to pass through a constellation, and nearly 26,000 to make the tour of the sky. If Mr Fagan is right in concluding that the oldest measured zodiac was defined by the star Aldebaràn in the exact middle of Taurus, then the Vernal Equinoctial Point of the northern hemisphere entered the constellation Taurus about 4139 B.C., entered Aries about 1953 B.C., when incidentally the cult of the ram-god Amun was becoming so important in Egypt, then entered Pisces in A.D. 220, the Fish being the symbol of the Christian Era, and will enter Aquarius about A.D. 2375.

Most astrologers think that the Aquarian Age will start earlier than that, perhaps indeed has already begun with the discovery of Uranus in 1784; but the transition must take one or two centuries, and Christianity did not become an official religion till about A.D. 330. Other modern astrologers give different dates, and having seen upon celestial globes unequal boundaries between the constellations, they leap to the conclusion that these boundaries are sacrosanct and of great occult significance, not realizing that they are only three or four hundred years old. In ancient times there were no accurate boundaries, except in the zodiac, which was divided for convenience into twelve equal divisions. The doctrine of unequal divisions, though sometimes true of the Indian and Chinese asterisms, is not true of the zodiac when used for measurement.

The interpretation of history in the light of planetary and precessional cycles was first conspicuously developed by Peter of Abano, who might therefore be regarded as the father of the present notion of the Aquarian Age, which is to last from now for the next two thousand years. His own historical schemes are highly implausible, but he was the first to give a reasonably accurate estimate of the speed of precession—one degree in 70 years, which is only 2 years short. He is best known, however, as a magician, indeed more souls are said to have been damned through reading his book than any other. Unfortunately the book surviving under his name is almost certainly spurious and, like all the blacker forms of magic, rather disgusting.

The method of medieval magic was largely concerned with the making of images, and much of this practice goes back to Thabit ibn Kurrah, or Thebit ben Corat, who was not an Arab but a Sabian, that is to say an old-fashioned pagan who had inherited the sparse remains of ancient Babylonian religion, combined with some of the many other religious influences of the Middle East in earlier times. He was also astrologer to the Caliph of Baghdad, and died in the same year as Alfred the Great. Like most other users of magical images, he maintains that each must be made under the appropriate sign of the zodiac, but unlike them he thinks the material of the image unimportant. Here is a sample from his book:

When you want to make an image for a man who wishes to become the head of a city or province, or judge of a prefecture or a town, the method is the same. First begin by making a mould in which to cast the image. Carve the head of the image when the Dragon's Head is in the Ascendant, and let the lord of the ascendant be a benefic, free from aspect of the malefics. Carve the body of the image under whatever rising sign the Moon shall be in, carve the shoulders and breasts with Venus in the ascendant, the haunches with the Sun rising in one of its dignities, the thighs with Mercury in the ascendant, and he must not be retrograde or combust, but should be unafflicted and in one of his fortunate places; and the feet under the ascendant of the Moon in conjunction with Venus.

When you have drawn out the figure thus, proceeding in order, you may start to cast it, of gold if you will, or any metal you like, under the ascendant of his birth if you know it, or else under the ascendant of the time when he asked the question. And you shall name the image by the name by which he is generally known. And see that the ascendant be fortunate, and its lord, and the tenth house, and that the malefics be remote from the ascendant and its lord, and let the lord of the eleventh be one of the benefics, in aspect of the ascendant and its lord; and let the lord of the tenth be in conjunction with the lord of the ascendant in a friendly conjunction or with complete mutual reception. When you have done this and made the image in this manner, he will obtain what he desires from his king and be given the post he seeks. Preserve the image as I have told you, and it will do the work if God wills.

Needless to say, there is another image for depriving a man of royal favour, but this, like those for creating friendship and enmity, must be buried with the recital of a magic spell. So must the image made with Scorpio rising to keep away scorpions. Sometimes instead of 'If Allah wills', Thabit says, 'Do this and you shall see marvels.'

Other effects supposed to be obtainable from the use of magical images were to give rheumatic pains, to heat baths at night, to congregate ten thousand birds or bees, and to prevent sexual intercourse in a given area. Roger Bacon believed in the value of astrological amulets, so did Albert the Great, Peter of Abano, Louis XI, and many others — and in modern times the great yogi Sri Yukteswar, guru of Yogananda.[13] Pope Boniface VIII valued highly a zodiacal seal made for him by Arnald of Villanova as an antidote to pains in the kidneys. This seal must have been made by some such procedure as the following, which Arnald gives as instruction for making the seal of Capricorn :[14]

When the Sun is in Capricorn take gold or silver and make a seal of it, and while it is being struck with the hammer say: 'Arise O Lord my God and set me free, for Thou art my hope and my patience from my youth up.' The psalm is *Deus in adjutorium meum intende*, etc. And carve upon it a figure of Capricorn while the Sun is in it, and around the edge thus: CHANARIEL, SANCTUS BARTHOLOMAEUS, and on the rest of the circumference the following inscription: Glory to GOD in the highest and on earth peace to men of goodwill; and in the middle JESU BRASIM. The virtues of this seal in general are:

57

It avails against the bites of poisonous beasts and mad dogs, and against gout in the knees.

Aquinas, that pillar of orthodoxy, without denying the virtue of gems, denies that it could be increased by carving figures on them, since words and figures are not material and cannot influence the constitution of matter. But this materialist explanation misses the point, since the effect of amulets, if there is any, might be psychological and not physical. Apart from this, Aquinas accepted the rule of superiors over inferiors, that is, the influence of celestial bodies over earthly bodies, saying that it was amply proved;[15] and he was inclined to admit that the planets were moved by angels, though he would not allow them to have soul and intelligence as Plato and Aristotle had thought.

Plato and Aristotle, though neither explicitly mentions the zodiac or the art of prediction from the heavens, are not irrelevant to the study of astrology. Indeed, in the Middle Ages they were supposed to be the head and fount of it — and not without a reason. Roger Bacon in the thirteenth century cannot be blamed for accepting as a genuine work of Aristotle *The Secret of Secrets*, which purported to be the essence of the teaching that Alexander the Great, between the ages of thirteen and sixteen, had received from Aristotle, who was his tutor. There is much good advice in this book, and only here and there is it explicitly astrological; for instance, 'When you wish to take a laxative, let the Moon be in Scorpio or Libra or Pisces, but be careful to avoid the Moon's application to Saturn, for then she makes the medicine and humours in the body to congeal.'

To make a talisman for lordship and dominion, let the ascendant be in Leo — this is quite right since Alexander the Great was born with the sun in Leo conjoined to Regulus — and let the sun be in 13° Aries, the Moon in 3° Taurus, Saturn in Aquarius, Jupiter in Sagittarius, and Mars in Virgo. You then melt together the metals of the planets (putting in as much of Saturn as will equal all the rest) on a Thursday morning in the hour of Jupiter, make a signet ring, inlay it with a red ruby, and engrave on it a black man riding on a lion, crowned, winged, and carrying a standard, and before him there should march six beardless men with the wings of birds.

In medieval myth, even the birth of Alexander was supposed to have been arranged by astrology. St Basil, who wrote in Greek before 379, had never heard of a king who took steps to have his son born under a favourable constellation; but Augustine, writing in Latin less than fifty years later, had heard of a sage who selected an astrological hour for intercourse with his wife, in order to beget a marvellous son. It seems to have been agreed that Nectanebus was a king of Egypt who used to defeat his enemies by conjuring armies out of the air by magic. Eventually, however, like Guido da Montefeltro, he found that the time had come when the planets were against him, so he disguised himself, emigrated to Macedon, and set up as an astrologer. His skill was so remarkable that he was soon known at court, and in the absence of King Philip he became intimate with the queen, Olympias. Thus he, rather than Philip, was the true father of Alexander. Needless to say, he achieved this by making a wax image of the queen, and appeared to her in the likeness of the god Ammon, with many other marvellous details. Finally when the day of the birth arrived he stood beside her and obliged her to hold back until the most favourable moment, crying: 'No, no! He who is born now will be ugly and unsuccessful! Do not let the child come forth!'

Another curiosity of the *Secret of Secrets* is that it speaks of the two zodiacs.[16] The eighth sphere, that of the fixed stars, is supposed to move by precession inside the ninth, which contains the equinoctial points and is immovable and invisible. We can no longer accept as genuine a work in which Aristotle advises Alexander to remember the story of Cain and Abel; but even in Aristotle's genuine works there is reason enough to make him the father of medieval astrology.

Perhaps the sidereal system of measuring the zodiac did not die out completely. In Italy there are astrological frescoes in various Renaissance buildings, for instance the Schifanoja Palace at Ferrara, the Palazzo della Ragione at Padua, and the Farnesina in Rome. The paintings in the Farnesina are by Baldassare Peruzzi, illustrating the horoscope of his patron Agostino Chigi. They are in panels all round and on the ceiling of the Sala di Galatea, and represent no fewer than eighteen constellations in addition to the signs of the zodiac and the planets.

The room runs almost due north and south, the northern end being canted a little towards the west. The painting at the north end represents Leo, and that at the south end Aquarius, while between them, running along the middle of the ceiling, are two larger pictures, the northern one portraying the Wain, the southern one Pegasus and Perseus. This gives us an approximate hour of birth; for when the meridian passes through Aquarius in the south, it also passes through the Wain and Pegasus, and of course Leo, which is invisible under the earth. Perseus is possibly emphasized because he was in the east, to provide another indication of the hour of birth, or perhaps only for mythological reasons: Pegasus sprang from a drop of blood when Perseus cut off the Gorgon's head.

In 1934 a little book on these frescoes was published by Fritz Saxl, with the horoscope computed by Arthur Beer. Both writers were rather keen to exhibit their contempt for their subject of study; hence Beer places Saturn neatly on the midheaven, while Saxl blandly speaks of Agostino Chigi's excellent horoscope! The frescoes give no hint of Saturn being on the midheaven, indeed from the position of the constellation Cygnus it seems rather more likely that the sidereal time was about 22 hours, and the hour of birth would therefore be about 5 p.m. Beer sets up his chart for 6.15 and calls it seven o'clock.

The date is given correctly as December 1st, 1466. This does not fit the tropical zodiac, which was thought to be the only one then in use; for in that system the Moon is in Libra and Venus in 0° Aquarius, whereas the frescoes show Venus in Capricorn and the Moon in Virgo. Beer gets over the difficulty by claiming that the signs are taken 'within their true limits', and gives a table of the extent of the constellations in tropical longitude in 1466. But if that were so, the horoscope would be purely visual and have no astrological reference at all. There is no record of astrologers bothering themselves with unequal constellations, although they too sometimes fall into the same fallacy, and speak as though the dotted lines drawn between constellations had some divine sanction.

But even the 'true limits' do not make Beer's example fit, for they put Jupiter in 3° Taurus, and Peruzzi, as can be seen from our frontispiece, took Jupiter to be entering Taurus but still in touch with Aries. Oddly enough, this is the precise position he occupied in the sidereal zodiac.

60

TABLE 1 *Longitudes of Planets in the Horoscope of Agostino Chigi*

Constellation	Extent (according to A. Beer)	Beginning (15th century)			Tropical Positions of Planets	Sidereal position of Planets
Aries	24° from	20°	trop. long.			29° 54′ Jupiter
Taurus	32°	44°	,,	,,	Jupiter 17°	
Gemini	34°	76°	,,	,,		
Cancer	20°	110°	,,	,,		
Leo	36°	130°	,,	,,		
Virgo	43°	166°	,,	,,		Moon 20°
Libra	20°	209°	,,	,,	Moon 8°	Mars 20°
Scorpio	27°	229°	,,	,,	Mars 7° Mercury 29°	Mercury 12°
Sagittarius	34°	256°	,,	,,	Sun 18½°	Sun 1°
Capricorn	24°	290°	,,	,,		Venus 13°
Aquarius	32°	314°	,,	,,	Venus 0°	
Pisces	34°	346°–20°	,,	,,	Saturn 26°	Saturn 9°

5. *The Twelve Gods: Plato and Augustus*

'WE tend,' says Aristotle, 'to think of the stars as mere bodies or items arranged in order, quite without soul or life. We ought rather to regard them as possessed of life and activity, for the consequences of this will not seem unreasonable ... We ought to regard the action of the planets as comparable to that of animals and plants.'[1]

And Plato says, in the Timaeus,[2] that mortal men were created by the lesser gods working with the Creator, in order that they should be partly not immortal.

> He divided the whole mixture into souls equal in number to the stars, and assigned each soul to a star ... and declared to them the laws of destiny, according to which their first birth would be one and the same for all—no one should suffer a disadvantage at his hands ... He who lived well during his appointed time was to return and dwell in his native star, and there he would have a blessed and congenial existence. But if he failed in attaining this, at the second birth he would pass into a woman, and if, when in that state of being, he did not desist from evil, he would continually be changed into some brute who resembled him in the evil nature which he had acquired, and would not cease from his toils and transformations until he followed the revolution of the same and the like within him, and overcame by the help of reason the turbulent and irrational mob of later accretions, made up of fire and air and water and earth, and returned to the form of his first and better state. Having given all these laws to His creatures, that He might be guiltless of future evil in any of them, the Creator sowed some of them in the earth, and some in the moon, and some in the other instruments of time; and when He had sown them, He committed to the younger gods the fashioning of their mortal bodies.

The 'younger gods' were thought in the Middle Ages to be an allusion to the signs of the zodiac. So it is not surprising that Plato and Aristotle should have been regarded as the great justifiers of astrology in those—as we now think—superstitious times.

Yet by condemning people for being unscientific we render ourselves incapable of understanding what their beliefs have meant to them. This is well illustrated by some words of Otto Neugebauer[3]:

> But there exists a third type (of astrology), standing between the omina type ('when this and this happens in the skies, then such and such a major event will be the consequence') and the individual birth horoscope, namely, the 'general prognostication', explained in full detail in the first two books of the *Tetrabiblos*. This type of astrology is actually primitive cosmic physics built on a vast generalization of the influence of the position of the sun in the zodiac on the weather on earth. The influence of the moon is considered as of almost equal importance, and from this point of departure an intricate system of characterization of the parts of the zodiac, the nature of the planets, and their mutual relations is developed. This whole astronomical meteorology is, to be sure, based on utterly naive analogies and generalizations, but it is certainly no more naive and plays no more with words than the most admired philosophical systems of antiquity. It would be of great interest for the understanding of ancient physics and science in general to know where and when this system was developed. The question arises whether this is a Greek invention, replacing the Babylonian omen literature, which must at any rate have lost most of its interest with the end of independent Mesopotamian rule, whether it precedes the invention of the horoscopic art for individuals or merely represents an attempt to rationalize the latter on more general principles.

By the fifth century A.D., when Proclus wrote his commentaries on Plato's *Dialogues*, astrology had become an ingredient of the whole culture of the Greco-Roman world, and Proclus, when discussing the *Republic*,[4] even gives rules for working out the relation between the horoscope of birth and that of conception, which later became known as the 'trutine of Hermes', or 'pre-natal epoch'. Although these rules cannot apply in the Arctic Circle, textbooks on them have been published in the twentieth century. In Greco-Roman times the horoscope of conception was often used, and sometimes thought more important, but the preference for the horoscope of birth does not rest only on the fact that the event is easier to observe. It is also the beginning of independent life, and furthermore no one has ever proved the somewhat unlikely proposition that the incarnating entity times its descent for the moment of conception; according to Buddhists it waits till six months before birth. On the other hand the horoscope is that of the personality, not of the immortal self.

All these points will have been discussed by Platonists, Neo-platonists, and other learned men of the Roman Empire, but to popularize astrology no one contributed more than the Emperor Augustus himself. 'While in retirement at Apollonia,' says Suetonius[5] —and this was when he was eighteen, just before Caesar's death— 'Augustus mounted with Agrippa to the studio of the astrologer Theogenes. Agrippa was the first to try his fortune, and when a great and almost incredible career was predicted for him, Augustus persisted in concealing the time of his birth and in refusing to disclose it, through diffidence and fear that he might be found to be less eminent. When at last he gave it unwillingly and hesitatingly, and only after many urgent requests, Theogenes sprang up and threw himself at his feet. From that time on Augustus had such faith in his destiny, that he made his horoscope public and issued a silver coin stamped with the sign of the constellation Capricorn, under which he was born.' (One of these coins is illustrated in Plate 4(a).)

The date of Augustus's birth is given as September 23rd, 64 B.C.; but the coin is evidence that it should probably be one day earlier. For Roman astrologers called a man Capricornian if he had the Moon in that constellation, whereas modern usage prefers to go by the Sun or Ascendant. The question is, which of five possible zodiacs did Theogenes use? Eudoxus had put the equinox in 15° Aries, Cleostratos of Tenedos in 12°, Naburiannu in 10°, Kidinnu (the founder of the Hellenistic zodiac) in 8°, and Hipparchus in 0°! And all these systems were still current.

In the modern tropical zodiac the Moon was in 27.3° Capricorn, but that zodiac had only been invented less than a century before

Augustus went to Apollonia, and not yet been popularized by Ptolemy. In the Spica zodiac the Moon's longitude would have been measured as 1·2° Aquarius, and in the Hellenistic zodiac, which is far the most likely for Theogenes to have used, the Moon's position would have been called 5° Aquarius. Further, the Moon at dawn on 23rd was going to the square aspect of Mars and Saturn, at which no astrologer would prostrate himself in worship! The obvious conclusion is that Augustus was born on September 22nd, when the Moon was unquestionably in Capricorn and strengthened by a beautiful and close opposition to Jupiter in its exaltation, both being in close aspect to the rising Mercury, which was also exalted. Granted Augustus' devotion to his horoscope, the date of 22nd is unescapable, and Illustration 4(a), which shows the Goat holding the Urn, should not be taken as conclusive evidence that the Moon was on the cusp between Capricorn and Aquarius. (The Ascendant was Mercury in Virgo, with the Sun a little below it just entering Libra.)

It is not probable that Augustus waited to act until the proper sign of the zodiac was rising, but Tiberius may have retired to Capri to escape the designs of maleficent planets. Suetonius wrote of him: 'He was rather neglectful of gods and religions, being addicted to astrology, and fully persuaded that all things are brought about by fate. Yet he was immoderately afraid of thunder, and if the sky became threatening he never failed to put on a laurel wreath, because of the common saying that that kind of leaf is never touched by lightning.'[6]

Astrology is known to have been practised in Rome in the third century B.C. — Plautus mentions it. It gained ground as representing Stoic rationalism and determinism against religion; rather the opposite of the present situation. No doubt Romans, like modern historians, often fell into the false antithesis of thinking that determinism excludes freewill, on the false premise that if anything is determined then everything must be. But apart from Augustus, the men who did most to popularize astrology were scholars of the first rank, Posidonius of Apamea, Nigidius Figulus, and Thrasyllus. Thrasyllus was the editor of the current edition of Plato's works; Tiberius met him in Rhodes in 6 B.C., brought him to Rome, and remained his personal friend for forty years, so that Thrasyllus, born an Alexandrine Greek, was for a long time the most influential man in the Roman Empire. In their time both Augustus and Tiberius expelled professional astrologers from Rome, which shows that then as now there was a distinction between scholarly study and the exploitation of public credulity.

By A.D. 11 astrology was so popular that Augustus made illegal the use of divination to discover the date of anyone's death, and published his own horoscope in order to show that it was not time for him to die. He died three years later, but of course the temptation remained, since the succession was so often uncertain, and under Caligula citizens whom the emperor did not like were commonly tried for treason on the excuse of illegal divination.

Nor was it always safe to be the astrologer, for the emperor might ask: 'And what of your own horoscope?' If the astrologer claims that all is well, he is put to death just to prove him wrong. Among various stories of this kind one is of an astrologer, possibly called Asclation, who answers: 'I am destined to be eaten by dogs.' The emperor therefore orders him to be crucified, but at the critical moment a torrential thunderstorm breaks out, the executioners run for shelter, so do the keepers of some ferocious circus dogs, and the astrologer has the satisfaction of disappointing the emperor. The best answer to this awkward question was perhaps discovered by Thrasyllus: 'I stand at this moment in the most imminent peril.'

Tiberius' hour of birth has not come down to us, but he had the Sun in Scorpio and the Moon in Libra, the Moon being in aspect of Venus and Jupiter, which makes for charm, but also of Mars and Saturn, which does the reverse. Evidently Mars and Saturn were more prominent than Jupiter and Venus!

Nero appears a rather worse character. He was born at exact sunrise with the Sun and Mars in conjunction in Sagittarius, both in square to an elevated Saturn; and the Moon in Leo closely square to Jupiter would account for his love of flaunting himself in theatres.

Seneca, who was Nero's tutor, writes: 'Aristotle says that we should always be respectful in the presence of the gods; and surely this is never more true than when we are discussing the planets.'[7] But he also complains that the Chaldeans only speak of the influence of five stars (apart from the sun and moon), and asks: 'Do you think the others shine for nothing? We must be under their influence too.'[8]

Cicero was less favourable to astrology, though he repeated Plato's argument for thinking the planets to be living and divine. 'The marvellous and incredible regularity', he says, 'of the stars in their eternal and unvarying courses, shows that they have divine power and intelligence, in fact anyone who cannot see that they possess the power of gods would seem to be quite incapable of understanding anything.'[9] In his book *On Divination*, however, he gives ten pages to an attack on astrology, calling it 'incredible mad folly which is daily refuted by experience', and argues that the weather, which it can at least feel, should have more influence on a new-born baby than the signs of the zodiac.

An attempt was even made to work out the horoscope of Rome. According to Plutarch, this was the achievement of an astrologer called Tarrutius in the first century B.C. Tarrutius dated the conception of Romulus to a total eclipse of the sun which occurred on 23rd Khoiak of the Egyptian calendar, in the first year of the second Olympiad, which corresponds to June 25th (Julian), 772 B.C.; and he put the birth on 21st Thoth at sunrise, which equates to March 25th. The eclipse he mentions actually occurred on June 24th. The foundation of the city he then gave as the third year of the sixth Olympiad (which would be 754 B.C., not 753), on 9th Pharmuthi, which would be October 4th, between the second and third hour.

It will be noticed that Romulus is supposed to have founded Rome at the age of nineteen. This is probably because Tarrutius knew the 'Metonic cycle', whereby new moons occur on the same day of the month after nineteen years, and perhaps he wanted both the foundation of the city and the conception of its founder to be marked by eclipses. As so often happens with these ancient and much-copied documents, the astronomical data do not fit, and one is left to guess which points are erroneous.

Manilius puts Rome under Libra, doubtless in the same way that Augustus was under Capricorn, for he says

Hesperiam sua Libra tenet, qua condita Roma
(Italy doth the Balance rule, the sign of Rome's foundation).[10]

To put Rome under Libra is symbolically right enough, for Libra is the constellation of law and administration. According to statistics more lawyers and administrators are born under Libra than under any other constellation, and Rome's great contribution to the civilization of Europe was her law and her administrative system. There is, however, one other characteristic of Rome which is as ancient and undying as her law, and that is her desire to have someone for whom to legislate, in other words her traditional imperialism. No city in the world can equal Rome in this, and she should therefore, along with Libra, have been founded under Aries or Leo, and preferably both.

The date usually given was traditional, namely the festival of the Parilia, which fell a.d.vii kal. mai., on April 21st, and we are further told by Solinus and Lydus that the Sun was in Taurus, Jupiter in Pisces, and the four remaining planets in Scorpio—which is physically impossible. There is no getting at 'the truth' in such a complicated state of affairs, but it is possible to calculate a horoscope of Rome for April 753 (the usual year) with the Moon in Libra. If the Sun be put on the midheaven in the imperialistic Aries, with the full Moon opposite, then the imperialistic Leo will rise. By a curious chance the sign and constellation Aries were both full of planets at the time, and the Libran full moon occurred on April 11th (Julian).[11]

TABLE 2 *Longitudes of Planets in Tarrutius' Horoscope of Rome*

	tropical longitude		*sidereal longitude (Spica 29° 0' Virgo)*	
Sun	13° 30'	Aries	26° 50'	Aries
Moon	14° 54'	Libra	28° 14'	Libra
Mercury	7° 48'	Aries	21° 08'	Aries
Venus	3° 48'	Aries	17° 08'	Aries
Mars	13° 12'	Pisces	26° 32'	Pisces
Jupiter	8° 42'	Aries	22° 2'	Aries
Saturn	15° 54'	Scorpio	29° 14'	Scorpio
Uranus	6° 30'	Aries	19° 50'	Aries
Neptune	17° 48'	Aries	0° 28'	Taurus
Midheaven	14°	Aries	27°	Aries
Ascendant	0°	Leo	13°	Leo

It is not surprising that a city should be thought to have a horoscope when we remember that the oldest form of prediction from celestial phenomena was for war or peace, plenty of dearth, in fact, for public and not for individual affairs. But the old astrologers had not the modern need to think of the planets as causes rather than significators. If a raven proclaimed the end of an epoch by alighting on the left, that would not make it, for them, the cause of the ensuing disaster, even if it quoth: 'Nevermore!' One could, at a stretch, imagine some causative influence at work in the horoscope of the foundation of a city, but why bother, when no causative influence can be adduced in the ancient practice of 'horary astrology'?

For the 'horary art' is astrological divination, or the art of answering questions by noting the time of asking. It differs from ordinary divination in that the practitioner is less free to choose what symbols shall be significant to his unconscious mind. Such are the rules that twelve astrologers, confronted with the same chart, ought to give twelve very similar answers; and although the basic quality of the answer, the yes or no of it, depends upon the planets, the details and circumstances are derived from a knowledge of the many associations of the signs of the zodiac.

Here for example is a question asked one Saturday morning in A.D. 479. The astrologer was Palchus, an Egyptian living in Smyrna under the emperor Zeno of Constantinople, and the date was the 20th Epiphi (Egyptian calendar) in the 195th year of the Era of Diocletian. In the Gregorian calendar the date was July 14th; the time, 8.30 a.m.

The question was of the safety of a ship bound for Smyrna from Alexandria, which had failed to arrive. With the omission of one or two technical terms, this is the astrologer's answer as translated by Richard Garnett[12]:

> Finding that the lords of the day and hour, being Saturn and Mars, were both in the ascendant, and observing that the moon was applying to an aspect of Saturn, I said that the ship had encountered a violent storm, but had escaped, inasmuch as Venus and the moon were beheld by Jupiter ... The nature of the question not having been disclosed to me, I said it concerned a ship, because the Part of Fortune was in Sagittarius, rising nigh Argo, and its lord was in a watery sign.

This, incidentally, would surprise modern astrologers, for Sagittarius is not now thought to have anything to do with shipping. The Part of Fortune is an imaginary point obtained by adding to the

Ascendant the difference in longitude between the Sun and Moon. Since it does not exist as a material body, some astrologers think better to do without it; and it was not, at the time, 'rising nigh Argo', but Argo would rise when its position came to the ascendant, about nine and a half hours later. Furthermore, the Part of Fortune was just passing out of Sagittarius and into Capricorn. That, however, is by the way.

Palchus continues:

And observing that the Ascendant was in a bi-corporeal sign, and that (several other technicalities) were one and all in bi-corporeal signs, I said that the ship's company would pass from one vessel to another. And as Venus, who has dominion over birds, was in opposition to Sagittarius, I said they would bring some birds with them. And because the moon was in the house of Mars and in the terms of Mercury, I said they would probably bring some books or papers, and some brazen vessels on account of the moon being in Scorpio.

Scorpio being the house of Mars, the vessels might equally well have been of iron; but we must always allow a diviner to use his intuition. The double-bodied signs are not only the Twins and the Two Fishes, but, since Ptolemy had such a mania for symmetry, the Archer, half man and half horse, and also the Virgin with her ear of corn. The Balance, with its two scales, ought to be 'double-bodied' but is not.

'And observing that Aesculapius was rising along with the moon' — this again means 'would rise when the moon rose', for the moon was far below the horizon; and 'Aesculapius' is the constellation Ophiuchus, the Serpent-bearer, well outside the zodiac — 'I said they would bring medicines.'

Being asked concerning the time of their arrival, I said that this would take place when the Moon entered Aquarius. They arrived accordingly, and being questioned respecting their detention, replied that it was owing to a violent tempest, and that, the sea being cloven, their prow struck against a rock and was broken, and that they were mightily tossed to and fro. But having made a harbour, they shifted into another vessel the cargo they had brought with them, which consisted of birds, and blank writing paper on account of Mercury being aphaeretic [i.e. he signified death rather than life], and cooking vessels on account of Scorpio, and a full medicine chest by reason of Aesculapius.

This is believed to be the earliest recorded reading of a horary chart, and if it all happened as described it certainly was a great success. By 'paper' is meant of course papyrus, which stood high on the list of Egyptian exports.

Palchus, who, as the reader can now judge for himself, was nothing if not brilliant, will also provide us with a splendid example of the use of the zodiac in making elections of favourable times for starting things. This is the technique of trying to ensure the success of an undertaking by beginning it at an astrologically favourable moment. It means that not only must the horoscope of the moment be good in itself, but, more important still, its comparison to the horoscopes of the people concerned must be favourable likewise. It is no use choosing a moment when the Moon is in conjunction to both the benefics, Venus and Jupiter, and failing to notice that the degree upon the Ascendant is the very same degree where Saturn stood at your birth! But if you are going mining, any astrologer would say that the Moon should be in Capricorn, which rules mines, or else in Taurus (the earth) and in aspect of Saturn. The Moon in an airy sign would mean no mining, and in a watery sign would threaten flooding.

The art of making elections has existed for two thousand years, yet many modern astrologers do not believe in it, having had experience of its failures. Sometimes it is downright impossible to find any moment at all which will favour the native in a particular direction before a certain date; and at other times the 'election' remains blandly ineffective. The reason for this is clear enough, even without abandoning the presuppositions of astrology. The real time of beginning any undertaking is when it is effectively decided upon, when there is no longer any question of going back, not the moment of birth of the idea, and not the purely formal moment of carrying out an already fixed intention, except in the case of official functions like the foundation of a city or the opening of a congress. But it can be seen from this that the effective time of the 'election' will not be the time you choose, but the time when you chose the time!

Here then is one of the earliest known examples of an 'election' which went wrong. It too is taken from Palchus.[13]

Pamprepios was a native of Egyptian Thebes who came to Athens and taught philosophy there in the fifth century A.D. He was one of those unreliable characters who are too clever by half, and bring interested in occult science had contrived to gain a reputation as a magician before he was expelled from the city. He then went to Byzantium, trying always to move in the highest circles, and having left there, not perhaps by choice, he met in Asia Minor a certain Leontios, whom he persuaded to set himself up as emperor in opposition to the legitimate ruler Zeno in Constantinople. This then is Palchus' account of the coronation of Leontios:

> He was crowned at a time elected by two astrologers, and at once lost both his kingdom and his luck ... Those who made the election much fancied the rising of Sun, Jupiter, and Mars, with Mercury succedent to them, and the good aspects of the Moon to Saturn and Jupiter. But they did not pay attention to the fact that Mercury, ruler of the day and of the next ensuing hour was in evil case; for he was at his greatest elongation from the Sun, which makes him to signify violent death, and his only aspect was to Saturn. Also Venus, being isolated, could not cure the evil, for the Sun intercepted her. Nor did they observe that the Moon, being the dispositor (or ruler) of the Sun, Ascendant, Jupiter, Mars, and the preceding new moon, was in her fall and afflicted. And the fact that the Sun, Ascendant, and Jupiter were together did not suffice to outweigh those other aspects and prevent them from working.

Modern astrologers would agree that the election was badly made, but in the main for different reasons. Though they would readily grant that bad aspects can interfere with good ones, the converse proposition might be less easy to defend. They would ignore the fact that Mercury rules the first hour on Wednesday, nor would they think it a sign of danger to find him so far away from the Sun. They would however be horrified to discover that the Moon was in her fall (that is, in Scorpio), beneath the earth, and applying to a conjunction of Saturn, which is a sure sign of failure! There are also at least two errors in the text, since the Moon is incorrectly stated to be in Cancer, and the longitudes of Mars and Jupiter are interchanged.

As it turned out, Leontios and his lieutenant Illus were defeated at the castle of Papyrion by a land and sea expedition under John the Scythian. They fled, and waited a long time in another castle for the brother of Illus, but on learning that he had been killed by John they realized that their astrologer had deceived them, so they cut off his head and hung his body from the battlements. And any modern astrologer would admit that, if he really chose a time when the Moon was going to conjunction of Saturn, he certainly deserved it.

If we recalculate with modern methods the horoscopes by Palchus to be found in various Greek manuscripts in Paris and Florence,[13] we find that the positions of the planets average, in most of them, 3 degrees less in longitude than is computed by our tables. This cannot be due to carelessness or inefficiency on the part of Palchus, for the error is consistently on the same side; it can only mean that Palchus was not measuring the zodiac from the equinox. His zodiac in fact was sidereal, not tropical, and his equinox lay in 27° Pisces.

In the Michigan Astrological Papyrus No. 1, of the second century A.D., we find the explicit statement[14]: 'The marking-points of the Sun are four, two equinoctial in the eighth degrees of Aries and Libra, and the tropics, the summer tropic in the eighth degree of Cancer and the winter tropic in the eighth degree of Capricorn.' This statement was long out of date; but again in the *Apotelesmatica* of Pseudo-Manetho, a work of the second to fourth centuries A.D. reflecting the older tradition, we are told:[15] 'The circle that turns the season of fiery summer is described in the sky by the all-seeing Sun in its course upon the eighth degree of Cancer.'

The eighth degree, however, was not universally accepted, for Manilius says at the very end of his third book:[16] 'So one degree in tropical signs is to be distinguished, which moves the world and alters the seasons ... Some place this power in the eighth degree, others prefer the tenth, and there has even been a writer who has allotted to the first degree the alteration and shortening of the days.'

And Columella, writing about A.D. 60, has a similar comment:[17] 'Winter which begins about viii kal.Jan. in the eighth degree of

Capricorn ... And I am not overlooking Hipparchus' argument, which teaches that the solstices and equinoxes happen not in the eighth but in the first degrees of signs. In this rustic science I follow the calendar of Eudoxus and Meton, which fits in with the public festivals.'

These quotations, with one or two others,[18] explain a difficulty which astrologers have had to overlook for centuries. For when they used to claim that their science was many thousands of years old, and also that the twelve visible constellations were much less important than the invisible 'signs', they had no sound way of explaining why the names of both were the same. For the date when the two zodiacs coincided must in any case be less than two thousand years ago, since the difference between them does not yet amount to 30 degrees; and if the names are older than two thousand years, it is hard to believe that they became tacked on to the visible constellations some time after they had been chosen to express the influences of invisible signs—especially since the name of the Twins does seem to refer to the two stars Castor and Pollux, and the name of the Scorpion to the curling tail seen in the eastern half of that constellation. And the only other explanation was to assume that the names had been given 26,000 years B.C., leaving a rather hungry gap in history.

To discover the precession of the equinoxes at all would in any case take several centuries; for if the vernal equinox were marked by the day when Spica rose at dusk—the acronychal rising, as it is called—then a century later this measurement would only be in error by a day and a half, and, allowing for variations of visibility, this might easily be disregarded, especially as it was difficult to check.

The actual time required for the making of the discovery seems to have been from about 500 B.C., when the Babylonian astronomer Naburiannu located the equinoctial point in 10 degrees of the constellation Aries, through the time of Kidinnu, who about 373 B.C. located it in 8 degrees of that constellation, until some time between 150 and 126 B.C., the end of Hipparchus' life.

But although precession had been discovered, it was not at once adopted and taken seriously by users of the zodiac. It was much easier to accept Kidinnu's statement that the equinoxes were in the eighth degrees of the constellations and then do nothing about it—

since they moved at a rate vaguely guessed to be one degree in a century, to ignore this and treat them as fixed. Thus arose the Hellenistic Zodiac, which was a tropical zodiac measured from its tropics in the eighth degrees of Aries, Cancer, Libra, and Capricorn. This is the zodiac used by Manetho and the Michigan Papyrus, and referred to by Columella, Manilius and Pliny. Correct about 373 B.C., it continued in common use in the time of Augustus, when it was already 5 degrees out, and indeed for some time after. The reason may have been that Greek astronomers did not know from which stars the zodiac had originally been measured. Possibly this key fact was kept as a religious secret by whatever Babylonian or Egyptian priest first divulged the practice of individual astrology.

Hipparchus was the founder of the Tropical Zodiac because he first suggested that it might be convenient to measure the zodiac from the tropical points. Ptolemy in his *Tetrabiblos* justifies this on astrological grounds, as if it were the proper way to analyse human character from the stars, but it seems more likely that Hipparchus adopted it for the same reason that the equinoctial 'First Point of Aries' is still used as the chief celestial measuring-point, namely as the best way of fixing the calendar conveniently to the seasons. The ancient world had long been bothered by its many lunar calendars, which were about eleven days short, as the Muslim calendar still is, and therefore had to be adjusted every two or three years with the insertion of a whole extra month—as the Muslim calendar is not.

The location of the equinox came in fact as a godsend to agriculture, which hitherto had been forced to time its operations by the stars—hence the traditional injunctions found in Virgil, Hesiod, and other agricultural writers. Hesiod was giving sound and valuable advice to farmers when he wrote:[19]

> Begin your harvest when the Pleiads come
> To rising, and your ploughing when they set.

But, after Julius Caesar's reform of the Roman calendar in 46 B.C., Virgil's corresponding instructions (in the rather engaging translation of John Jackson) were an archaism:[20]

Twice men gather the teeming produce; two are the seasons of harvest; either so soon as Taÿgete the Pleiad has shown her fair face to the earth, and spurned beneath her foot the despised streams of Ocean, or when she flees before the sign of the watery Fish, and descends from heaven—a sadder maid—into the wintry waves.

The Pleiades are invisible for about forty days while the sun is in the end of Aries and in Taurus, but the exact length of time depends on the latitude, the visibility, and the nature of the horizon. The name is thought to mean 'The Sailing Stars', because their morning rising marks for Hesiod the beginning of the season of navigation. The Greeks, however, thought it might mean 'The Doves'. The Hyades on the other hand, which the Greeks took to mean 'The Rainy Ones', may possibly mean 'The Little Pigs', which was their name in Latin.

The next step was the invention of parapegmata. A parapegma (with a long E in the Greek) was a stone tablet with 360 holes arranged in rows of thirty, corresponding to the Sun's longitude in the Tropical Zodiac, and thus forming a zodiacal calendar. It was presumably put up like a public notice-board in the agora of any Greek town, and every day the responsible official would put in the proper hole a stick, which might be marked on the head with the date in the civil calendar. Thus the 22nd of Hecatombaion would be marked with the letters $\Theta \, \Phi$ (meaning '9 waning', since the days in the last third of the month were numbered backwards), and this would be inserted into whatever degree of the Cancer row was appropriate that year. The normal length of the Athenian year was 354 days, and New Year's Day was kept as close as possible to the summer solstice by inserting a month called Second Poseideon whenever necessary.

Plate No. 3 shows part of a broken parapegma found at Miletus.[21] A translation of the right-hand column of fragment B follows. The large isolated Λ at the beginning means '30', referring to the thirty days of Aquarius (some signs have thirty-one days), and thirty holes can be counted in this column, but nine of them occur over the word 'Andromeda' because for nine days there would be no risings or settings to observe; the rest, by chance, fall for the most part on successive days, but altogether there are eighteen blank days out of thirty, signified by the eighteen holes between the lines of text, and twelve holes at the beginnings of lines:

Λ

∘ Sun in Aquarius

∘ (Leo) begins its morning setting

and Lyra sets

∘ Bird's evening setting begins

∘ Andromeda begins morning rising

∘ Waterbearer in middle of rising

∘ Horse begins morning rising

∘ Centaur completes morning setting

∘ Hydrus completes morning setting

∘ Cetus begins evening

setting

∘ Arrow sets, west winds

constant

∘ Bird completes evening setting

∘ (Arcturus) evening rising

The invention of the parapegma was ascribed to the philosopher Democritos, the 'laughing philosopher' and principal exponent in ancient Greece of atomic materialism — strange though it seems nowadays that a materialist should laugh. He was indeed a man of very wide knowledge, but the invention may equally well have been made by one of the contemporary astronomers, perhaps Meton or Euktemon. The date of it must in any case have been about 400 B.C., and this shows that the zodiac, as a calendar, must have been already known in Greece at that date.

The zodiac at this stage was a division of the ecliptic circle into twelve equal divisions of 30 degrees each, but we cannot assume that these divisions had the characteristics which we associate nowadays with the twelve signs. They may well have had no ruling planets and

77

no supposed influence on human character, for horoscopic astrology was possibly unknown in Greece in 400 B.C. And in any case the precession of the equinoxes was still undiscovered, so no distinction will have been made between signs and constellations, and the constellations of that time will have been twelve equal divisions, the tropics and equinoxes being in the eighth degrees of the first, fourth, seventh and tenth of them.

The earliest allusion to horoscopic astrology in Greek literature was probably that passage of Eudoxus in which he expressly dissociated himself from the astrological predictions of the 'Chaldeans'. But the passage has not survived, and we only have the statement on authority of Cicero, some four centuries later.[22]

Plato was a contemporary of Eudoxus, born twenty years earlier and dying eight years later, so he must at least have heard of predictional astrology, since Eudoxus came to stay in his house. But Plato's zodiac is not by any means all that modern astrologers might desire; for it suggests that the rulership of planets over signs was not yet irremovably established, if indeed established at all; and thus conceivably the art of personal astrology was still only in an early stage of growth, or had as yet been only partly revealed by the initiates of Babylon or Egypt.

Plato's use of the zodiac can best be illustrated by direct quotation:[23]

Zeus, the mighty lord holding the reins of a winged chariot, leads the way in heaven, ordering all and caring for all; and there follows him the heavenly array of gods and demigods, divided into eleven bands; for only Hestia is left at home in the house of heaven; but the rest of the twelve greater deities march in their appointed order. And they see in the interior of heaven many blessed sights; and there are ways to and fro, along which the happy gods are passing, each one fulfilling his own work; and anyone may follow whom he pleases, for jealousy has no place in the heavenly choir.

The eleven companies have been supposed to refer to the zodiac of only eleven signs, in which the Scorpion's claws occupied the space allotted afterwards to Libra; but no less probably Plato meant that Zeus the sky-god should go first, leading eleven companies besides his own. For Plato speaks of the planet Mercury as 'the planet sacred to Hermes',[24] showing that, for him, Hermes was a divine power to which, incidentally, a planet was dedicated. Only later did Zeus in Greek and Jupiter in Latin come to be thought of no longer as the supreme god of heaven, but simply as the power of a particular planet. This loss of their principal gods, who became no more than the mechanical powers of planets, may be one reason why the Greeks and Romans welcomed so eagerly the gods of the Orient, Cybele, Iris and Osiris, Sarapis, Mithra, who were genuinely potent and had not been devalued by either astrology or rationalism.

Plato knew also that men could be born under the influence of a god. He says in the *Phaedrus*:[25]

Now the lover who is the attendant of Zeus is better able to bear the winged god [i.e. Eros], and can endure a heavier burden; but the attendants and companions of Ares [i.e. Mars], when under the influence of love, if they fancy that they have been at all wronged, are ready to kill and put an end to themselves and their beloved. And in like manner he who follows in the train of any other god honours him, and imitates him as far as he is able while the impression lasts; and this is his way of life and the manner of his behaviour to his beloved and to every other in the first period of his earthly existence. Everyone chooses the object of his affections according to his character, and this he makes his god, and fashions and adorns as a sort of image which he is to fall down and worship. The followers of Zeus desire that their beloved should have a soul like him; and, therefore, they seek some philosophical and imperial nature, and when they have found him and loved him, they do all they can to create such a nature in him ... But those who are the followers of Hera seek a royal love, and when they have found him they do the same with him; and in like manner the followers of Apollo, and of every other god walking in the ways of their god, seek a love who is to be like their god, and when they have found him, they themselves imitate their god, and persuade their love to do the same, and bring him into harmony with the form and ways of the god as far as they can; for they have no feelings of envy or mean enmity towards their beloved, but they do their utmost to

79

create in him the greatest likeness of themselves and the god whom they honour.

So here is Plato genuinely saying that 'followers of Mars'—which may or may not mean persons born under Mars—are capable of murder when crossed in love, but that 'those who have the nature of Zeus' (who is not of necessity the same as Jupiter) are more patient. And the 'followers of Hera' may be those born under Aquarius.

But it is most important to distinguish Plato's spiritual attitude to the zodiac from the more mechanical attitude of the average astrologer. Plato had no use for the angry assumption which is sometimes vented in the words: 'I did not ask to be born.' He was convinced, on the contrary, that the soul chooses to descend, and even if it chooses unwisely it is none the less responsible for its presence here. Hence the 'followers of Zeus' are not those born under the mechanical influence of a celestial sign or planet, but those who have chosen to manifest according to, or to be guided principally by, that particular mode of the Creative Force which among the Greeks was called Zeus. All the gods are part of God, but some express one aspect and some another, and so do we ourselves.

Further, though Plato calls the planets 'visible gods', and 'animals', that is to say living powers, the rulers of the twelve signs are not for him the planets, since they are specifically stated to be invisible;[26] they were the twelve principal manifestations of the Creative Force which runs the universe.

So the Twelve Gods of Plato are neither the planets nor the signs of the zodiac. They are the Dodeka Theoi, the twelve Greek gods who were pictured on the central milestone of Athens, from which all distances were measured. And Plato is not the only one to tell us of the Twelve Gods; the full list comes from Manilius:[27]

Pallas rules the woolly Ram, and Venus guards the Bull,
Apollo has the handsome Twins, and Mercury the Crab,
Jove, with the Mother of the Gods, himself is Leo's lord;
The Virgin with her Ear of Corn to Ceres falls; the Scales
To Vulcan's smithy; while to Mars the warlike Scorpion cleaves;
The Hunter's human part Diana rules, but what's of horse
Is ruled by Vesta, with the straitened stars of Capricorn;

Aquarius is Juno's sign, as opposite to Jove,
And Neptune owns the pair of Fish that in the heaven move.

This list of gods is arranged so far as possible in opposite pairs, and is not inappropriate, except that Vesta, who is Hestia the hearth-goddess, has no particular connection with horses or goats. The attribution of Cancer to Mercury, though it may shock modern astrologers, comes from Egypt, and is further justified by the myth in which the infant Hermes, while still in his cradle, found a tortoise at the mouth of his cave on Mount Cyllene and made its shell into a lyre, on which he immediately played. And Cancer, though called the Crab by the Greeks and Babylonians, is basically just a hard-shelled creature, a tortoise to the Chinese and a scarab to the Egyptians.

Pallas Athene, or in Latin Minerva, is perfectly suitable for Aries, which rules the head and is a warlike sign, since she sprang fully armed from the head of Zeus. For the Ear of Corn no ruler could be more suitable than Demeter-Ceres. Diana as the huntress is obviously correct for Sagittarius, and her brother Apollo, the spirit of music and prophecy, rules the opposite sign. The many-breasted 'Diana of the Ephesians' would equate with the Mother of the Gods and be placed in Leo. Taurus and Scorpio have their usual rulers, and the Scales, as the only manufactured object in the list, are naturally given to Vulcan the craftsman. As for the Fishes, their allotment to Neptune ought to be welcomed by astrologers, who have been trying for the past hundred years to hand them over to the planet of that name!

The Twelve Gods are illustrated in a most beautiful wellhead sculpture (Plate 6) now in the Capitoline Museum in Rome,[28] and also on the Altar of Gabii now in the Louvre.

The division into twelve evidently fascinated Plato, as it has so many others, and he stipulates: 'We will divide the city into portions, first founding temples to Hestia, to Zeus, and to Athene, in a spot which we will call the Acropolis, and surround with a circular wall, making the division of the entire city and country radiate from this point. The twelve portions shall be equalized by the provision that those which are of good land shall be smaller, while those of inferior quality shall be larger.' And later: 'There are to be twelve hamlets in the twelve country districts, each with a temple to the proper one

F

of the Twelve Gods, but Zeus, Athene and Hestia have temples everywhere.'[29]

Zeus has temples everywhere as the supreme god of the present world — though he is not the Creator. If he ruled any sign of the zodiac in Plato's time, it was still Leo and not Sagittarius. Athene has temples everywhere as patron goddess of Attica and Athens, and Hestia as goddess of the home. But Plato was not quite satisfied with the list of the Twelve Gods, and suggested that the god of the underworld, Pluto or Hades, ought to be included. 'The law will say', he writes,[30] 'that there are twelve feasts dedicated to the Twelve Gods', and he adds that Pluto is to have his feast in the twelfth month and not be excluded as a denizen of the underworld, for warlike men should realize that he is the best friend of man.

The twelfth month, both at Athens and for Plato,[31] would be that preceding the summer solstice, and since he begins his list with Zeus, who rules over Leo, perhaps he meant to substitute Pluto god of the underworld for Hermes ruler of Cancer, the guide of souls to the world below. Yet one cannot help feeling that the power to be excluded should have been Hestia, the hearth-goddess, who according to the passage in the *Phaedrus*[32] 'alone remains in the house of the gods' and does not make the circuit of heaven with the others. By this means Pluto could have ruled Capricorn, which was then the place of the winter solstice and, as the lowest part of the sun's path, the natural symbol of death and resurrection.

Modern astrologers would like Pluto the planet, discovered in 1930, to rule either Aries or Scorpio, and they can quote Plato's statement that Pluto the god is 'the best friend of warlike men'. But planets and gods should not be equated too easily. Uranus, whose name means 'heaven', has fitted well enough to Aquarius the sign of the rain-cloud, but Neptune the planet, though commonly allotted to Pisces, has shown no evidence of affinity for the sea, and Pluto the planet may yet turn out to have no connection with the underworld either through Scorpio as the sign associated with death or through Capricorn as the sign of the descent into hell.

And Capricorn, being the sign of the lowest depths, is also the sign of reascent. In Porphyry's essay 'On the Cave of the Nymphs', written towards A.D. 300, we are told that souls descend into generation in Cancer and begin their return to heaven in Capricorn.

Cancer is warm and moist, the sign of the summer tropic, when the material world is most powerful; Capricorn is stony and hard, where material seductions are overcome by deep thought and aspiration. There is a picture by Blake which illustrates the Cave of the Nymphs, from the passage in the *Odyssey* where it is described.[33]

Plato, who taught reincarnation, certainly knew of these astrological speculations, but to say so is not to accuse him of 'being' an astrologer, nor of 'believing in' astrology, as the superstitious materialist may fear. The average modern scholar ignores the gods, and thereby becomes incapable of understanding Plato when he talks about them; his nearest approach to understanding involves the mental substitution for the word 'gods' of some such phrase as 'the forces of the unconscious'—which of course is not far out, but does imply an attempt to devaluate the gods and get them so far as possible under control of the conscious rationalizing intellect. This will work so long as the weather is fair and you are alone in your study, but the intellect is not an impenetrable bomb-proof shelter against the earthquakes of the unconscious. To Plato the gods were certainly not dead; his modern admirers think they are. In consequence they worship them under other names: the Earth-Mother has been rechristened Matter, Hermes is called Science or Rationalism, and so forth.

The object of such renaming is evident; it rises from that fear of the unconscious which always infects the conscious mind when the latter is striving for exclusive control and trying to pretend that Reason is the only tool that it possesses. Instead of admitting God to be Wisdom, Love, and Power, it likes to pretend that logical analysis can keep the world under control, that the human mind will never have any more capacities than it has at present, and that the only reality is what it can understand, namely that static half of Wisdom which can be boiled down and safely catalogued as technique and information. The advantage of saying 'Science' instead of 'Hermes', and 'Matter' instead of 'Demeter', is the implication that there simply is no power or love to bother about, only facts, only information. And as if this defence against the power of creation were not enough, some thinkers assure us that the mind does not exist, but is simply a misleading word to describe certain phenomena. But 'Matter is the only Reality' only makes sense if we translate it

'Demeter is the only Reality', for only in virtue of the Power inherent in material phenomena do we have any material experience at all. Materialism is just the worship of the Great Mother under another name.

To a universal mind like Plato's there is no invidious distinction between science and religion, or between psychology and astronomy. The problem is to adapt ourselves to the world in which we live, and any religion which enables us to do this is a true religion, and of necessity in harmony with science and astronomy and psychology. When an astronomer hates astrology, or a materialist hates religion, he is uncritically copying the intolerance of the monotheistic Church, which claimed that there was only one valid adaptation to life. To Greek astronomers the zodiac may have been only a calendar, and to astrologers only a mechanical method of divination, but that it had a spiritual significance for the greater minds is shown by a remark put into the mouth of Aristophanes in the *Symposium*:[34] 'Hoar-frost and hail and blight spring from the excesses and disorders of this element of love, which to know in relation to the revolutions of the heavenly bodies and the seasons of the year is termed astronomy. Furthermore all sacrifices and the whole province of divination, which is the art of communion between gods and men —these I say are concerned only with the preservation of the good and the cure of the evil love.'

In other words, all human problems are of relationship, and all relationships are symbolized in the zodiac, where the twelve types make all possible combinations as they circle round the focus of life; and divination is the art of reconciling conscious and unconscious, whether by the interpretation of dreams, as in psycho-analysis, or by ritual, as in religion. Divination is now despised in obedience to the negative superstition that no such thing can be possible, or else exaggerated by the positive superstition that one can extract from the unconscious, by methods which do not emerge from it, such as numerology, mere facts which are not in it in any case, such as the date of the next election or the winner of the two-thirty. The divination mentioned by Aristophanes is the reconciliation of conscious and unconscious, and this is closely allied to the reconciliation of God and man.

Plato, at the end of his life, or one of his immediate pupils, wrote a short dialogue called *Epinomis*, the aim of which, according to Mr Harward, was to reform Hellenic religion by substituting the worship of the planets for that of the Greek gods and goddesses — although, of course, this aim is only put forward in very guarded terms, in order not to offend the Delphic Oracle. More probably Mr Harward's opinion should be attributed to the monotheistic prejudice which for so long has obliged classical scholars to pretend that the Greeks found their gods unsatisfactory. If we cannot recognize the divinity of Athena, Plato certainly could.

That the zodiac had been brought to Greece about 400 B.C. and used for parapegmata is certain. Whether it came from Babylon or Egypt we shall consider in a later chapter. Meanwhile the *Epinomis* only tells us that Plato at the end of his life accepted the zodiac as an archetype, a deeply religious symbol of the harmony of the Many and the One; and that is exactly what it is.

TABLE 3 *Plants of the Signs and Planets* according to the Greek astrologers

(from the *Catalogus Codicum Astrologorum Graecorum*, VIII (3), 151 (best), 139 foll.; VII, 232; VIII (2), 159; XII, 126; VIII (4) 253–262.)

ARIES	Sage (*salvia triloba*); water milfoil (*myriophyllum spicatum*).
TAURUS	Vervain (*verbena officinalis*); clover (*trifolium*).
GEMINI	Holy vervain (*v. supina*); wild *gladiolus*.
CANCER	Comfrey (*symphytum bulbosum*); *mandragora officinalis*.
LEO	*Cyclamen graecum* or *neapolitanum*; another unidentified.
VIRGO	Calaminth (*calamintha*).*
LIBRA	Scorpion-tail (*scorpiurus sulcata*); 'needle-plant' (*belonike*).
SCORPIO	*Artemisia*; houndstongue (*cynoglossum*).
SAGITTARIUS	Pimpernel (blue or red) (*anagallis*).*
CAPRICORN	Sorrel (*rumex patientia*); stinking tutsan (*hypericum hircinum*), which smells of goat.
AQUARIUS	Edder-wort (*dracunculus*); fennel (*foeniculum*); buttercup (*ranunculus*).
PISCES	*Aristolochia* (long- or round-leaved birthwort).

* Other(s) unidentified
See *Wild Flowers of Attica*, by S. C. Atchley (Oxford, 1938).

85

SATURN   Asphodel (*asphodelus*); white heliotrope (*h. euro-paeum*); houseleek (*sempervivum*); frothy poppy (*silene viscosum*).

JUPITER   Agrimony (*eupatorium*); 'chrysacanthus'.

MARS   Lambstongue (*arnoglossum*); butterburr (*petasites*); *peucedanum* (hog's fennel).

SUN   Sunspurge (*euphorbia helioscopia*); chicory (*cichorium intybus*).

VENUS   Vervain (as Taurus); white rose (*r. sempervirens*); man orchis; Venus's allheal, i.e. maidenhair fern (*adiantum capillus-Veneris*).

MERCURY   Mullein (*verbascum*); cinquefoil (*potentilla*).

MOON   Paeony (*paeonia*); helenium (*inaula h.*; but this would seem to be a solar plant).

6. *The Zodiac in China*

NOT so long ago, if you asked a Chinese his age, he would reply simply with the name of an animal. He would say, for example: Dog, Rat, or Monkey—naming the year of his birth. Twelve animals—the Rat, the Ox, the Tiger, the Hare, the Dragon, the Serpent, the Horse, the Sheep, the Monkey, the Cock, the Dog, the Boar—formed the Chinese 'circle of animals'; and, except for the Ox falling into second place, it does not bear much resemblance to our Western zodiac. There is, however, a partial resemblance. The star Spica (Alpha Virginis) was called by the Chinese Kio (also spelt Chio and Güo) and regarded as the lower Horn of the Dragon, the upper horn being Arcturus; and if we therefore equate the Dragon with Libra, which adjoins Spica, we shall have the Serpent for Scorpio, which is very appropriate; the Horse for Sagittarius, which is right; the Sheep for Capricorn, which is again suitable since the Chinese regard goats and sheep as much the same animal; then the Monkey in place of the Man with the Urn, which is not far out; and the Tiger very properly in the place of our Lion. The Hare, however, which would thus correspond to Virgo, does not equate to our constellation Lepus the Hare, for the latter is not in the zodiac but lies south of Orion's feet.

At first sight, it seems, no Chinese scholar is likely to thank us for this comparison. For in the first place it leaves six of the animals unaccounted for—the Rat, Ox, Hare, Cock, Dog, and Boar—even if we accept the Dragon in place of the Scorpion's Claws which are commonly called Libra. Secondly, it is an hour-circle, and therefore like any clock is numbered clockwise, whereas the zodiac is numbered widdershins; hence any resemblance to the zodiac should be in reverse order. Thirdly, it is closely related to the twenty-eight *hsiu* (asterisms, or mansions) of Chinese astronomy, which are not a zodiac. Fourthly (if more reasons were needed), the Chinese equate the Rat with Aries, the Ox with Taurus, and so on round the circle. The Rat rules the third watch of the night, just after midnight, noon is the hour of the Horse, and sunset that of the Cock.

If the circle of animals is transferred from service as marking the twelve months, and used instead to signify the twelve double-hours of the day, a reversal of order of the signs is only to be expected. Scorpio is visibly to the left of Libra when we look at the nocturnal sky, and if Libra culminates in the south at sunset, Scorpio will follow two hours later; hence the same sequence seems to apply. On the other hand from noon to 2 p.m. the sun has moved one-twelfth of a circle to the right, hence the hands of a clock move to the right, and the hour-circle of animals must be counted in that direction. The Chinese day began at midnight, so if Aries as the first sign is given the first double-hour and the direction North, Taurus will rule from 2 till 4 a.m. and correspond to the direction NNE, although visibly Taurus lies to the left of Aries, not to the right.

Thus there ought really to be two circles: an annual circle, the zodiac, counted from right to left, the direction of motion of the sun and moon among the stars; and a diurnal circle, or hour-circle, counted from left to right, the direction of motion of the sun across the sky. And in China both exist.

Our Western zodiac has been known there for several centuries, having been introduced, to all intents and purposes, by the first Jesuit mission under Matteo Ricci, who reached Peking in 1601. Knowledge of it had come through earlier by way of the Central Asian caravan-route, but the Chinese did not use our zodiac until the Jesuits arrived and were able to teach them something of practical value concerning it.

Native Chinese astronomy was based, as we should expect, on different ideas from those of Egypt and Babylon. Instead of paying their chief attention to the ecliptic, of which no more than one-half is ever visible at one time, the Chinese seem to have relied originally on the circumpolar stars, which, weather permitting, are visible all night every night of the year.

The Chinese Empire called itself The Middle Kingdom as being the earthly counterpart of the Middle Kingdom of Heaven, the region of the never-setting stars. The Emperor gave audience seated facing south because he represented the very centre of the central kingdom, namely the Pole Star. This suggests that the custom arose at a date when, as today, there was a star of perceptible brightness very close to the pole; perhaps 3067 *i* Draconis (*T'ien-yi*) which was pole star about 2668 B.C., or else either 42 or 184 Draconis (*T'ai-yi*) about 2260 B.C.[1]

Around the Middle Kingdom the Chinese divided the sky into four palaces, called by the names of the four cardinal points. But in terms of remoteness from the equator the Northern Palace was no more northerly than any other; and the Eastern Palace, comprising the constellation of the Green Dragon, centred on Antares, cannot in the nature of things be any more easterly than any other part of the sky, except when it happens to be rising.

The doctrine of the Palaces is rather obscure, and it has even been claimed that the asterisms within them were counted clockwise in two of them and widdershins in the other two, thereby explaining (with some considerable effort) why the months in the primitive Turkish calendar were named after numbers, but the numbers run in the wrong order![2] Yet this is not impossible, if we remember that the Green Dragon, which corresponds to Spring and the element of Wood, has its head to the south and tail to the north, and so does the White Tiger, which corresponds to Metal and Autumn; but the Red Bird (Fire and Summer) and the Black Tortoise (Earth and Winter) both have their heads to the west and tails to the east, although they are on opposite sides of the sky.

Not until the first or second century A.D., in the time of the later Han, do we find the Chinese giving a name to the ecliptic. They then honoured it with the title of The Yellow Road (*hoang-tao*), the equator being called The Red Road; thus they recognized at that time the superior importance of the ecliptic. However, the 28 asterisms are older than this period, and were not divisions of the ecliptic but of the equator, therefore they cannot rightly be called a zodiac. Further, they were not originally called by the names of animals, any more than were the twelve divisions of the year.

The Mongol chief Argoun wrote to Philippe le Bel in the year of the Ox, which was 1289, as 1955 was for Tibetans 'the year of the Wood Sheep'. This use of a cycle of animals for numbering years appears to be later than their use for numbering months or hours. And if the animals are not an arbitrary list, but had some original appropriateness, then they are likely to have been used first of all to describe the months.

In fact, according to Gustave Schlegel, the choice of animals was made from the seasons at which their activity was most conspicuous. The Cock, for example, is bellicose, and was therefore chosen for October, when preparations for war are made. (The Cock is the Pleiades.) The ape *semnopithecus schistosus* gives birth in November, the tenth month of the Chinese year, when the full moon would, about 1000 B.C., rise near the asterism of Shên the Ape, which is Orion's head. In a similar way the Horse gives birth during the twelfth moon, Snakes come out of the earth at the end of winter (first moon), Hares give birth in March and April, Tigers migrate in April and May, Rats are commonest in July, and Pigs were put out in August to trample and manure the water-logged ground.[3]

That a race should have named its months after the natural phenomena of the seasons is not improbable, and thus far Schlegel may be right; but his actual explanations are not acceptable now because they are thought to put the origin of the animals names too early. We cannot, in order to make Chinese astronomy look ancient, claim that it influenced Babylon rather than the other way round, or that the contact happened in a gratuitously remote antiquity.

According to Carl Bezold,[4] Babylon and China had the same names for the constellations of the two Bears, Draco, Coma Berenices, Orion, and Andromeda. He also showed a distinct Babylonian influence on the astrology of the *Shi-ki*. For in this book, as on Babylonian omen-tablets, sentences are found in which an if-clause describing some celestial phenomenon (for instance 'if there be a halo round the full moon in Fang') is followed by a prediction in one word: 'hunger', 'war', or the like. Mars in Fang (which is part of Scorpio) has the same effect as Mars in Scorpio in Babylon, and Bezold gives seven examples of this, in one of which Mars is actually called by the name of the constellation Boötes; and it was a Babylonian custom to call a planet by the name of a star or constellation whose influence was supposed to be similar. This is the normal type of Babylonian celestial prediction, and was already ancient and traditional when Asshurbanipal built up his great library at Nineveh in the seventh century B.C. Nothing leads us to suppose that this typically Babylonian method was of Chinese origin, so it seems more natural to conclude that it came to China from Babylon; and

Bezold thought that this must have happened before the end of the sixth century B.C.

A similar interchange of names or symbolism is implied in those texts which speak of Venus being worshipped as the White Emperor, Jupiter as the Green (or Blue) Emperor, and the star Denebola (Beta Leonis, the Lion's Tail) as the Yellow Emperor.[5]

The regular Chinese names of the planets are these, with their elements and directions:

TABLE 4

Jupiter	suei-sing	wood	east
Mars	yong-ho	fire	south
Saturn	chen-sing	earth	centre
Venus	t'ai-po	metal	west
Mercury	ch'en-sing	water	north

A purely Chinese type of political prediction, though of later date, is given in the sixth century A.D. by Wei Shou, who describes the traditional catastrophes attributed to various animals.[6] These occur whenever a monster is born on earth, or a miraculous beast is seen in the sky. A two-headed calf means that the temple of the ancestors will be destroyed. A horse in the sky means war, and a cock with horns prefigures the usurpation of royal prerogative by a minor official. The Calamities of the Goat signify that the ruler is not enlightened and makes mistakes in government—nowadays we should expect this every year!—but the Calamities of the Pig are said to be even worse: 'Of all the signs of evil augury, these are much the most common; they signify that a person holding public office is perverse.'

A more cheering view of life is taken in the following passage from a Buddhist text of uncertain date and Central Asian origin:[7]

When the twelve animals have accomplished their meritorious work, they make a solemn vow in the presence of all the Buddhas to see to it that night and day there shall always be one of them travelling, preaching, and converting, while the other eleven remain quietly practising goodness. The Rat begins on the first day of the seventh moon, and converts all beings who have the form of rats. He persuades them to give up evil actions and exhorts them to do good. The others in succession do the same, and when the thirteenth day comes the Rat begins again. In the same way they go on until the end of the twelve months, and the twelve years, with a view to bringing all living beings under the Rule. It is for this reason there are so many meritorious actions upon the earth, since even the animals preach and convert, teaching the unsurpassable doctrine of the Buddha.

To go back, however, to earlier times, a purely solar calendar is not convenient for primitive peoples, since the sun makes the stars invisible, and a purely lunar calendar, though much easier to observe, is useless as a guide to the seasons. To reconcile the two the Chinese had, according to Saussure,[8] a particularly simple self-operating system. With them the full moon to the right of Kio was always the last of the year, and the full moon to the left of it was always the first, regardless whether the year had twelve or thirteen moons. Kio, which was called The Root of Heaven and Chief of the Asterisms, was the star Spica; and it is curious that Spica was also the sidereal marking-star of the zodiac, as we shall later see. This may be only chance, but the Chinese could equally well have chosen several other equatorial stars, particularly Markab, Altair, Antares, Alphard, Procyon, Betelgeuze, the Pleiades or Hyades.

Again, for primitive peoples, to count the number of full moons in a year, and arrange to meet for the autumn fair after a given number, is not so easy, nor so reliable seasonally, as to arrange the meeting when the moon shall be full in conjunction with a particular group of stars. For this purpose the Chinese chose two constellations, Scorpio and Orion. When the Moon was full in conjunction with Antares (Hsin, the Heart of the Green Dragon) they met for the festival of the Renewal of Fire in spring; and the convocation of vassals for the harvest festival, and the execution of criminals at the end of the year, was timed by the full moon near Orion.[9]

At present the full moon of Antares falls about May 31st, and that of Orion about December 17th, which shows the effect of precession, for both these dates are far too late. In the twenty-fourth century B.C., the ostensible date of the Canon of Yao, they would have been about March 30th and October 18th. This, however, does not enable us to date the system at all accurately, since the constellations are so large and the climate may have somewhat altered.

The Chinese had another simple dodge for making the calendar regulate itself. At first, allegedly since the time of the Yellow Emperor, their year had had 366 days, but this was shortened under the Chou to 365¼, and thenceforward the Chinese circle of the sky was divided not into 360 degrees but into 365¼ *tou*, this being a closely approximate average to the daily motion of the sun.

The subdivision of the seasons also became more accurate, through the invention of a method supposedly due to Chou-kong, brother of the first Chou emperor. A 'circle of declination' is drawn from pole to pole of the sky, passing through the sun at the winter solstice, and this is called The First *Chong-ki*. Then the twelve *chong-ki* are intervals of 30·4375 days, twelfth-parts of the circle of 365¼ days, and the fourth, seventh, and tenth of these gave the official (but slightly inexact) Chinese dates of the two equinoxes and the summer solstice.

However, the moon's synodical revolution (her period from new to new) is distinctly less than 30·4375 days, being in fact 29 days 12 hours 44 minutes 2·9 seconds; it could therefore happen that an entire moon, or month, would pass without containing a *chong-ki*. Such a month was regarded as an extra or intercalary month, and bore the same name as the preceding month, followed by the hieroglyph of the 'Prince-between-two-doors'.[10] By this means an extra month was put in whenever required, and the lunar calendar was kept in harmony with the solar seasons. This method is much superior to the ancient Greek system of inserting one or even two extra months whenever the calendar was found to be badly out.

Being a time system and not a spatial system, the *chong-ki* do not provide equal divisions of the ecliptic, and so cannot properly be called a zodiac; but their use suggests that a division into twelve was practised under the Chou, perhaps as early as Chou-Kong himself (1111 B.C.), and possibly even earlier.

When we come to look into the matter of dates, there are four questions to be answered. What is the earliest Chinese record of the 28 asterisms, of the 12 divisions of the sky, and of the two sets of animal names?

The earliest Chinese astronomical document is the Yao-tien, or Canon of Yao, which forms the first chapter of the Shu King, or Book of History, supposedly compiled by Confucius in the early fifth century B.C.[11] This was, so to speak, the first press-cutting book on record, for it consisted of famous speeches and enactments; but in its present form it was long thought to be of early Han date, and merely a reconstruction from memory, with perhaps a few fragments discovered in remote localities; for it was assumed that no Chinese book could be older than the Burning of the Books in 213 B.C.

More recently, with a better knowledge of the evolution of the Chinese language, scholars have decided not to believe in the total destruction of China's early literature. This does not mean, however, that we can take any ancient text at its face value; for Chinese scholars did not copy their texts in the perfunctory manner of medieval monks, without bothering to understand what they were writing; being scholars, and not merely scribes, they made sense of their texts, brought them up to date, and sometimes wrote commentaries on them. In consequence, of course, no Chinese text can be relied on as a verbatim expression of the thought of its ostensible author.

Further, in the early centuries A.D. Chinese astronomers were learning to compute backwards what the appearance of the sky would have been at epochs in the past, and having done so they thought it only natural to insert into ancient books statements of what they knew to have been the case. Hence the allegations of scholars that such statements are largely 'forgeries' of the sixth century A.D. or even later.

This is why we cannot take too seriously the statement that in the twenty-ninth year of Lu-siang, which would be 544 B.C., the cold winter was attributed to the fact that Jupiter had gone too far, and instead of being in *Sing-ki* (Sagittarius–Capricorn) had gone on into *hiuen-hiao* (Capricorn–Aquarius). We can, however, parallel the phenomenon, which is only due to the slight eccentricity of Jupiter's orbit; for

in December	1931	Jupiter turned retrograde in	22½°	Leo	tropical
in January	1933	„	„	„	„ 23°	Virgo	„
in February	1934	„	„	„	„ 23°	Libra	„
in March	1935	„	„	„	„ 23°	Scorpio	„
in April	1936	„	„	„	„ 24°	Sagittarius	„
in May	1937	„	„	„	„ 27°	Capricorn	„
in June	1938	„	„	„	„ 2°	Pisces	„

omitting Aquarius altogether.

94

In its final form, however, the Canon of Yao has come down to us as follows, describing how two pairs of brothers were appointed by Yao to observe the cardinal points:

He separately commanded the second brother Hsî to reside at Yü-î, in what was called the Bright Valley, and (there) respectfully to receive as a guest the rising sun, and to adjust and arrange the labours of the spring. 'The day', (said he), 'is of the medium length, and the culminating star is Niâo;—you may thus exactly determine mid-spring. The people are dispersed (in the fields), and birds and beasts breed and copulate.'

He further commanded the third brother Hsî to reside at Nan-kiâo (in what was called the Brilliant Capital), to adjust and arrange the transformations of the summer, and respectfully to observe the exact limit (of the shadow). 'The day', (said he), 'is at its longest, and the star is Hwo;—you may thus exactly determine midsummer. The people are more dispersed; and birds and beasts have their feathers and hair thin, and change their coats.'

He separately commanded the second brother Ho to reside at the west, in what was called the Dark Valley, and (there) respectfully to convoy the setting sun, and to adjust and arrange the completing labours of the autumn. 'The night', (said he), 'is of the medium length, and the star is Hsü;—you may thus exactly determine mid-autumn. The people feel at ease, and birds and beasts have their coats in good condition.'

He further commanded the third brother Ho to reside in the northern region, in what was called the Sombre Capital, and (there) to adjust and examine the changes of the winter. 'The day', (said he), 'is at its shortest, and the star is Mâo;—you may thus exactly determine mid-winter. The people keep in their houses, and the coats of birds and beasts are downy and thick.'

The Tî said, Ah! you, Hsîs and Hos, a round year consists of three hundred, sixty, and six days. Do you, by means of the intercalary month, fix the four seasons, and complete (the period of) the year. (Thereafter) the various officers being regulated in accordance with this, all the works (of the year) will be fully performed.

This text goes back to a time when the determination of the seasons was still regarded as difficult, and the dates implied are as follows[12] (in the astronomical era, by which −2357=B.C. 2358):

Mao	=Pleiades	−2357
Niao	=Alphard	−2152
Huo=Fang	=Beta Scorpii	−2619
or else	Delta Scorpii	−2477
Hsü	=Beta Aquarii	−1858

These dates, however, cannot be taken seriously, for several reasons. The constellations Huo and Niao are far too large to provide any date at all. Hsü and Mao are smaller, but differ in date by half a millennium. Hence it is an illusion to suppose that one can date the Canon of Yao by the precession of the equinoxes. For if, as does seem to be the case in the opinion of most reputable sinologists, the marking-stars of the 28 asterisms were chosen to coincide with an already existing set of circumpolar marking-stars, then the precession of the equinoxes has nothing to do with the case. The main difficulty is that the literary and archaeological evidence all points to Chinese astronomy having grown up in the Shang period, roughly between 1600 and 1100; but if we take the Pleiades seriously as a seasonal marker, there is no escaping from the twenty-fourth century.

Of course the mention of four asterisms in the Yao-tien does not imply that the whole system of 28 was known. Stars are mentioned on the oracle-bones discovered at Anyang, and from these it seems certain that the Four Palaces were recognized as early as 1300 B.C., in the reign of Wu Ting. Particular mention is made of the Bird Star (Niao hsing, Alphard) and the Fire Star (Huo hsing, Antares).

A little later comes the Shih King, or Book of Odes, also supposedly compiled by Confucius, but containing poems now thought to date from the ninth and eighth centuries. It mentions at least eight of the asterisms. Next in date comes the Yueh Ling, which may be as old as 850 or as late as 420 B.C. It mentions all but five of the asterisms. And finally the full list was almost certainly in existence by 350.[13]

The Yueh Ling speaks in this style: 'In the first month of spring the Sun is in the constellation Ing Shih (Pegasus); Shen (Orion) culminates at sunset, and Wei (the Scorpion's tail) at dawn. In the

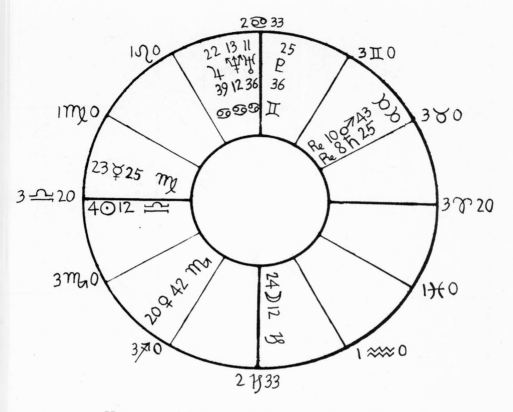

1. Horoscope of the Emperor Augustus, calculated in the
Hellenistic zodiac (*see pages* 39 *and* 64–5)

Born at sunrise, September 22nd, 63 B.C. The date usually given is
September 23rd, but this is impossible because Suetonius says that the
astrologer fell down and worshipped Augustus because of his wonderful
horoscope; and on the 23rd the Moon was in square to Mars and Saturn,
which makes a very bad horoscope indeed. On the 22nd, however, she was
in sextile to Venus and in opposition to an exalted Jupiter, which quite
explains Theogenes' behaviour. Besides, everyone knows from his coins
(Illustration 4(a)) that Augustus had Moon in Capricorn, and on the
23rd it went into Aquarius.
Calculated with Hynes' and with Bryant Tuckerman's tables, but Pluto's
longitude has not been corrected for perturbations, so it must be regarded
as approximate (Noesselt's tables).

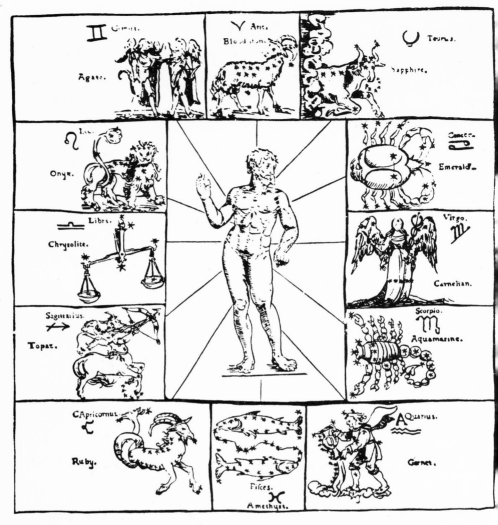

2. Medieval zodiacal man, with appropriate gems

3. Medieval biped Sagittarius

4. (*facing page*) Zodiacal coins and gem
(*see pages* (*a*) 64–5 *and* (*b*) 177)

d

u

a

b

c

c

e

f

g

5. (*above*) Parapegma found at Miletus (*see page 77*)
6. (*right*) Poseidon and Hermes (Neptune and Mercury) on the Puteal Albani

second month of spring the sun is in K'uei (Andromeda with Pisces); Hou (Canis Major and Argo) culminates at sunset, and Kien (the head of Sagittarius) at dawn; equinox, the swallows arrive.'

Each month has its agricultural and social duties, depending on the season—to plough or to sow, not to pull down nests or kill pregnant animals, to care for the aged by providing them with walking-sticks, and so forth—and there are many other correspondences. In the second month of autumn, for instance, the divine ruler is Shao Hao, its animals are the hairy ones, its smell is metallic; one sacrifices to the spirit of the gate and puts the liver on top. The Son of Heaven wears white and goes out in the war-chariot drawn by white horses with black manes and tails, and decorated with white flags. He eats sesame and dog's flesh out of rectangular dishes.[14]

He orders the Grand Recorder to guard the statutes and maintain the laws, and especially to observe the motions in the heavens of the sun and moon, and of the zodiacal stars in which the conjunctions of these bodies take place, so that there should be no error as to where they rest and what they pass over; that there should be no failure in the record of all these things, according to the regular practice of early times.

The astronomical information in these books has of course been brought up to date in the usual Chinese manner, and now corresponds to a date A.D. rather than to its own ostensible time; but the asterisms are not yet alluded to by their animal names. Indeed it is not quite certain how early these occur, but unless they originated in Turkestan, as Chavannes suggested,[6] then they probably came from the West about the time of Alexander the Great. It is known that trade relations between India and China expanded in the third century B.C., and it has been thought that the name China (Sanskrit *Cina*, and in similar forms, sometimes with S instead of C, in many Western languages) perpetuates the name of the Ch'in Dynasty, which ruled from 249 to 206 B.C.

The best-known minister of that dynasty, and probably the first low-born capitalist to become a nationally important figure in China, was Lü-pu-wey, who was appointed Grand Counsellor in 250, and dismissed, to the delight of his many enemies, in 237.

Legend tells that he seduced the queen and so became the father of the ensuing emperor, the notorious Cheng, who called himself Shih-Hoang-Ti—First Yellow Emperor—although the original Yellow Emperor had reigned some four-and-twenty centuries earlier. It was Cheng who committed the historic crime of decreeing the Burning of the Books.

Lü-pu-wey had realized that the Ch'in Dynasty, and its whole province, was backward and uncultured compared to the rest of China, which it had recently conquered, and he therefore assembled scholars from many parts and caused them to compile a book of annals, including a vast amount of miscellaneous information. Then, with the vanity of the self-made, he himself assumed the authorship, calling it Lü-shih Ch'un Ch'iu—'Mr Lü's Spring and Autumn'.[15]

Lü-pu-wey, being a wealthy merchant and importer, may well have been interested in foreign parts; he was a Taoist, and Lao-tse the founder of Taoism was said to have travelled to India and the West, perhaps even to the Caspian Sea; and we are told in the *Spring and Autumn* that in ancient times the empire was governed by 71 sages, an unlikely number which recalls the Indian doctrine of 71 divine rulers to a *manvantara*, or phase of manifested life. This being so, it seems possible that knowledge of the circle of animals may first have come to China in the time of Lü-pu-wey.

Lists of asterisms in China begin either with Kio (Spica), which is the native system, or else with Mao (the Pleiades), which is the Indian method. Lists beginning with Mao were compiled under Buddhist influence, for when the first Buddhist missionaries arrived from India, certainly no later than the third century B.C., they most likely brought with them the traditional Indian list, in which Krittika (the Pleiades) stood first. It was already long out of date, and precession has since obliged the Hindus to transfer the head of the list successively backwards to Bharani, then to Açvini, and now to Revati. But before precession was known it would not occur to anyone that the reference-points of the sky were becoming gradually obsolete.

The Chinese, however, had always measured their year from the winter solstice—in so far as they showed any preference for one of the four cardinal points—and their calendar began halfway between the winter solstice and the vernal equinox, in the middle of February.

Why then this choice of Kio as the first asterism, which it never was in India? Saussure thought it was chosen because the first full moon of the year appeared there in Shang times, and Shinjo suggested because the handle of the Big Dipper points towards it, the Big Dipper's handle being used as a seasonal marker according as it points east or west, up or down. With these two possible alternative reasons, it would be rash to lay too much stress on the use of Spica as the original marking-star of the zodiac, which would imply that a system essentially Chinese was measured by a fiducial imported from the Middle East.

The Chinese constellations have little in common with those of Europe; of the 48 in the Ptolemaic canon, only 10 were found by Professor Needham to have positive resemblances in China.[16] On the other hand we do discover in Censorinus,[17] a Latin writer of the third century A.D., a twelve-year cycle of predictions of plenty and scarcity of the fruits of the earth, which is closely paralleled in the Chi Ni Tzu.[16]

Besides the circle of 28 asterisms, the *hsiu*, there existed in China a circle of 12 divisions which may have been even older. These are called the Twelve Kung, and their principal use was apparently to predict plenty or scarcity, peace, or war, in the provinces they ruled, from the colour, brilliance, and course of the planet Jupiter when passing through or in opposition to them. The rulership of a sign over a province was determined by the constellation chiefly worshipped in each. In Sung, for example, the people worshipped Ta-Ho, the Great Fire, which is part of Scorpio, and in Tsin (Shansi) Orion's Belt. In contrast to modern times, Jupiter's influence was not supposed to be good in itself, but depended on the appearance of the planet.

It has been thought that this cycle took its origin from Jupiter's twelve-year period.[18] On the other hand the number 12 is unavoidable in astronomy because of the $12\frac{1}{2}$ lunations in the tropical year; and it is equally possible that the twelvefold division may have come from Babylon, as Bezold believed, and was originally a month-number rather than a year-number. That 'Twelve is the number of Heaven' is warranted in the Li-ki by the fact that the emperor's sacrificial robe was embroidered with the sun, moon and stars, and his crown bore twelve strings of pearls.

TABLE 5 *The 12 Kung*

Name	Meaning of Name	Beginning in the asterisms	Extent	
hsing-chi	recording star	tou 12°	30°	Winter Palace, North, water
hsüan-hsiao	empty depth	nü 8°	30°	Dark Warrior or Tortoise
chü-shih	?	wei 16°	31°	
hsiang-lou	?	k'uei 5°	30°	Autumn Palace, West, metal
ta-liang	great splendour	wei 7°	30°	White Tiger
shih-ch'en	Orion	pi 12°	31°	
shun-shou	head of the red quail	ching 16°	30°	Summer Palace, South, fire
shun-huo	body of the red quail	liu 9°	31°	Red Quail
shun-wei	tail of the red quail	chang 18°	30°	
shou-hsing	longevity (Spica)	chen 12°	31°	Spring Palace, East, wood,
ta-huo	great fire (Antares)	ti 5°	30°	Green Dragon
che-mu	the ford(?), or woodcutting	wei 10°	31°	

The 12 Kung, also called Tzhu, correspond to the 12-year cycle of Jupiter.

Besides the divisions into 12 and 28, the Chinese have a division of the year into 24 'solar terms', given by Giles as follows:[19]

TABLE 6

Begins about		Name	Meaning of name	Sun in tropical sign
February	5th	li ch'un	spring begins	Aquarius
,,	19th	yü shui	rain water	Pisces
March	5th	ching chih	excited insects	,,
,,	20th	ch'un fên	vernal equinox	Aries
April	5th	ch'ing ming	clear and bright	,,
,,	20th	ku yü	grain rains	Taurus
May	5th	li hsia	summer begins	,,
,,	21st	hsiao man	grain fills	Gemini
June	6th	mang chung	grain in ear	,,
,,	21st	hsia chih	summer solstice	Cancer
July	7th	hsiao shu	slight heat	,,
,,	23rd	ta shu	great heat	Leo
August	7th	li ch'iu	autumn begins	,,
,,	23rd	ch'u shu	limit of heat	Virgo
September	8th	pai lu	white dew	,,
,,	23rd	ch'iu fên	autumn equinox	Libra
October	8th	han lu	cold dew	,,
,,	23rd	shuang chiang	hoar-frost descends	Scorpio
November	7th	li tung	winter begins	,,
,,	22nd	hsiao hsüeh	little snow	Sagittarius
December	7th	ta hsüeh	heavy snow	,,
,,	22nd	tung chih	winter solstice	Capricorn
January	6th	hsiao han	little cold	,,
,,	21st	ta han	severe cold	Aquarius

The number 28 looks like an attempt to provide one asterism, or 'mansion', for every night of the moon's revolution; and so it might be, in a sufficiently backward state of culture. But it could not be accurate enough to serve as the basis of a calendar, since the length of the moon's sidereal revolution (between two successive conjunctions to a given star) is only 27 days 7 hours 43 minutes—an inexactitude of nearly one-third of a day in every month, or four days in a year.

Further, the Chinese asterisms were not originally intended to serve this purpose, since they follow the equator rather than the ecliptic. The moon can be near, but never actually in, the *hsiu* of the Ape, since the Ape is part of Orion, where the moon never goes. More probably, therefore, they were intended to serve as hour-markers for telling the time at night.

In Han times (from 206 B.C.) and perhaps earlier, the Chinese divided the day into 60 parts, beginning from midnight,[20] and this system is found also at Babylon and in the Vedas. Furthermore, both the Vedas and the Chinese give the proportion of the longest day to 24 hours as 18 : 30, and this works out at 14 hours 24 minutes, which is exactly the length of the longest day at Babylon as computed by Claudius Ptolemy in the second century A.D. So here is evidence of the transmission of astronomical knowledge and tradition, rather than fresh observation, from the Hellenized region of the Middle East to India and China.

Is it possible that the 28 mansions spread in the opposite direction, from China across Central Asia, and reached the Middle East via Turkestan and Persia? For the Parsees and Arabs have such systems, as well as the Hindus. Of the 28 asterisms, there are only 5 peculiar to China; 17 the Chinese have in common with the Hindus, and 18 in common with the Arabs; which suggests that the Arabs did not derive them from the Hindus. Or conceivably they could have originated in Persia, and spread thence to China, India, and Arabia.

The Chinese marking-stars, as Burgess and Chu Kho-Chen have shown,[21] follow the equator of the twenty-fourth century B.C. more closely than they do the equator of any later time, and more closely than do the Arab or Indian marking-stars. It is therefore possible that the Chinese system of asterisms grew up in or some time after the twenty-fourth century B.C. as an equatorial system of hour-divisions, chosen to fit in with the upper and lower culminations of circumpolar hour-stars which were already in use. But while it is true that the Chinese marking-stars follow the equator of the twenty-fourth century better than they do that of any later time, they do not follow it very closely. In particular, seven in succession (Nos. 6 to 12), all selected from the zodiacal constellations Scorpio, Sagittarius, Capricorn and Aquarius, were at that date no less than 13 degrees to the south of the equator; and since there are several stars bright enough to be used instead, standing higher in the sky and nearer to the equator—especially Altair, Eta Ophirichi, Lambda Aquilae and Epsilon Pegasi—it seems almost possible that some of the determining stars may have been altered to mark the zodiac rather than the equator. However, a curve drawn through the determining stars of the *hsiu* can only be rough at the best of times, and it may be rather more plausible to agree with Professor Needham that this curve can be taken to fit the sixteenth century as easily as the twenty-fourth.[22]

In any case the circle of animals is not the original Chinese system, and hardly anyone believes that it can be traced there so early as the sixth century B.C.; the fourth or third century is much more likely. The question remains, which is the older, the hour-circle of 12 animals, or the circle of 28? In order to solve this problem we must scrutinize the two lists.

TABLE 7   *The Twelve Branches, or Horary Circle*

	Hour	*Direction*	*Name*	*Meaning of Name*	*Animal*
1.	midnight	North	tzŭ	a child	Rat
2.	1–3 a.m.	NNE	ch'ou	(uncertain)	Ox
3.	3–5 a.m.	ENE	yin	to revere (?)	Tiger
4.	5–7 a.m.	East	mao	to burst forth	Hare
5.	7–9 a.m.	ESE	ch'en	a lucky time	Dragon
6.	9–11 a.m.	SSE	ssŭ	(uncertain)	Serpent
7.	noon	South	wu	noon (?)	Horse
8.	1–3 p.m.	SSW	wei	not yet (?)	Sheep
9.	3–5 p.m.	WSW	shen	continuation	Monkey
10.	5–7 p.m.	West	yu	ripeness, completion	Cock
11.	7–9 p.m.	WNW	hsü	(uncertain)	Dog
12.	9–11 p.m.	NNW	hai	(uncertain)	Boar

These animals are often represented in Chinese art, for instance on old mirrors, or carved in jade. The first, fourth, and tenth names have an obvious reference to the hour of the day, and such may well be the origin of all. But this does not apply to the animal names. The Cock does not, as with us, signify dawn, and even if it did, what hour would the Sheep or Tiger signify? Since these names have no obvious appropriateness, they may be derived from some other system.

The 28 asterisms are as follows—their numbers are given in both the Chinese and Buddhist systems, but they will be alluded to by the latter, following the practice of earlier writers. They are not equal in extent; the largest covers over 30 degrees, the smallest about 2 degrees. (See Table 8 on pages 104–5.)

Of these 28 asterisms, only the Deer and the Ox (Nos. 9 and 26) bore animal names originally; and these were preserved when the full cycle of animal names was devised. The descriptive names, being unsystematic, are clearly older; in some cases the meaning has been forgotten, and fancied resemblances are to be found in Nos. 8, 14, 18, 19, and 22, and possibly also in Nos. 15, 17, and 27.

But if we look down the list of 28 animals, we may well be struck by a certain duplication of ideas, as if this were an expansion of an originally smaller number of names. There are two adjacent dragons, then serpent and worm adjacent, and two kinds of deer with a horse between them; monkey and ape make a pair, followed by three birds together, then dog and wolf. It is often assumed that the twelve animals of the hour-circle were selected in reverse order from the 28, but this pairing makes it appear more probable that the 28 are an inflation of the 12. In that case J.-B. Biot may have been right to suppose that the original number of asterisms was 24, though not for the reason that he gave. He suggested that the extra four might have been put in to mark the equinoxes and solstices in the time of Chou-kung (1100 B.C.). They would then have had to be Nos. 24, 3, 10, and 17, and the dates indicated would be as follows:

Vernal Equinox, no. 17, Wei (pheasant)   =35 Arietis R.A. 0° in 1031 B.C.
Summer Solstice, no. 24, Liu (muntjak) =Delta Hydrae R.A. 90° in 913 B.C.
Autumn Equinox, no. 3, Ti (badger)=Alpha Librae R.A. 180° in 1280 B.C.
Winter Solstice, no. 10, Nü (bat) =Epsilon Aquarii R.A. 270° in 1009 B.C.

TABLE 8 *The 28 Chinese Asterisms, or Hsiu*

Chinese Number	Buddhist Number	Animal	Name	Meaning of name	Extent	Principal Stars
18	1	Cock	Mao	(uncertain)	11°	Pleiades
19	2	Raven	Pi 畢	handnet; writing-tablet	16°	Hyades
20	3	Monkey	tsüi	lips	2°	λφ Orionis
21	4	Ape	shen	(uncertain)	9°	Orion's head and shoulder
Southern Palace 22	5	Tapir	ching	the well	33°	μ Geminorum
23	6	Sheep	kuei	the spirits or ghosts	4°	θ Cancri
24	7	Muntjak	liu	the willow-tree	15°	δ Hydrae
25	8	Horse	hsing	the star	7°	α Hydrae (Alphard)
26	9	Deer	chang	the hornless deer*	18°	κνμ Hydrae
27	10	Serpent	i	the wings of a bird	18°	α Crateris
28	11	Worm	chên	to revolve†	17°	γ Corvi
Eastern Palace 1	12	Hornless Dragon	kio	the horn	12°	Spica
2	13	Dragon	k'ang	strong, violent; neck	9°	κλ Virginis
3	14	Badger	ti	to hang down (?); root	15°	αβ Librae
4	15	Hare	fang	the room	5°	βδπ Scorpii
5	16	Fox	hsin	the heart	5°	Antares
6	17	Tiger	wei 尾	the tail	18°	εμ Scorpii
7	18	Leopard	chi	spread out fanwise‡	11°	γ etc. Sagittarii

Northern Palace	8	Gryphon	tou	the (southern) dipper	26°	μφ Sagittarii
	9	Ox	niu	the ox; the herd-boy	8°	αβ Capricorni
	10	Bat	nü	the woman, serving-maid	12°	ε Aquarii
	11	Rat	hsü	empty	10°	β Aquarii
	12	Swallow	wei 危	precipitous, rooftop	17°	α Aquarii
	13	Boar	shih	the mansion	16°	α Pegasi
	14	Porcupine	pi 壁	the fortified wall	9°	γ Pegasi
Western Palace	15	Wolf	k'uei	legs	16°	βζη Andromedae
	16	Dog	lou	the tether	12°	αβ Arietis
	17	Pheasant	wei 胃	the stomach	14°	35 Arietis

* or, extended net † or, chariot-platform ‡ or, winnowing-basket

The mean date of this table 1096 B.C., and the margin of error $183\frac{1}{2}$ years on either side (just over 3 degrees). This is evidently possible, but there seems no reason to accept it, rather the contrary, since at that epoch the system of *hsiu* had hardly settled into its final shape. Further, there would be no need to insert four extra asterisms unless the original system had contained four which had been supposed to mark the equinoxes and solstices in earlier times. And although Dr Chatley [23] declares that the four marking-stars of the equatorial belt in early times were Alphard, Antares, Beta Aquarii, and the Pleiades, these stars can only have been used as a rough guide before the birth of exact celestial measurement, for the dates when they would have been exact are centuries apart:

Hsing (Alphard) marked the summer solstice in 2153 B.C.
Fang (Beta Scorpii) marked the autumn equinox in 2620 B.C.
Hsü (Beta Aquarii) marked the winter solstice in 1859 B.C.
Mao (Pleiades) marked the vernal equinox in 2219 B.C.
Antares marked the autumnal equinox in 2922 B.C.

It is thus not at all probable that the *hsiu* were ever combined with a system of seasonal marking-stars; and the four which would have marked the seasons in 1100 B.C. are all too large to be later insertions.

But, to return to the later period when the animal cycle had been imported, there is surely some significance in the intrusion of the horse between two deer. Should we reduce the 28 to 24 by excising the Horse and every seventh therefrom? If we do this, we lose the Hare, Rat, and Cock, and the remainder form an uninterrupted sequence of twelve pairs, which we can compare with the horary circle:

TABLE 9   *Asterisms and Hour-circle compared*

24 *Asterisms*	12 *Branches*	24 *Asterisms*	12 *Branches*
1. Two dragons	5. dragon	7. dog and wolf	11. dog
2. badger and fox	4. hare	8. raven and pheasant	10. cock
3. tiger and leopard	3. tiger	9. monkey and ape	9. monkey
4. gryphon and ox	2. ox	10. sheep and tapir	8. sheep
5. bat and swallow	1. rat	11. deer and muntjak	7. horse
6. boar and porcupine	12. boar	12. serpent and worm	6. serpent

All but two of these pairs are obvious; for the muntjak is a kind of hornless deer; the porcupine's name in several languages means 'spiny pig'; and the bat and swallow both fly round the house. So obvious, in fact, is the principle of pairing that is seems hard to discredit it even by the oddly assorted couples sheep and tapir, gryphon and ox. Are the words rightly translated?

The word *han* 犴 translated by Giles as 'tapir' in reference to the asterisms, in other connections means 'a wild dog like a fox but smaller', or else a watchdog or possibly a jackal. Since we already have both dog and wolf in the circle, this can hardly apply: Giles is doubtless right to translate the word differently. In the third century B.C., however, the meaning may not have been what it is today, and the Chinese are also capable of having seen a resemblance not obvious to the Westerner.

The animal *hsieh* 獬 is 'a fabulous animal with a single horn like a unicorn. It dwells in the desert, and being able to discriminate right from wrong, gores wicked people when it sees them. It eats fire in its ravenous fury, even to its own destruction'. Thus Giles, enlarging upon the Chinese Imperial Encyclopaedia, the *Ku-chin T'u-shu Chi-ch'eng*, where the animal is illustrated.[24] Like most Chinese dragons, it resembles a Pekingese dog more than anything else, and the horn is placed on its nose. More terse than Giles, the Encyclopaedia says: 'like a sheep one horn four feet' — and a sheep, of course, means equally a goat. Not unnaturally Couvreur translates it 'unicorn'.

But a unicorn is found in the horary cycle of the Mimaut Papyrus! Hence it, too, may have come from the West; and if so, one would expect it to be paired with the Sheep rather than the Ox. The Ox, however, is one of the only two asterisms which had an animal name originally; there could therefore be no question of altering the Ox, but the Unicorn, if it needed a place, could fit in beside it since both are horned. The difficulty about the Tapir and the Sheep remains, but can hardly be held to cancel out the whole principle of pairing.

To return, then, to the comparison from which we started, the circle of animals would seem to have come to China, and the Far East generally, in the following form, which has a significant resemblance to the zodiac:

TABLE 10   *The Far Eastern Circle of Animals*

Dog	Dragon (in Thailand Great Dragon; in Persia crocodile)
Pig (in Japan Boar)	Snake (in Thailand Small Dragon) (♏)
Rat or Mouse	Horse (♐)
Ox (in Thailand Cow)	Sheep or Goat (in Thailand Goat) (♑)
Tiger (in Mongolia Panther)	Monkey or Ape (in Japan long-tailed monkey) (♒)
Hare (in Thailand Rabbit)	Bird (Cock or Hen in Japan, Persia and Thailand)[25]

When these names were applied to the already existing set of asterisms, there was no difficulty in making them fit, for there was only one name in common, namely the Ox, which was located at Alpha and Beta Capricorni. But had it been our zodiac, as a year-circle, which was imported into China, then after the equation of the Bull with Niu the Ox (No. 20), we should have had the Twins, instead of the Boar, equated with Shih the Mansion (No. 24), and the Crab instead of the Dog given to Lou the Tether (No. 27). Three things show that the idea which came to China was not at first the year-circle of the zodiac, but the hour-circle, or dodeca-oros: first, the equation of the animals being counter to the order of the asterisms; secondly, the circle being exclusively animal, without any human figures; and thirdly, though it bears a partial resemblance to our zodiac, the Chinese circle of animals is patently not our zodiac and was not put to the same use.

In favour of there having at first been 24 asterisms, not 28, the evidence is the list of pairs obtained by excising the Horse, Hare, Rat, and Cock, and the fact that, if one were merely trying to inflate the 12 up to 28, it is not at all clear why the Bat and Swallow, two flying creatures, should be chosen as fit companions for the Rat. But a formidable difficulty remains: the four excised animals correspond to the most ancient marking-stars of Chinese astronomy, which we cannot suppose to have been omitted from the original list of asterisms. Nor is it really likely that the four large asterisms which marked the cardinal points in 1100 B.C. were merely afterthoughts. And the table of twenty-four pairs really proves nothing, since in order to inflate the twelve up to 28 the obvious procedure is to invent a pair for each and then add four; and since we have seen already that it was the circle of 12 hour-animals which came to China, one can hardly doubt that this procedure was followed.

How then do we explain the extra four? The Cock and the Hare take no explaining, for each is part of a regular trio, three birds in the one case, and in the other three animals which haunt the fringes of cultivation. Nor is the Horse so intrusive as it appears; it is part of the hour-circle, and the two Deer come next to it because one of them was there already, being one of the only two asterisms which had an animal name. The Rat or Mouse, for all its resemblance to a Bat, does look out of place between two flying creatures, but it appears to be the original member of the group, and one can at least say of all three that they haunt the house without being reckoned domestic animals.

Why then does the Rat come first in the Chinese circle? Perhaps because the Chinese day began at midnight, which happened to be the hour of the Rat. This, if true, would explain why the Rat, ruling the first hour, was equated to Aries the first sign. But how did midnight come to be the hour of the Rat? Possibly for no particular reason, since we know that in the dodeca-oros the sequence of animals was much less constant than in the zodiac. In the Middle East, however, where the hour-circle originated, the day was reckoned to begin not at midnight but at sunset, so the first hour would be, in summer, from about 7 to 9 p.m. We can imagine this being ruled by whatever animal corresponded to Aries and came first on the list; but if we are right to put the Dragon in Libra, this must have been the Dog. And if the Dog rules at 8 p.m., the Rat will rule at midnight.

In conclusion, then, the number of asterisms would seem to have been originally 28 in China, not 27 or 24, and this may have been an accident, determined by the number of convenient groups of marking-stars which had been chosen, or it may have been decided under Indian influence, or it may have grown up as a set of moon-stations in such ancient times that its inexactitude would not have mattered. The Indian *nakshatras* existed as a system by about 800 or possibly even 1000 B.C.; but there is no proving whether they had an influence on Chinese astronomy or conversely, for the system of *hsiu* grew up about the same time, and the two may have been independent. The animal circle was not Chinese in origin, but was imported about the third or fourth century B.C.

It is worth remembering that all the most ancient zodiacs began with the Pleiades and ended with the asterism Al Butain, 'the belly', whose longitude was Aries 17° 09'.

7. *From Mexico to Tibet*

WHEN Alexander von Humboldt returned from Mexico and published, in 1816, his great travel-book *Vues des Cordillères*,[1] he claimed to have discovered a striking similarity between the zodiac of Mexico and that of Tibet. This idea is extremely surprising, since the Mexican calendar is not based on the numbers 12, 28, and 30, like most calendars of Europe and Asia, but upon 13 and 20. The solar year consisted of 18 'months' of 20 days each, making 360 days; more important, however, was the period of Venus, which consists astronomically of 584 days, but ritually was made to consist of 260, that is, 13 of the 'months' of 20 days. The 20 days bore, of course, names instead of numbers—the notion of merely numbering things. and otherwise leaving them anonymous, had not yet been invented—and the months also bore names, which according to Bowditch[2] had the following meanings:

TABLE 11   *Mexican Month-names*

pop	=mat	yax	=green, fresh
uo	=frog	zac	=white
zip	=error, swollen, rotten tree, or sunset (?)	ceh	=deer, flint knife for killing deer
zotz	=bat	mac	=lid
tzec	=chastisement or scorpion	kankin	=yellow sun
xul	=end	moan	=cloudy day or head of a bird
yaxkin	=beginning of summer, new sun, rainy season	pax	=a drum
		kayab	=song or turtle
mol	=a claw; to collect	cumhu	=thunder
chen	=a well or spring	uayeb	=bed, repose

These names for the most part are patently seasonal, and give no handle for any connection with the zodiac. The 20 names of the days, however, are taken mostly from animals, and are therefore more promising. Each day had also its ruling god or goddess, but if

Fritz Roeck can be relied on, these did not always fall in the expected places; Quetzal-coatl, for instance, the Feathered Serpent, ruled the second day, called Wind, and not the fifth day, which was called Coatl (serpent); the fire-god ruled the day called Water, and the god and goddess of death ruled the day called Dog, not, as one might have expected, the day called Skull. With their mania for human sacrifice the Mexicans naturally wanted a day of this name, and they had two feasts of the dead in successive 'months'.

The calendar systems of pre-Columbian peoples often seem to have a good deal in common, and it may be that astrology, in some form or other, was widespread, for in 1698 the bishop of Chiapas, F. Nuñez de la Vega, wrote as follows in a pastoral letter referring to the Nagualists among the Quiché: 'They believe that the birth of men is regulated by the course of the stars and planets; they observe the time of the day and of the month at which a child is born, and predict the conditions of its life and destiny, both favourable and unfavourable. And the worst of it is that these perverted men have written down their signs and rules and so deceive the erring and the ignorant.' Too bad!

But although the bishop was writing more than 200 years after Columbus, it does not seem certain that these perverted wizards were putting into practice in southern Mexico astrological rules imported by Spaniards who had studied the writings of King Alphonso the Wise (1252–84), or of Firmicus Maternus and Peter of Abano. Possibly they had their own methods. Among the Nagualists, for example, a boy was given at his initiation into manhood a protecting spirit in animal form, and although the nature of this spirit was sometimes discovered by the local magician in a dream, the animals used may have an astrological connection with the 31 animals which gave their names to the days of the Nagual calendar. It has been suggested by Roeck, on the strength of this, that totemism may have an astrological origin, but this, like some of his other conclusions, is more enthusiastic than convincing.

If prediction by astrology did exist in pre-Columbian America, it was probably found only in the higher cultures. The Navaho,[3] for example, have no knowledge of the zodiac, and though a few of them will use for their 'sand-paintings' an occasional theme of astronomical inspiration, most regard the subject of constellations as too difficult to be interesting. But Toltec astronomy did have something in common with Chinese, in so far as both divided the world into five directions instead of four—north, south, east, west, and centre. Further, the four outward directions were ruled, as in China, by four cosmic creatures comparable to the Four Holy Creatures of Christianity and Judaism—the Bull, Lion, Eagle, and Man that are associated with the evangelists. Roeck[4] has the following comparative table which he believes to indicate some continuity of cultural contact, rather than just the expression of similar archetypal ideas in different places:

	EGYPT	Magic papyrus	TIBET	CHINA	MEXICO
	The Four Sons of Horus	(Berlin) (Parthey II, 101)	Spirits of the Seasons	Four Cosmic Beings (Constellations)	Ritual Masks of the 4 Regents
South	Hawk	Hawk (fire)	Garuda-vulture	Red Bird	Vulture
West	Jackal	Crocodile (water)	Black Dog	White Tiger (originally Spotted Dog)	Dog
North	'Black-faced Ape' (i.e. dog-headed baboon)	Horus-child on lotus (earth)	Horse and Rider	Black Warrior on Tortoise	Death's-head
East	Man	Snake (air)	Man-dragon	Green Dragon	Crocodile

This table is not above criticism, as can be seen. When however we come to the comparison of the animal names of the Chinese and Tibetan asterisms with the Mexican names of the 20 days, Roeck's equations are not very persuasive, any more than those of Humboldt with the twelve Tibetan months. (The Tibetan animal cycle is the same as the Chinese.) It would be guesswork to try to establish any definite theory of Toltec astronomy being copied from that of China or derived from Babylon, although some influence may have percolated. However, for the sake of comparison with the zodiacs of the old world, a list is given here of the 20 Mexican[5] day-names and the 31 animals of the Nagual calendar.

7. (*left*) T'ang mirror with circle of animals

8. (*below*) Mithraic zodiac (*see pages* 118 *and* 120)

9. Macara the Indian Capricorn and Kumbha the Waterpot (*see page* 141)

(*facing page*)

10. (*left*) Comparison of Sagittarius, Capricorn, and Aquarius in
Babylon and Egypt

11. (*right*) Scorpion-man on a boundary-stone of 12th century B.C.
(*see page* 167)

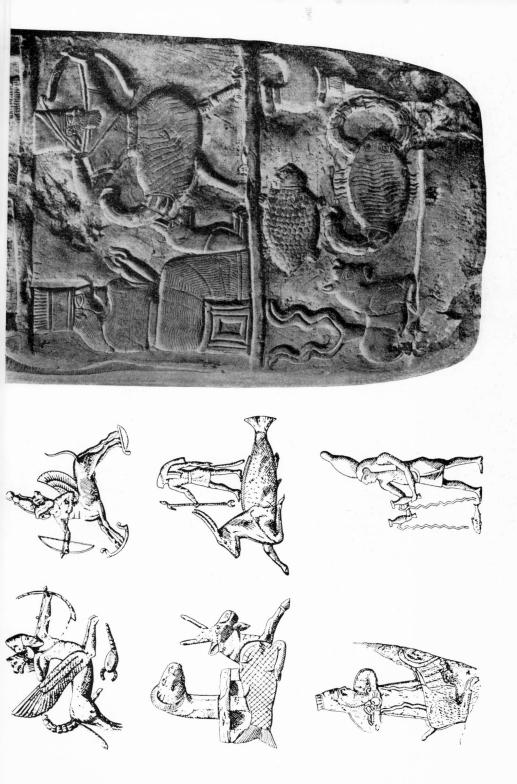

12. The Babylonian God-with-Streams (*see pages* 167–8)

13. Virgo the grain-goddess in the Persian period (*see page* 171)

TABLE 12 *Toltec and Nagual Day-names*

Toltec		Nagual	
* 1.	cipactli=swordfish or alligator	1.	'lion', i.e. puma
* 2.	èēcatl=wind	* 2.	snake
3.	calli=house	3.	stone
4.	cuetzpalin=lizard	* 4.	alligator
* 5.	coatl=snake	5.	cotton-tree
6.	miquiztli=death's-head	6.	quetzal-bird
7.	maçatl=stag	7.	stick
* 8.	tochtli=rabbit	* 8.	rabbit
9.	atl=water	* 9.	cord
10.	itzcuintli=dog	10.	leaf
11.	ocomatli=ape	11.	red cattle
*12.	malinalli=straw rope	12.	parrot
*13.	acatl=reed	*13.	flower
*14.	ocelotl=jaguar	14.	frog
*15.	quauhtli=eagle	15.	maggot
*16.	cozcaquauhtli=vulture	16.	treestump
17.	olin=movement	17.	arrow
*18.	tecpatl=flint	18.	broom
19.	quiauitl=rain	*19.	jaguar
*20.	xochitl=flower	20.	maize
		21.	flute
		*22.	greenstone
		23.	crow
		24.	fire
		25.	pheasant
		*26.	reed
		27.	opossum
		*28.	storm-wind
		*29.	vulture
		*30.	hawk
		31.	bat

An asterisk (*) in either list signifies that a very similar name will be found in the other.

Eleven of the Toltec names are found in the Nagual list, but nine are not, and this suggests imitation and cultural contact rather than the handing on of an actual tradition. Comparison with the Chinese cycle shows that the Chinese have at most 6 names in common with the Toltec list and 8 with the Nagual list, but only 3, the snake, the rabbit or hare, and the jaguar or leopard, in common with both.

H

The Chinese and Tibetan list, being restricted to animals, naturally has little in common with the American lists, which are not. Further, if we compare these American lists with the 28 'signs' given in the British Museum Papyrus 121, written in Egypt about the third century A.D., we find that the Toltec list has only 4 names in common with the Egyptian list (the stag, dog, leopard, and vulture), while the Nagual list has 6 or 7 (the lion, leopard, snake, ox, vulture, and hawk, and possibly the staff, being equated to the stick of the Naguals).

One cannot therefore seriously pretend that the American lists of signs are derived either from Egypt or from China. Can we claim that the idea behind them originated at one place on the earth's surface? Even that is not too plausible, for the natural procedure, when one begins to classify the stars, is to group them into convenient small groups and label each with the name of some object which it may possibly resemble, or of some seasonal phenomenon which it may annually indicate. There may be a seasonal significance in the Toltec names 'water', 'wind', and 'rain', or in the Nagual names 'fire' and 'maize'. But on the whole it is very rare for a constellation to resemble anything on earth except a winding river or snake (which occurs in all the lists), a triangle, a curve such as the Crown or the Scorpion's tail, a box or house (which occurs in Mexico and China), and a dipper (a box with a handle, which does equally well for a wain with shafts). There is no difficulty in seeing further resemblances, the difficulty lies rather in pretending that the Lion cannot equally well resemble a knife, which is what the Egyptians called it, or that the square of Pegasus is any more like a horse than a house.[6]

The American names may therefore quite well be of indigenous origin; and we cannot easily suppose that the whole notion of naming constellations was imported. The question is not so much of the origin of these apparently very capricious lists of names, but rather why and from whence the Chinese, Tibetans, and other peoples drew the idea that the names should be restricted to animals.

8. *Persia and the Four Elements*

PERSIA lies just east of Babylonia, on the way to India by land, and also at the beginning of the golden road to Samarkand and on to China. Geographically, therefore, it was well placed to take part in the spread of ancient ideas about astronomy. Its early history, however, is much less known than that of the Babylonian lowlands. The Amādai and the Parsua, that is to say the Medes and Persians, first come to our knowledge in 837 B.C., in an inscription of Shalmaneser III, King of Assyria. The Median Empire was established by Cyaxares (in his own language Huvakhshatara) between 633 and 584, and transferred to the Persians by Cyrus (Kurash) in 550. Medo-Persian art and civilization were mainly derived, through Assyria, from Babylonian models, but Persian religion was not of Babylonian origin and was not astrological. The supreme and omniscient Good God was Ahura-Mazda, opposed by the Evil God Angra-Mainyu or Ahriman, who was not omniscient. The goddess Anâhita, representing the planet Venus, first begins to be important in the reigns of Artaxerxes II and III (404–336), and at that period the people also worshipped the four elements, light, water, earth, and wind, of which light was divided into the light of the sun and that of the moon.

The Magi seem to have been originally a tribe who specialized in religious observances, like the Levites in Israel. No sacrifice was valid unless attended by a Magus. But later they became a caste, and in the Sassanian period (A.D. 224–642) the Chief of the Magi was appointed by the king, and himself appointed his assistants. By this time astrologers were, with physicians and poets, a regular class of the Persian bureaucracy; but their astrology was not distinguished from that which had spread to India from the Hellenistic world. Further, it was not till near the time of the Muslim conquest that some of the oldest surviving texts of the Persian religion were collected into the book we know as the Bundahish; hence the following account of the creation cannot claim any great antiquity.[1]

Auharmazd produced illumination between the sky and the earth, the constellation stars and those also not of the constellations, then the moon and afterwards the sun, as I shall relate. First he produced the celestial sphere, and the constellation stars are assigned to it by him; especially those twelve whose names are Varak (the Lamb), Tora (the Bull), Dopatkar (Gemini), Kalakang (the Crab), Ser (the Lion), Khusak (Virgo), Tarâzuk (the Balance), Gazdûm (the Scorpion), Nimasp (the Centaur), Vahik (Capricorn), Dûl (the Waterpot), and Mahik (the Fish); which, from their original creation, were divided into the twenty-eight subdivisions of the astronomers, of which the names are

unfortunately corrupt, and can therefore only profitably be discussed by an expert on the Pahlevi language. However, the third of them corresponds to the Pleiades, hence the first must equate with Açvini, which in the Indian system stood first when the equinox was there, that is, about the first century B.C. and for at least five hundred years thereafter.

In Sassanian times, and perhaps earlier, the Persians seem to have acknowledged four 'chieftains' of the four quarters of the sky. The chieftain of the north was called Haptôk-ring and can be reliably identified with the Wain; hence Vanand, chieftain of the south, may be Fomalhaut, because this star stands in the south when the Wain is underneath the Pole Star. Tishtar, or Tishtrya, chieftain of the east, was Sirius,[2] and this leaves Antares as the most probable identification of Satavês the chieftain of the west.

Tishtar, however, had an adventure which suggests that he was not only a star, but an angel whose home was in a constellation. This adventure is described in Chapter 7 of the Bundahish; it is a flood story, but without an ark.

The second conflict was waged with the water, because, as the star Tishtar was in Cancer, the water which is in the subdivision they call Avrak[3] was pouring, on the same day when the destroyer rushed in, and came again to notice for mischief (*avarak*) in the direction of the west. For every single month is the owner of one constellation; the month Tir is the fourth month of the year, and Cancer the fourth constellation from

Aries, so it is the owner of Cancer, into which Tishtar sprang, and displayed the characteristics of a producer of rain; and he brought on the water aloft by the strength of the wind. Co-operators with Tishtar were Vohuman and the angel Hôm, with the assistance of the angel Burg, and the righteous guardian spirits in orderly arrangement. Tishtar was converted into three forms, the form of a man and the form of a horse and the form of a bull; thirty days and nights he was distinguished in brilliance, and in each form he produced rain ten days and nights; as the astrologers say that every constellation has three forms.

Tishtar has become the guardian deity of Cancer, and there is a reference to the three decans, which in Egyptian astrology have presiding spirits with animal heads.

The wind, however, then blew the waters away, and so formed the ocean all round the edge of the world, but

the noxious creatures remained dead within the earth, and their venom and stench were mingled with the earth, and in order to carry that poison away from the earth Tishtar went down into the ocean in the form of a white horse with long hoofs. And Apâôsh, the demon, came meeting him in the likeness of a black horse with clumsy hoofs; a mile away from him fled Tishtar, through the fright which drove him away. And Tishtar begged for success from Auharmazd, and Auharmazd gave him strength and power, as it is said, that unto Tishtar was brought at once the strength of ten vigorous horses, ten vigorous camels, ten vigorous bulls, ten mountains, and ten rivers. A mile away from him fled Apâôsh the demon, through fright at his strength; on account of this they speak of an arrow-shot with Tishtar's strength in the sense of a mile.

Then, with a cloud for a jar—but the word for jar (*khumb*) is not the usual Pahlevi word for the waterpot of Aquarius—Tishtar made it rain once more for ten days and nights in order to wash away the venom of the noxious creatures which had been drowned; but he was not entirely successful, and the water remained salt. Evidently this myth is intended to explain the creation of the sea, which the Persians in their original mountain home would not have known.

A very similar story is told in the eighth Yasht of the Avesta, but there the purpose is merely seasonal, to explain the origin not of the ocean but of rain, and Apâôsh is accordingly the demon of drought.

The three shapes of Tishtar in the Avesta are 'a man of fifteen' (the ideal age according to the Persians), a bull with golden horns, and a white horse with golden ears and a golden caparison. In another part of the Avesta there is frequent reference to 'the star Tishtrya, the radiant, the glorious, and the Moon, which contains the seed of cattle in its beams'. This is because in old Persian myths a cloud, as a source of fertility, was compared to a bull; and the Moon, being masculine in both Zend and Pahlevi, and connected in the popular mind with rain, could therefore easily be compared to a bull. This is enough to make any astrologer recollect that the Moon is exalted in the sign of the Bull; and it is perhaps significant that the sacred bull of Mithraism, which was the reputed origin of all fertility, came also from this part of the world; for Mithra was a member of the Persian and Indian pantheons before he became established in a religion of his own. There were sacred bulls in Egypt too, but they were symbols of strength as well as fertility, and not especially connected with the Moon.

We seem, then, to be on the track of the Bull as a celestial symbol. But we cannot safely claim that its origin was among the Aryan peoples, because Persian civilization is so relatively late in time and so dependent on its predecessors. The Avesta seems to represent the religion of the Median Magi in the period just preceding Alexander the Great; but this religion was not that of the people, and did not become the State religion until the time of Shapur II (A.D. 310–79). By then the Zoroastrian mania for symmetry had decided that since the stars were created by Ormuzd, and were therefore good, the planets could only have been created by Ahriman, and were therefore all wicked.

There exists in the Avesta a Sirozah, or list of the thirty gods which rule the days of the month, but since a similar list is known from Assyrian times this cannot claim to be a Persian invention.

Again, in the thirty-fourth chapter of the Bundahish we learn that each sign of the zodiac is to reign for a thousand years; but as they follow each other in direct and not retrograde order, this cannot have any reference to the precession of the equinoxes.

Another Pahlevi text will serve to illustrate a use to which the zodiac was put in many countries other than Persia, namely the measurement of the calendar by means of noonday shadows. 'When the sun enters Cancer the shadow is one foot of the man, at fifteen of Cancer it is one foot; when the sun enters Leo it is one foot and a half, at fifteen of Leo it is two feet', and so on up to ten feet at the entry of Capricorn. This table, combined with other measurements found in the Bundahish, proves to have been computed in latitude 32° North, which is the latitude of Yazd, the last part of Persia where any Zoroastrians were to be found. A further table follows, stating that every thirty days the sun's midday shadow increases by one and a third feet, and here the shadow at the beginning of Leo is given as seven and a half feet, and at the beginning of Capricorn fourteen and two thirds. Every 'constellation' is allowed the same amount of increase or decrease, regardless of its obliquity.[4]

Thus the Zoroastrian religion adopted the zodiac, and in consequence it is accepted today among the Parsees of India, though their sacred books oblige them to consider the signs good and the planets bad. But the Persian contribution to the history of the zodiac was almost certainly the lore of the four elements. Fire, Earth, Air, and Water, before Claudius Ptolemy forced them into a neat scheme, had already been associated with the twelve constellations in various irregular ways, but the original worshippers of the elements appear to have been the Magi. To the Greeks and Romans they were known as fire-worshippers, but in fact they considered all four elements holy, and declared that none of them must be polluted by the contact of a corpse. Corpses therefore might not be buried, burnt, or thrown into rivers, and under the Sassanian dynasty, when this prescription had become law, they were exposed to the vultures; but this was not the law nor common practice under Darius and Artaxerxes.

Although the belief that a corpse could pollute fire does suggest that fire was regarded as a material substance, it is important to observe that, as far as the zodiac was concerned, the four elements are not and never were material substances, as our present mechanomorphic philosophy likes to believe. They were more nearly the four principles of the physically perceptible world, namely solidity, liquidity, gaseous conditions, and light.

The other Persian influence on the history of the zodiac was Mithraic. The great popularity of astrology in the Roman Empire was due in part to Mithraism, which was derived from the old Persian religion by a process of fermentation no longer easy to explain. For although the planets are regarded as wicked in the Bundahish, being creations of Ahriman, they were worshipped by the initiates of Mithra, and on the floor of a mithraeum at Ostia, near Rome, could still be seen the seven stations of the priests, in which, it is thought, they stood to invoke the planetary spirits.[5]

The earliest famous devotee of Mithraism was that Mithridates King of Pontus whom nobody could poison. He was eventually overcome by the Romans in 66 B.C., but his religion began to flourish at Rome in the following century, and was finally suppressed under Theodosius, soon after 394. Mithras was not officially a sun-god, but a hero who overcame the sun and then made friends with him. He conferred fertility on the earth by the slaughter of a bull, and sculptures of this sacrifice show it happening in the presence of a dog, serpent, scorpion, cup, and crow, all of which were among the constellations known to the Romans; often also a lion, and sometimes a cock, which is not a constellation. Probably the serpent is a symbol of earth, the cup of water, the crow of air, and the lion of fire.

The two dadophoroi, or torch-bearers, who stand on either side, suggest the alternate lengthening and shortening of the days, since one holds his torch upwards and the other down. They are certainly connected with the Two Pillars of Freemasonry and Kabbalism, which tradition says were copied by Solomon from the mysteries of Tyre.

It is hard not to believe that the exaltation of the Moon in Taurus comes from this cycle of thought. Equally, since Scorpio rises when Taurus sets, it is natural enough for a scorpion to be present at the death of the Bull. This is like the Greek story, also of astronomical origin, that Orion died of a scorpion's sting.

Mithraism was a military religion which made no place for women, but it carried belief in astrology to the remotest garrisons of the Roman Empire; for the signs of the zodiac were represented in every mithraeum; and by the time of its extermination by Christianity the zodiac had become deeply engrained in the

European mind. Having nothing plainly heretical about it, it was naturally not condemned.

Sculptures of the bull-sacrifice, or 'tauroctony', often show the signs of the zodiac, and sometimes in reversed order. One of the best known was found at the Walbrook in London, and another, surrounding a bust of Mithra born from the rock, at Housesteads in Northumberland.[6] On this one Sagittarius is shown as a man instead of a centaur.

Another Mithraic style was to draw the entire zodiac on the breast of the lion-headed god representing time, who is akin to Zervan and to the Orphic Phanes. Sometimes one sees this figure, naked except for the serpent wound spirally up him, with Aries and Libra on his breast and Cancer and Capricorn on his loins. The serpent, even though it has not its tail in its mouth, implies eternal recurrence, as in Plate 7.[7]

9. *The Bible and Birthstones*

In the Bible there is less astronomy than one might expect. Of the planets only two are mentioned, namely Saturn (*kijjûn*, which should be the same as the Assyrian *kaimanu*) in Amos v 26: 'Ye have borne Siccuth your king and *Chiun* your images, the star of your god, which ye made to yourselves'; and the morning star, which must be Venus, in Isaiah xiv 12: 'How art thou fallen from heaven, O daystar, son of the morning! how art thou cut down to the ground, which didst lay low the nations!'[1]

And of the constellations and stars Orion and the Pleiades are almost the only ones which can be identified with reasonable certainty. Mention has been alleged[2] of Boötes, Antares, Corvus, and the Hyades, but the latter two are almost certainly wrong.

The most famous reference occurs in the Lord's speech out of the whirlwind in the thirty-eighth chapter of Job: 'Canst thou bind the cluster of the Pleiades, or loose the bands of Orion? Canst thou lead forth the Mazzaroth in their season? or canst thou guide the Bear with her train?'

And there is a similar passage in the ninth chapter, verse nine, where Job says of God: 'Which maketh the Bear, Orion, and the Pleiades, and the chambers of the south.'

Also the prophet Amos exhorts us (Chapter v 8): 'Seek Him that maketh the Pleiades and Orion, and turneth the shadow of death into the morning, and maketh the day dark with night.'

Among these allusions, the 'chambers of the south' may well be the six southern signs of the zodiac, although we cannot be sure, for Mowinckel identified them, somewhat improbably, with the constellation Corvus. Similarly 'Mazzaroth' may mean simply the constellations in general, or a single constellation, or it may refer to the zodiac specifically. *Kimah*, the word translated 'Pleiades', is probably correct and seems to mean 'the heap'. *Kesîl* also is almost certainly correct as Orion, but not within the same boundaries as today. The word means 'fool', not however a silly fool, but the hubristic, insolent, or godless one whom the Arabs call *al-Jauza'*, the Giant; and the same accusation of disrespect to the gods is found in the Greek myth of Orion the hunter. But among the Arabs, as in Babylon and doubtless among the Hebrews, the constellation of the twins consisted only of the two stars Castor and Pollux, and the other stars of what we call Gemini were included in Orion.

As another example of changed boundaries in the sky, only the learned among the Arabs speak of *al-Hamal*, the Ram; popularly the constellation is limited to the three stars in the Ram's head, which are known as *al-Ashrat*, 'the mark', or *ash-sharatain*, 'the two marks'. And the Hebrews, like the Arabs and Babylonians, may well have made of Leo a large constellation extending from the middle of Cancer to the middle of Virgo. This, at least according to J. J. Hess,[3] is the meaning of the word *'ayish*, translated in the Book of Job as 'The Bear'.

For the zodiac one naturally turns to the forty-ninth chapter of Genesis, where Jacob blesses his sons; for we should expect there to have grown up, sooner or later, a standard identification of the twelve tribes with the twelve signs, and it would have to be based on this passage. In fact, however, the position is not so simple, for the blessings had not originally any astrological intention; Professor Skinner, who wrote the volume on Genesis in the *International Critical Commentary*, does not consider them all to be of the same date. Some seem to be based on etymology, others on tribal emblems; those on Zebulun, Gad, and Asher are of geographical origin, since Asher had fertile soil, Zebulun lived by the sea, and Gad was on the landward frontier; and those on Reuben, and on the twins Simeon and Levi, are curses, not blessings, referring supposedly to historical events.

The only easy identifications with the zodiac are those of Judah ('a lion's whelp', as in the fifth chapter of Revelation), Dan, who as a serpent must be equated with Scorpio, and Issachar—'a bony ass crouching between the panniers', which may refer to the two asses and manger in the constellation of Cancer.

However, comparing this list with that in the thirty-third chapter of Deuteronomy, where incidentally two other tribes are compared to lion and lioness, namely Dan and Gad, Skinner found in both one twin sign (either Simeon and Levi, or Ephraim and Manasseh) and one feminine, for which Jacob's daughter Dinah could be brought in to correspond to Virgo. Further, the animals mentioned are all found in or near the zodiac, including the Wolf to which Benjamin is compared; and Skinner concludes accordingly that there may be some astrological reference. If so, it can hardly have been meant in the original version of the text.

In equating the tribes with the signs, the Jewish Encyclopaedia places Judah in the east between Issachar and Zebulun, in opposition to Aries, Taurus and Gemini. This would make Judah correspond to Scorpio, and Issachar to Libra. Reuben stands in the south between Simeon and Gad, and in opposition to Cancer, Leo and Virgo; so the obvious attribution of Reuben to Aquarius is upheld. Ephraim, Manasseh and Benjamin occupy the west, so that Ephraim corresponds to Taurus, suitably enough in view of the remarks about Joseph in Deuteronomy xxxiii. And the north is the place of Dan Asher and Naphtali, Dan being Leo as Deuteronomy suggests.

This is a little surprising, the Lion of Judah being so well known; but then Jewish thought does not seem to have taken the zodiac too seriously. Medieval Jewish writers agree that the righteous Jew is above being influenced by the constellations, in view of Jeremiah x 2: 'Thus saith the Lord, Learn not the way of the nations, and be not dismayed at the signs of heaven; for the nations are dismayed at them.' And to consult or depend on astrologers seems at variance with the Jewish religion on account of Deuteronomy xviii 10–12: 'There shall not be found among you any one that maketh his son or his daughter to pass through the fire, one that useth divination, one that practiseth augury, or an enchanter, or a sorcerer, or a charmer, or a consulter with a familiar spirit, or a wizard, or a necromancer. For whosoever doeth these things is an abomination unto the Lord.'

Star-worship is condemned in 2 Kings xxiii 5; but inevitably zodiacal symbolism found its way into Jewish literature, and it was quite permissible to use it in a calendrical sense, as was done for instance by the famous liturgical poet Eleazar Kalir in a prayer for rain which he composed at the end of the eighth century, mentioning the signs of the zodiac in order in every other stanza:[4]

In God's hand is the key; without it can no one open; He maketh water to gush forth in the depth, to loose the bonds of him who is bound [that is, Isaac].

At the testing he poured out his heart like water; may his *Lambs* remain ever in life.

Be ever gracious to the people chosen in the beginning; may water increase corn and new wine on the fields of the firstborn; the meadows are green, *Oxen* and fat cattle multiply.

May his rich store in the rainy vault of heaven fill with rich water the valleys of the ox-lamers. [That is, Simeon and Levi, see Genesis xlix 6.]

The kindly and friendly one hearkens to our lovely song, may he not be angry for the murmuring at the waters of strife.

Well-pleasing be the prayer as acknowledgement of the *Twins* [that is, Moses and Aaron].

May water be allotted to the sowers in the music of the wheel of the Sun ...

The zodiac and planets were likewise adopted into the Qabalah, twelve of the thirty-two Paths of the Concealed Glory being given zodiacal correspondences; and the same correspondences occur in the 22 Tarot trumps, which are of Qabalistic origin. These are perfectly valid for the practising mystic who knows how to use them in meditation, but there is no point in describing them here; the fact that philosophical thinkers have never managed to agree upon an interpretation of the world bears witness to the existence of numerous paradoxes which mere thinking cannot resolve. Any valid system of meditation must, without abandoning thinking, make it possible to explore the further realm of direct realization, and thus to understand in experience the resolution of paradoxes which cannot be thought out. The Qabalah is such a system, but its correspondences to the zodiac represent stages of experience through which the human spirit passes time and again on many different levels. The nature and consequence of these experiences is often far from obvious, and hence to try to summarize them would only be misleading. Realization, to those who have not had it in the same form, often appears unlikely and unconvincing.

A correspondence to the four 'fixed' signs of the zodiac is often assumed in the four 'holy living creatures' from the first chapter of Ezekiel; they are often identified with the four evangelists, and frequently appear in Christian iconography. They are also represented on the 21st Tarot trump. 'Irenaeus seems to have been the first to play with this fancy', writes Dr Cooke; 'he identified the man with Matthew, the lion with John, the ox with Luke, and the eagle with Mark. A different series of identifications, however, became more popular: man—Matthew, lion—Mark, ox—Luke, eagle—John.'[5] This in fact is the version of Victorinus, but two further different versions were put forward, by Athanasius and by Augustine.

Astrologers, when they make the equation with the four fixed signs, use the eagle instead of Scorpio, and pretend that it represents the higher side of that maligned constellation. Yet the Eagle's longitude places it not close to Scorpio but over the junction of Sagittarius and Capricorn, to both of which it is symbolically appropriate, since the motto of Sagittarius is 'Onward and upward', and Capricorn is the goat which climbs to the mountain-top.

It was Zimmern[6] who first suggested that the Cherubim in the first chapter of Ezekiel represent the cardinal constellations of the third and fourth millennium B.C.; but he inevitably pointed out, what astrologers have since ignored, that if this Babylonian derivation is justified, then the Man does not represent Aquarius, but is the Scorpion-man of the Babylonian boundary-stones (see Plate 11); and the Eagle, of course, was used because Altair, its brightest star, standing consistently about 6 degrees north of the equator, was a more convenient seasonal marker than the stars of Aquarius, which are both dimmer and less high in the sky. So when we admire in the British Museum the 'winged bulls' or 'cherubim', which have a human head, the forefeet of a bull, the hind feet of a lion, and eagle's wings, we ought to remember that the human head represents Scorpio, not Aquarius, and the eagle's wings represent Altair, which was put in to make a fourth with Antares, Aldebaràn, and Regulus.

The four cherubim—the word means 'intercessors' according to Cooke and Langdon—occur again in the fourth chapter of the Revelation of St John, and are among the many supposedly astrological references in that book. But these references, even when developed by so able a scholar as Boll,[7] remain exceedingly unconvincing. Since we are told in the last verse of Chapter i that 'the seven stars are the angels of the seven churches', it seems improbable that the author was primarily interested in developing an astrological symbolism. Admittedly both Philo and Josephus[8] found a connection between the seven-branched candlestick and the seven planets; and Josephus also states that the twelve loaves of shewbread in the Temple refer to the signs of the zodiac. Further, the reference to the four Living Creatures being 'full of eyes' may indicate that they were originally constellations. And in Zechariah iv 10 the planets are apparently alluded to as 'the eyes of the Lord'. But on the other hand when we try to work out astrologically various passages in Revelation we are apt to be disappointed.

For instance, in the beginning of Chapter vi, the third and fourth horsemen can very easily be equated with Libra and Scorpio, since the fourth is Death and the third carries a balance; but if this is so, the first and second should correspond to Leo and Virgo, which they show no sign of doing. Similarly the scorpions in verses 7 to 10 of Chapter ix have been said to suggest the scorpions on Babylonian boundary-stones; and if Scorpio thus becomes the First Woe, the Second and Third should be Sagittarius and Capricorn respectively, which they can be in view of the mention of horses in the Second and an earthquake in the Third; but one cannot feel sure that the author intended anything of the kind.

It has also been thought[9] that the four-and-twenty elders of Chapter iv verse 4 are of astronomical Babylonian origin, and correspond to the 24 stars, or star-gods, which according to Diodorus Siculus[10] were allotted to the zodiac, twelve visible ones in nothern latitudes to rule the living, and twelve, more frequently invisible, in southern latitudes, to rule the dead. This equation has been accepted by some scholars and rejected by others. Dr Charles, who edited the book in the *International Critical Commentary*,[11] finds it too far-fetched, and explains the elders as the heavenly counterpart of the twenty-four priestly orders in 1 Chronicles xxiv 7–18.

An outstanding passage of possible zodiacal interest is the first six verses of Chapter xii of the Revelation:

And a great sign was seen in heaven; a woman arrayed with the sun, and the moon under her feet, and upon her head a crown of twelve stars; and she was with child: and she crieth out, travailing in birth, and in pain to be delivered. And there was seen another sign in heaven; and behold, a great red dragon, having seven heads and ten horns, and upon his heads seven diadems. And his tail draweth the third part of the stars of heaven, and did cast them to the earth: and the dragon stood before the woman which was about to be delivered, that when she was delivered, he might devour her child. And she was delivered of a son, a man child, who is to rule all the nations with a rod of iron: and her child was caught up unto God, and unto His throne. And the woman fled into the wilderness, where she hath a place prepared of God, that there they may nourish her a thousand two hundred and threescore days.

This period of 1,260 days is exactly three and a half years of 360 days, and is no doubt the same as the 'time, times, and a half' mentioned in verse 14 of the same chapter. But again one cannot feel sure that this has not merely a political reference, since 1,260 days is not an astronomical period of any significance. The ten horns of verse 3 seem to be traditional,[12] and are certainly not astrological; the destruction of a third part of the stars sounds astronomical, and a similar story is found in the Bundahish,[13] but does not appear to correspond to anything observable in nature.

The woman clothed with the sun represents, according to most interpreters, the spiritual Israel as the spouse of God. For various reasons scholars have decided that she is an adaptation of an earlier sun-goddess, either the Egyptian Hat-Hor, who is crowned with the sun, or the Greek Leto, who wears[14] a veil of stars, or the Babylonian Damkina, the mother of Marduk,[15] or finally the 'Assyrian' Juno, who according to Martianus Capella wore as a crown the twelve precious stones listed in the table at the end of this chapter.[16] However, the allusion of the twelve stars to the zodiac is usually admitted, and might be regarded as the only certain reference to the zodiac in the Bible, were it not that we cannot call it certain. On the analogy of the seven spirits of the seven churches, the twelve stars may only mean the spirits of the twelve tribes of the spiritual Israel, and be no more astrological than the sun, moon, and eleven stars in Joseph's dream.[17]

We have to remember that the author of Revelation was deeply

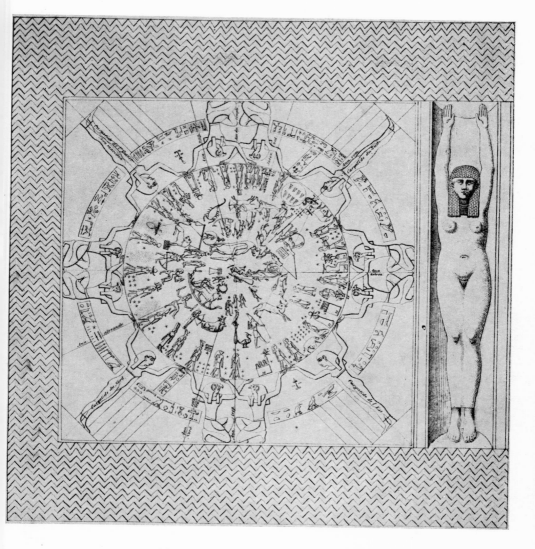

14. Circular zodiac of Denderah (*see page* 180)

15. Horoscope from Athribis
(*see page* 182)

16. (*below*) Standard Diagram of Decans with Orion. Sirius and Planets
(*see pages* 186–7)

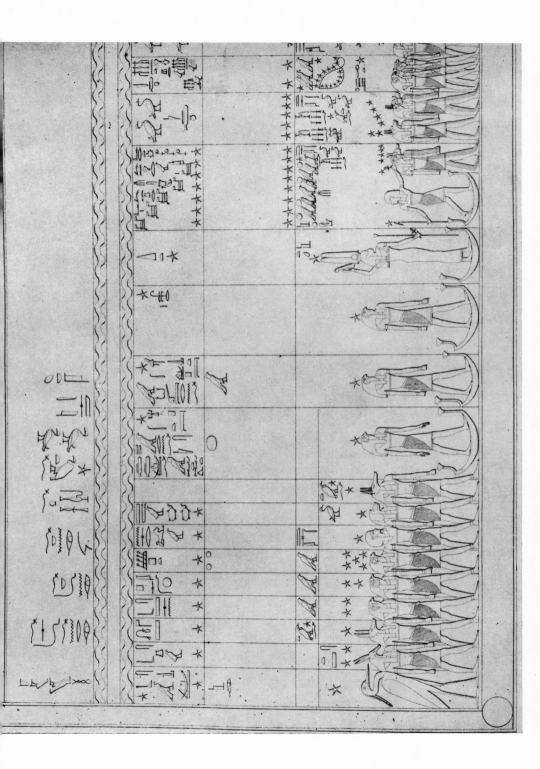

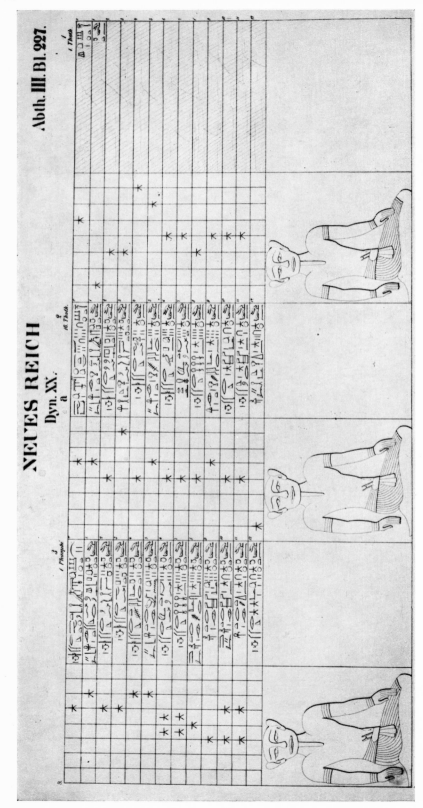

17. Hour-stars and target-priest on a temple roof (*see page* 190)

read in the Jewish apocalyptic literature of the last centuries B.C., and may fairly be expected to have a point of view not very different from that of the Book of Enoch or the Book of Jubilees. Jubilees is a calendrical work, written within about half a century of A.D. 1. It strongly condemns the traditional lunar calendar of the Jews, and urges the adoption of a solar year of 364 days.[18] The zodiac and planets are not even mentioned. Enoch is of slightly older date, and also advocates a solar year, but we learn that among the wickednesses of the fallen angels 'Barâqîjâl taught astrology. Kôkabêl taught the constellations,' and various other angels taught the knowledge of the signs of clouds, of the sun and moon, and so forth.[19] The author's astronomical knowledge was not great, as he shows by his endeavour to explain the varying length of the day;[20] and he frequently speaks of the fallen angels as fallen stars, which suggests a metaphorical rather than a literal approach to his subject-matter. But since astrology is classed with magic as a sin, it is not unlikely that the author of Revelation may have been equally opposed both to the zodiac and to astrology.

This will not prevent astrologers and others from trying to equate the twelve precious stones, which are the foundations of the New Jerusalem in Chapter xix 19–20, with the Twelve Tribes in the order enumerated in Chapter vi 5–8, and also with the signs of the zodiac. It is quite possible that an author of that date would have had the idea of making such a correspondence; but Dr Charles believed that the author's object was, on the contrary, to avoid any astrological reference, and show the Holy City 'as having nothing to do with the ethnic speculations of his own and past ages regarding the city of the gods'. As evidence of this Dr Charles points out that the stones are mentioned in reverse zodiacal order, beginning with Jasper (The Fishes) and ending with Amethyst (The Ram). He did not realize that the reverse order of the signs is the direct order of the Sun's progress through the houses which correspond to them; hence this does not weaken the possibility of an astrological interpretation. The fact which does militate against the astrological view is that the angel in Chapter xxi measures the city neither clockwise nor anticlockwise, but taking the sides of the square in the order East North South West (verse 13); and this order does suggest a wish to break the circle of astrological analogies.

I

But the equation of stones and signs which Dr Charles accepted is taken from Athanasius Kircher, who claimed that it could be found on Egyptian and Arabian monuments;[21] and when we reflect that his book, *Œdipus Ægyptiacus*, was published in 1653, this begins to seem doubtful. Further, if we accept the stones as running in the same manner as the gates of the city, in the order East North South West, we find ourselves with a diagram in which Aries and Libra stand next to one another in the north-west corner, and Virgo with Pisces similarly in the south-east, which is in plain defiance of astronomical fact. Thus it seems not improbable that the author of Revelation was indeed trying to avoid the astrological parallel.

The original list of twelve precious stones is of course that of the high priest's 'breastplate' or pouch in the Book of Exodus (xxviii 17–20 and xxxix 10–13). This list has also been interpolated in a garbled form into a passage of Ezekiel (xxviii 13).[22] The author of Revelation does not follow either list; and his catalogue of the Tribes (vii 5–8), which omits Dan and Ephraim in favour of Joseph and Manasseh, differs in both order and composition from the list in Ezekiel xlviii 31, where Ephraim and Manasseh are omitted; and both disagree with the much older list in Numbers ii, which omits Joseph and Levi.

There is no reason to suppose that any astrological reference was intended by the writer of Exodus, any more than by the authors of the forty-ninth chapter of Genesis. And we can only obtain an astronomically coherent scheme in Revelation if we assume that the order East North South West was an early copyist's error, and that the order intended was some circular order; though this might be East South West North, as in Numbers ii, or North East South West as in Ezekiel xlviii, or even East North West South. Dr Charles, however, has shown a possible reason for the order stated,[23] in putting first the six sons of Leah, then those of Rachel, and last those of Leah's handmaid.

In view of all this confusion we may just as well ignore Kircher's equation of amethyst with the Ram, and if we also ignore the order East North South West, we can take the first foundation to be Aries and run straight through the list. This is probably the origin of the popular catalogue which ends with amethyst for the Fishes.

To make matters worse (if that were necessary) Josephus gives two somewhat different lists of the correspondences of the stones with the Tribes, which are taken in order of birth. And the words he uses, when he refers the high priest's breastplate to the zodiac, are worthy of note.[24] He says: 'The two sardonyxes that were in the clasps on the high priest's shoulders indicate to us the sun and moon. And for the twelve stones, whether we understand by them the months, or the twelve signs of what the Greeks call the zodiac, we shall not be mistaken in their meaning.' In fact Josephus regards the zodiac as a Greek innovation rather than a Jewish tradition, but at the same time accepts the symbolism of the number 12 as corresponding to the months of the Hebrew calendar no less than to the twelve tribes.

The two *shoham*-stones which represented the sun and moon, and are here called sardonyxes, have been variously identified as reddish-brown onyx or possibly topaz (by Charles), as very dark (in the Midrash Bemibdar), and as aquamarine-beryls (by Kunz).[25]

But although Josephus, Philo of Alexandria, and others accepted the equation of the twelve jewels with the zodiac, the wearing of special birthstones is not too well attested in ancient times. Kunz suggests that it arose in Poland in the eighteenth century, among the Jewish population there, and mentions that Catherine de' Medici possessed a girdle of twelve stones which may or may not have been zodiacal. In view of her period (1509–89) we shall probably not be wrong in assuming that they were (see Plate 2).

Nor is it in the least unlikely that zodiacal stones were worn under the Roman Empire; for among surviving classical gems one may find a heliotrope bearing the head of Sarapis surrounded by the zodiac,[26] a green jasper bearing the symbols of the Moon, Capricorn, and Taurus, obviously in reference to the owner's horoscope, and a jewel which belonged to Tiberius and bore his sign of Scorpio as well as that of Capricorn for his predecessor Augustus (see Plate 4).

The most common list of birthstones is derived from that in the Book of Revelation, beginning with St Peter, Aries, and the month of March, and assuming the jasper for that month to be red. But in the course of time several alterations have been made, and lists discoverable in different countries often disagree. There is no possibility of finding an authentic list because there has never been one, and also because of the differences which have arisen in course of time and through the difficulty of identifying the stones. As examples of these difficulties, the Authorized Version has reversed the order of the third and fourth stones in the Book of Exodus; the *topazion* is said by Pliny to have been a greenish stone, so that it cannot be our modern topaz; and the Apostles were supposed to be attributed to the twelve jewels of the Apocalypse in the order in which they occur in the synoptic Gospels, but the synoptic Gospels do not all give the names in the same order!

The most futile of all lists is that authorized by the National Association of Jewellers at its meeting in Kansas City in 1912 or 1913. This is nothing but a piece of unfounded salesmanship, and is wrong in principle because it ignores tradition and commits such solecisms as making aquamarine an alternative to bloodstone, including the pearl which is not a mineral, and using various stones not known in antiquity. If birthstones are to be worn at all, one would think that they should at least correspond to the signs of the zodiac, which are supposed to have some occult virtue, and not to the months, which are mere calendrical divisions and have none. To wear a month-stone is as meaningless as to wear the civic arms of one's birthplace. The use of a birthstone ought to imply a belief in the Law of Correspondences, and therefore like anything else should be done properly or not at all. And oddly enough Kunz, though he condemns the Kansas City lists so roundly, attributes the emerald to Aries and the carbuncle to Pisces!

Colour has notoriously a strong psychological effect on the mind. If there is to be an astrological correspondence as well, there should be something in common between the symbol and the thing symbolized. One cannot symbolize the Ocean or the Fishes by a red stone such as the carbuncle. Camillo Leonardi's *Speculum Lapidum*, published in Venice in 1502, attributes to the constellation of the Eagle a zodiacal influence comparable to that of the Crab. As symbology this is impossible; but an inspection of Leonardi's other attributions suggests that he did know what he was about, and hence Cancer is probably a slip for its opposite sign Capricorn, which would be correct.

The basic symbols are archetypal, that is to say, the human mind thinks in those terms and cannot be prevented from doing so. Gold, being the colour of the sun, represents the highest value, or God;

red, not blue, is the colour of blood, bloodshed, ferocity and energy; blue, not yellow, is the colour of the sea and therefore of the feminine aspect of God; and green, as the colour of growth, suggests peace and plenty. Regardless whether jewels can be consecrated with spiritual force or magnetized by the power of a personality, these laws of symbolism must be observed or there will be a conflict of opinion between the conscious mind, with its arbitrary wrong symbolism, and the unconscious, which cannot help knowing better. Even among Muslims the unconscious will not accept a green stone as a symbol of war in general, nor therefore of the constellation Scorpio which has produced so many famous soldiers.

The chemical composition of the various gems is not much help, since ruby, emerald, amethyst, and topaz are now all classed as varieties of corundum; emerald and aquamarine are greener and bluer varieties of beryl; and the various different-coloured chalcedonies, including carnelian, agate, chrysoprase, catseye, jasper, sard, and others, are all classed as quartz. For this reason we are almost entirely reduced to making the attributions by colour.

A 'correct' list of stones for the twelve signs would have to be one which was psychologically easy to associate with their other corres-pondances, and in accordance with tradition and the Qabalah. Such a list might run somehow as follows:

Aries must obviously have a red stone, hence red jasper would be a good choice; and ruby, traditionally a solar stone, suits the exalta-tion of the sun here.

Taurus: green jasper; emerald; malachite.

Gemini in the Middle Ages was thought to deserve a mixture of red, white, and dark stones, hence the best would be some variegated stone such as onyx (banded agate) or a striped chalcedony.

Cancer, in view of its association with the Moon and the sea, might well have moonstone, sea-green beryl, or turquoise.

Leo must have a yellow stone, presumably topaz, zircon, yellow jasper, or fire-opal.

Virgo, as sign of the green corn, could have the apple-green chrysoprase, chrysoberyl, which is much the same colour, or green felspar, which was associated in ancient Egypt with fertility. If thought of as a sign of purity, diamond or an uncoloured chalcedony would be required. But since ripe corn is also a suitable colour for Virgo, one could use light brown agate or onyx.

For *Libra* the correct stone would be jade, from its use in treating kidney-disease in China, the kidneys being 'ruled' by Libra; also chrysolite and peridot (olivine), which are transparent green stones, green being required because Libra is ruled by Venus.

Scorpio: bloodstone or haematite; carnelian (red chalcedony).

Sagittarius should for Qabalistic reasons have a blue stone, hence sapphire or star-sapphire; and this suits quite well in the sidereal zodiac, where the constellation is a mixture of air and earth, and associated with flight. Those who prefer the tropical zodiac, and think of this as a fiery sign, might choose rose-quartz.

For *Capricorn* tourmaline is appropriate by reason of its light-excluding qualities, in any colour including the dark blue indicolite; also the black opal.

Aquarius as the sky sign should have a sky-blue stone, but since it is a more watery sign than Sagittarius perhaps it should have the paler stone, aquamarine rather than sapphire. It might also have lapis lazuli, which was much prized in antiquity and so ought not to be omitted.

Pisces: the amethyst, though attributed here for the wrong reason, suits very well on account of the Jupiterian colour and also because it was supposed to be a preventive of drunkenness, which is associated with the planet Neptune and the Fishes. The opal also seems to belong here, and there is a purple fluorspar which much resembles amethyst.

The terminology of gems is not always reliable. Jacinth meant originally a hyacinth-blue stone, probably the sapphire, but the name is now used of an orange stone, which is ridiculous. Further, some gems found in jewellers' shops are dyed, the original colour having been removed by heating. This may not matter from the point of view of appearance, but obviously no person using a gem for magical purposes would choose a dyed stone.[27] This remains part of the curious lore of gems, despite the widespread belief that because one cannot work magic oneself, therefore no one else can! Those who try ought at least to do it properly.

TABLE 13   *Jewels of the High Priest's Breastplate*

As translated in Exodus xxviii 17–20 and xxxix 10–13, Revised Version:

sard	topaz	carbuncle
emerald	sapphire	diamond
jacinth	agate	amethyst
beryl	onyx	jasper[28]

As in a model made in India in 1927 for the late Rev. G. A. Cooke, D.D., Regius Professor of Hebrew at Oxford (cp. Notes 5 and 22 of this chapter):

carnelian	peridot	emerald
carbuncle	lapis lazuli	sardonyx
brown agate	banded agate	amethyst
topaz	turquoise	aquamarine

TABLE 14 *Some Symbols, Animals, Colours and Gems attributed to the 12 Signs*

	Altar of Gabii (Louvre).	Varaha Mihira, Pancha Sidd. I. 20.		Martianus Capella, Teubner, p. 34.	CCAG XII 68.	Theosophical Society (1912)	'777', by A. Crowley (2nd ed. 1955).
ARIES	Minerva / owl	sheep / amethyst / red	blood-red	dendrites	siderite	sardonyx	ruby / geranium / tiger lily / topaz / mallow
TAURUS	Venus / dove	cattle / jacinth / dark	white	heliotrope (stone)	yellow jacinth	carnelian	alexandrite / tourmaline
GEMINI	Apollo / tripod	apes / chrysoprase / yellow	green	keraunos (reddish onyx)	diamond / heliotrope	topaz	magpie, orchid / amber / lotus
CANCER	Hermes / tortoise	water-creatures / topaz / blue (cyaneus)	darkish red	lychnis (fiery red)	green jasper, euchite	chalcedony	
LEO	Jupiter / eagle	forest beasts / beryl / golden	smoky white	astrites (?catseye)	agate / selenite	jasper	catseye / sunflower
VIRGO	Ceres / basket	green / dogs / chrysolite	variegated	emerald	corallite, dendrite	emerald	peridot / lily
LIBRA	Vulcan / bonnet	birds / sard	black	Scythian-emerald	sardine, emerald	beryl	emerald / aloe
SCORPIO	Mars / wolf	purple / birds of prey / sardonyx / black	golden	jasper	hematite, pyrites	amethyst	snakestone / cactus
SAGITTARIUS	Diana / hound	military beasts(!) / emerald / flame-colour	yellow	rock crystal	amethyst	jacinth	jacinth / rush
CAPRICORN	Vesta / lamp	ruminants / chalcedony / white	whitish yellow	water-coloured gems	ophite / chalcedony	chrysoprase	black diamond / thistle / Indian hemp / glass (sic) / coconut
AQUARIUS	Juno / peacock	marine beasts / sapphire / deep blue	darkish white(!)	diamond	magnet	crystal	
PISCES	Neptune / dolphin	marsh and river beasts / jasper / ash-colour	fish-colour	hyacinth	beryl / jacinth	sapphire	pearl / opium

10. *India and the Asterisms*

'AN astrologer', says Varaha Mihira, 'ought to be of good family, friendly in his appearance, and fashionable in his dress; veracious, and not malignant. He must have well-proportioned, compact and full limbs, no bodily defect, and be a fine man, with nice hands, feet, nails, eyes, chin, teeth, ears, brows, and head, and with a deep and clear voice; for generally one's good and bad moral qualities are in unison with one's personal appearance. Now, good qualities in a man are: that he is pure, clever, free, eloquent, ready-witted, able to discern time and place, good in the highest sense of the word; not timid in society, unsurpassed by his fellow-students, skilful, not addicted to bad passions, well versed in the arts of expiation, of procuring prosperity, of incantation, and of anointing; further, that he is regular in worshipping the gods, in his observances and fasts; that he is able to raise the prestige of science by the wonderful perfection of his branch of study, and to solve satisfactorily any question, except in cases where supernatural agencies baffle human calculation; finally, that he knows both text and meaning of the works on mathematical astronomy, natural astrology, and horoscopy.'[1]

Modern Western astrologers do not realize that they need lessons in deportment and voice-production, and a manicure once a month! But India is of all countries that where astrology has stood highest in repute; marriages there are still made by astrological principles and, we are told, are almost always happy. Astrology has enjoyed in India not only high social standing but also a reputation for being incredibly ancient. The date of the most famous astronomical textbook, the Surya Siddhanta, is stated to be 2,163,102 B.C. ![2] However, the immense age claimed for Indian astronomy and astrology is finding fewer and fewer supporters, even in India. Nor is this due only to a naive pursuit of the fashion for discounting the antiquity of antiquity; the scholarly principle of believing nothing beyond the evidence leads straight to error only in such a study as the Mystery Religions, where the evidence is that the evidence is insufficient.

But the difficulty with Hindu star-science is its incurable vagueness. Both Sir William Jones in the eighteenth century and Albiruni[3] in the eleventh—his travel book on India was published in 1031—found it impossible to obtain clear-cut answers to astronomical questions from their Hindu informants. India is supposed to be under Capricorn, the symbol of which is a crystal, hard and lucid; and this accords with the pre-eminence of Indian thinkers in the deep realms of religion and philosophy: but religion, in which India particularly excels, is under Sagittarius, where Mercury, the planet of accurate measurement, is at its weakest. (Hence the supposed quarrel between science, which measures regardless of meaning, and religion, which having found meaning does not trouble to measure.)

Indian astronomy abounds in enormous periods of time. The present epoch of history, the Kali Yuga or Iron Age, began at midnight—or perhaps at dawn, for Aryabhata was ambiguous on this point—on Friday, February 18th, 3102 B.C. at Ujjain in Central India; it will last 432,000 years. According to another tradition, the Kali Yuga began when all the planets were in conjunction in 0° Aries; but this did not happen in 3102 B.C. In any case the Age of Brass, which preceded the Age of Iron, was twice as long, the Silver Age before that was three times as long, and the Golden Age, when men were twenty-one cubits tall and lived four hundred years, was four times as long. For 432,000 years is only one-tenth of a *mahayuga*, and 1,000 *mahayugas* make a *kalpa*, at the end of which the world is destroyed by fire and recreated. Thus a *kalpa*, according to Brahmagupta, who wrote in A.D. 628, lasts for 4,320,000,000 years. This is longer even than the Pre-Cambrian Age, which recent geologists have put at a thousand million years!

It has been suggested that these long periods arose because Indian astrologers wanted to claim experience of all possible combinations of planets and signs of the zodiac. But the real reason was that they did not feel at home with fractions, and so instead of saying, as we do, that the length of the synodical month is 29 days 12 hours 44 minutes 2·8 seconds, they preferred to say that the sun and moon return to exactly the same relative position after a given number of whole days. But of course the shorter this period, the less accurate it would be; so they sought greater accuracy, just as we do, by adding to their figures. The difference is that we use a decimal point.

Another difference is that Hindu astronomers measured celestial distances by co-ordinates which are not at right angles to each other — which has rather naturally earned them the disapproval of modern scientists. They used the ecliptic, but the pole of the equator instead of the pole of the zodiac; hence their references are distinguished by the names of 'polar longitude' and 'polar latitude'.

Recent scholars have deducted a good deal from the age of the Surya Siddhanta. It is now thought to be mostly of the sixth century A.D., and to be a compendium of Indian astronomical knowledge after the influence of Alexandria had become established. Alexandria was not founded till 332 B.C., and remained the capital of the learned world until the Muslim conquest in 640.

Its influence on Indian astronomy and astrology was enormous. Many Greek technical terms were taken over directly, for instance *lipta* for minutes, *trikona* for trigon, *jamitra* for diameter (or opposition), *panáphara* for rising; and it is significant that the art of calculating a horoscope is called *hora*, Greek for hour. The great names in Indian astronomy are almost all subsequent to the spread of Greek learning: Aryabhata, 'the father of Indian epicyclic astronomy', lived at the end of the fifth century A.D., Varaha Mihira died in 587, Brahmagupta was thirty years old in 628. Earlier than any of these, writing about 378, was Pulisa of Saintra; and when we remember that Alexander becomes Sandro in Italy and Sandy in Scotland, this may well be Paulus of Alexandria. Alexandria itself was called in India Yavanapura, meaning simply The Ionian City, and Varaha Mihira knew the difference in longitude between Yavanapura and Ujjain, which was the Greenwich of Hindu astronomy.[4]

The great period of immigration of Greek knowledge must have been between the birth of Christ and A.D. 400; and it must have begun before Claudius Ptolemy wrote his Great Construction (A.D. 140) because the constants used in Indian astronomy are never quite the same as those of Ptolemy, with one exception: the Romaka Siddhanta quotes the length of the tropical year in the same figures as were given by Hipparchus. One reason for such differences is that the Indians preferred to convert the Greek figures into long periods of whole days, in their usual style, and another is that they used sidereal and not tropical periods. Some of Ptolemy's discoveries, for instance the evection of the moon, are found in the Siddhantas, but sometimes their constants are more accurate than his: the Surya Siddhanta gives precession as 54 seconds per annum, against Ptolemy's 36″, and the correct figure nowadays is 50·2. The Surya Siddhanta also gives a more accurate estimate of the longitude of the sun's apogee, though this of course may have been improved with time; the climate of India does not readily preserve millennary manuscripts.

Despite efforts to prove the contrary,[5] heliacal risings, which were so useful to Greek farmers and sailors, and were the basis of Hesiod's *Works and Days* and of the parapegma shown in Plate 5, seem not to be mentioned in India before the time of Aryabhata. As late as A.D. 80 Hindu astronomers believed the moon to be farther away than the sun,[6] and it is quite possible that the names of the signs of the zodiac were then still unknown, although the existence of a twelve-fold division is mentioned in the Mahabhārata.[7]

The Alexandrian origin of the zodiac, or at least of its subdivision into 36 *drekkana* or decans, is suggested by such casual phrases as the following—from Varaha Mihira's astrological textbook the Brihat Jataka, in the picturesque translation of B. S. Row:[8]

> The first drekkana of Mesha [i.e. Aries] represents a man with a white cloth round his waist, dark complexion, pretending to protect, fearful red eyes and a lifted axe. The second drekkana of Mesha is sketched by Yavanas [i.e. Greeks] as representing a woman with red cloth, fond of ornaments and food, pot-belly, horse-face, thirsty and single-footed. The third drekkana of Mesha represents a man cruel, skilled in arts, yellowish, fond of work, unprincipled, with a lifted-up stick, angry and covered with purple clothes.

Another sign that the zodiac is not of Hindu origin is the existence of two sets of names, one transliterated from the Greek, presumably before the meanings were known, and the second a translation:

TABLE 15   *The Hindu Zodiac*

Greek name	Spelt in Sanskrit	Sanskrit name	Meaning of Sanskrit name
Krios	Kriya	Mesha (or Aja)	(Ram or Goat)
Tauros	Taurusi	Vrisha	Bull
Didumoi	Tituma	Mithuna	Couple (man and wife)
Karkinos	Karka	Karkata	Crab
Leōn	Leya	Simha	Lion
Parthenos	Pâthena	Kanya	Virgin
Zugos (=yoke)	Juka	Tulā	Balance
Skorpion	Kaurpya	Vrischika (or Ali)	Scorpion (or Bee)
Toxotēs (=archer)	Taukshika	Dhanus	Bow
Aigokerōs (=goat-horned)	Akokero	Makara (or Mriga)	Sea-monster or (Antelope)
Hydrokhoös (=water-pot)	Hridoga	Kumbha	Pot
Ikhthues	Ithusi	Mina	Fish

We shall see in the Babylonian chapter that *makara* the sea-monster is not likely to be a verbal corruption of *akokero*. By origin Capricorn is a sea-monster. Rather surprisingly, *Makara* is called 'the Indian Cupid', but this can be justified astrologically if we remember that the goat in Greece was a symbol of lust and that Mars is exalted in Capricorn; for Mars stands for creative energy, of which desire (Latin *cupído*) is the expression.

The Hindus, incidentally, have put the zodiac to a commoner use than any other people, in that they employ the twelve names to describe arcs of 30 degrees on any circle and not only along the ecliptic.

Before the influence of Alexandria began to be felt, Hindu cosmology had supposed a flat earth with the sun, moon, and planets circling an enormous mountain called Mount Meru. When this had to be modified, the earth-ball was imagined hanging in the centre of the world-egg, and Mount Meru became its axis, a golden mountain on which the gods lived at the north pole and the Asuras at the south pole.

Another halfway-house in the progress of ideas was the doctrine of the libration of the equinoxes. When it was found that the spring point did not remain stationary in Aries, someone suggested that perhaps it swung to and fro through an arc of 27 degrees to east and west of the beginning of the sidereal zodiac.[9] The time before it returns to this point is given in the Surya Siddhanta as 7,200 years. At the same period, before the theory of epicycles had been adopted to account for the retrogradation of the planets, the behaviour of Venus and Mercury in alternately preceding and following the sun was explained by saying that they were pulled this way and that with ropes of air by beings who were said to be forms of time.[10] The learned Westerner, if he likes to scorn such ideas, would do well to remember that in religious thought he is still far behind the Hindu, perhaps is hardly even an apprentice; and Hinduism includes atheism as a branch of religion.

What then did Indian astronomy amount to before the Hellenistic period? Did it owe anything directly to Babylon, and had the Hindus discovered the precession of the equinoxes?

Before the excavation of Mohenjo-Daro and Harappa, the Vedic period in India was variously dated between 4500 B.C. and A.D. 880. It is now generally agreed that Vedic literature grew up between 1500 and 1000 B.C. Before this time the Aryan-speaking tribes had not apparently entered the country; but their predecessors will have had the usual reasons for observing the stars. Thus B. G. Tilak discovered hints of the vernal equinox occurring in the neighbourhood of Orion (Mriga),[11] which would justify the earliest date suggested.

Sengupta says:[12] 'The chief requirements for the performance of Vedic sacrifices were to find as accurately as possible the equinoctial and solsticial dates, and thence to find the seasons. The Vedic months were synodic months and reckoned from a full moon to the next full moon.' Thibaut on the other hand[13] thought that the year at that epoch consisted of 12 months of 360 days with an intercalary month inserted whenever necessary. The fact is that the Hindus early started to use a period of 1,830 days, which is 67 lunations, and one cannot be sure whether this means 5 years of 366 days, or 5 years of 360 days plus one intercalary month of 30. At any rate in the literature of the Vedic period, which includes the Brahmanas and Samhitas, the sun and moon are the only heavenly bodies definitely mentioned; and since the Brahmanas are full of number symbolism, and the number 5 has no particular importance in them, it seems unlikely that the five planets were recognized as such.

But observation of the seasonal sacrifices in Vedic times did oblige men to notice certain changes due to precession. In the earliest period, according to Burgess and Sengupta, the winter solstice occurred when the moon was full in the constellation Maghâs, of which the principal star was Regulus. This gives as a date the year — 2344, with a margin of error of several centuries either way, since the moon might be up to 6 degrees away from the star. At the same time the Pleiades rose due east — exact in — 2926 — and spring began one day after the new moon nearest to Spica. All this would agree with a date perhaps as early as the thirty-first century: but we shall not need to go so far back for the origin of the zodiac.

The asterism Māghas gave its name to the month of Māgha, which at first was supposed to run from the full moon in conjunction with Regulus to the following full moon between Denébola and Spica; but owing to precession it became necessary, if the month of Māgha was to remain close to its proper asterism, to reckon it from the preceding new moon instead of from the full, and later still to make it end with the full moon of Regulus instead of beginning there.[14]

Dr R. Shama Sastry, followed by M. Raja Rao and others, has tried to maintain that in the Vedic era the Hindus could calculate the periodical return of eclipses in different parts of the zodiac.[15] It is difficult to feel certain of this, for not all myths can be interpreted as descriptions of external natural phenomena, especially among an introverted people such as the Hindus, with whom a religious and psychological interpretation is never unlikely. Shama Sastry, however, gives an entirely astronomical interpretation to the myth of Rohita and to the Śunahśepa hymns: Aditi, the mother of the gods, whose name means Unity, is interpreted as the 58-year eclipse cycle, Rohita becomes a reddish-coloured eclipse recurring in one thousand days, and the fact that Visvamitra cursed 50 of his 101 sons is explained because 50 of the 101 eclipses in a twenty-year cycle are invisible from any given place. Shama Sastry also says that the first day of the Kali Yuga was a total solar eclipse, and as confirmation shows that the 239th day of 3101 B.C. was a nearly total lunar eclipse.

After the Vedic period astronomical knowledge continued unchanged until the early centuries A.D. The chief work was the wearisome technique of calculating the places of the sun and moon in the *nakshatras*; but the word *nakshatra*, which in the Brahmanas had only meant a star or constellation, no matter which, was now specialized to mean one of the set of 27 or 28 asterisms into which the circle of the zodiac was divided. We read for instance in the Mahābhārata:[16] 'I went out with the moon at the Pushya and have returned with the moon at the Sravana.' Pushya is the sixth asterism counting from the Pleiades and its principal stars are Gamma, Delta, and Theta Cancri; Sravana is the twenty-first, marked by Beta and Gamma Aquilae; so the speaker tells us that he was absent for just over half a sidereal month, and owing to the moon's varying speed this might be anything from twelve and a half to fourteen and a half days. He also tells us that he measures time sidereally by the moon's place among the stars, and not synodically by her amount of light. The Babylonians would have done it the other way.

The first known mention of the asterisms as a complete set is in the Atharva Veda.[17] The passage is rather tedious since it lists all 28 in similar terms, but it begins as follows: 'Marvellous all together, and brilliant in the sky are the swift serpents of the firmament! Desiring the friendship of the twenty-eight, I worship in my song the sky and the days. May Krittika be to me a subject of fortunate invocation, and also Rohini; may Mrigaçiras be propitious to me, Ardra fortunate, Punarvasu amiable, Pushya beautiful, Açlesha light, and Māgha a path for me; may the Former and both Phalgunis be that which is pure, and Hasta likewise ... '

But whereas in this prayer all the asterisms are asked to be propitious, sooner or later tradition grew up about their individual influence, just as with the signs of the zodiac. For instance, a late fragment of debased Sanskrit discovered in Turkestan reads:[18] 'A formula of medical herbs ... In this respect effective are Chitra, Mrigaçira, Sravana, Nidhana ... Causers of misfortune are Krittika, Phalguni, Ashadha ... Causers of success in this respect are Purva-Phalguni, Purva-Ashadha, Purva-Bhadrapada ... The fourteenth day again has Yama for its deity.' (Yama is the god of death.) Modern use of the asterisms is of course similar, but more detailed.

As we saw, the asterisms are not mentioned in China before the third century B.C.; and the Arabian system is very much later. It seems then, in default of any evidence from Babylon, that their country of origin must have been India, unless we prefer to think

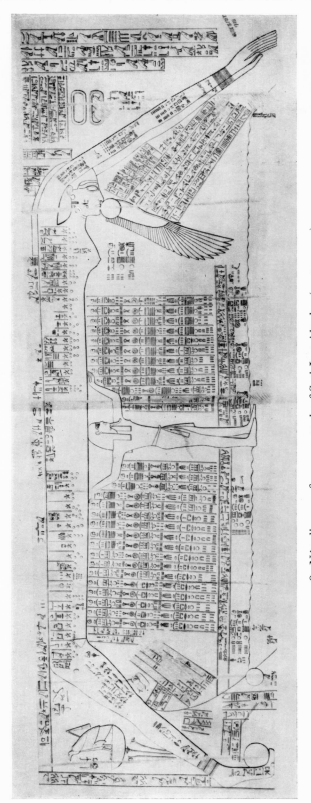

18. Nût diagram from cenotaph of Seti I at Abydos (*see page* 193)

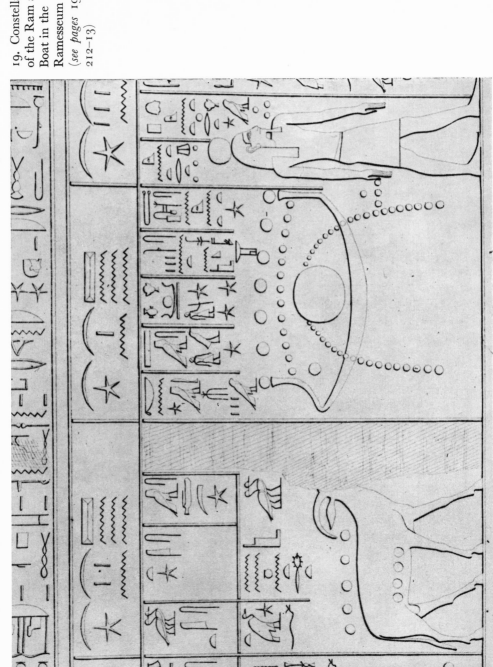

19. Constellations of the Ram and Boat in the Ramesseum (*see pages* 192, 200, 212–13)

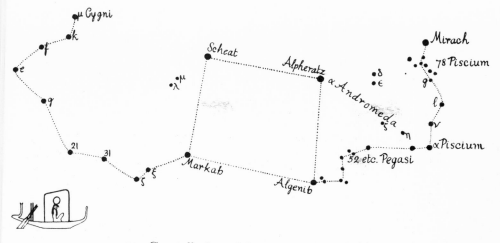

20. Constellation of the Boat (*see page* 200)

21. Marble plate from Egypt, Greco-Roman period, showing
zodiac and hour-circle

Modern. Medieval. Demotic. Hieroglyphic.

22. The Sigla of the 12 Signs

with a number of scholars including Thibaut[19] and Needham,[20] that they grew up separately in the two different countries. It is conceivable that the number may originally have been 24, since 6 of the Indian *nakshatras* are composed of pairs bearing the adjectives Former and Latter (Purva and Uttara). But most probably the total varies between 27 and 28 for the same reason that so many peoples used to use an intercalary month, and that our own year varies between 365 and 366 days. Not for nothing is the optional asterism, Abhijit, which bears the number 22 and not 28, marked by a star well outside the zodiacal belt—none other than Vega, which lies $61° 45'$ north of the ecliptic.

The Chinese have to a far greater extent than most peoples the civil-service mentality; they could hardly think of astronomy without imagining its use for administration, and to them the engaging vagueness of a system which varied between 27 and 28 divisions was psychologically repugnant. If they received this system from India, they will have decided to use always an even number of asterisms because it is more convenient for accounting. There is something after all in the attribution of the Chinese to Libra, the sign of administration; for even Confucius and Mencius, who, being sages, ought to have known better, wanted to be administrators.

Originally, then, and perhaps as long ago as the twenty-third century B.C., the asterisms will have been simply a set of small constellations lying near the path of the moon, having no standard length or recognized dividing lines. Later they were provided with *yogataras*, that is, 'junction stars', at or near which each began, and later still they became 27 arcs of $13° 20'$ each, the *yogataras* no longer marking the boundaries.

Of the pre-Alexandrian period of Indian astronomy hardly any books remain. There are fragments of the Garga Samhita, too corrupt and incomplete to be safely translated, and the Jyotisha Vedanga.[21] This little work makes no mention of the planets; it is entirely concerned with calculating the times of the full and new moon festivals, and the unexpected mention of Pisces (*mînât*) near the beginning, as first sign of the circle, is probably to be explained as an interpolation, since the zodiac is otherwise not referred to. At any rate this isolated reference is no safe basis for a theory that the zodiac was known in India at the time this book was composed; for the winter solstice then fell in the first degree of Sravishtha, the summer solstice in the middle of Aslesha, the vernal equinox in 10° of Bharani, and the autumn equinox in 3° of Visakha; and this points to a date about the sixteenth or seventeenth century B.C.

During this phase few of the fixed stars seem to have attracted attention outside of the zodiacal belt; we only hear of Agastya, which is Canopus, and the Seven Rishis, which are the stars of the Great Bear. The five-year cycle of 1,830 days was in use, and there were five names, instead of numbers, for the individual years within the cycle. But towards the end of the period another system of calculation along the zodiac was invented, the *tithi*, which was the length of time the moon takes to gain twelve degrees of longitude over the sun. A *tithi* may be a little more or a little less than a day, according to the speed of the moon.

In all the earliest writings the first of the asterisms is Krittika, the Pleiades, and this is generally taken to mean that the vernal equinox fell near it. But since Krittika means 'razor', Erard Mollien suggested in 1852[22] that the name might metaphorically signify 'the dividing-line'; for the original Sanskrit name of the Pleiades was *bahulah*, meaning 'very many' — and this, rather than 'sailing stars', may be the meaning of the Greek word Pleiades. He added that the opposite asterism Visakha, marked by Alpha and Beta Librae, means 'divided in two', and gives for it the symbol ⊖, which bears a certain resemblance to the glyph of the constellation Libra ♎. Furthermore, Kartikeya the war-god, who was suckled by the Pleiades and takes his name from them, was created by Shiva in order to vanquish (according to Mollien) the two giants Taraka (meaning 'constellation') and Kraoncha (meaning 'obliquity'). Not only so, but almost the first act of Kartikeya was to conquer an enormous Ram!

All this sounds very zodiacal. On the other hand Varaha Mihira makes no mention of precession in the Pança Siddhantika, which is of the sixth century A.D., and the Surya Siddhanta still accepts the theory of the libration of the equinoxes. So it seems impossible to suppose that precession was recognized in India before Alexandrian times.

Albiruni in the eleventh century blames Varaha Mihira for not having understood precession, alleging that 'he had no knowledge of the motion of the fixed stars towards the east. The solstice has kept its place, but the constellations have migrated, just the very opposite of what Varaha Mihira has fancied.'[23] This, however, is only an earlier example of the controversy that burst out in the nineteen forties, when Western astrologers were confronted with two zodiacs and began to wonder which of the two was fixed and which had moved. It is of course a question of point of view. A farmer would naturally conclude that the stars move against the fixed background of the seasons; an astronomer might think that the seasons move against the fixed background of the stars. Only since they discovered that neither is really fixed have astronomers made the seasonal measuring-point official.

The same controversy continues to this day in India, where some astrologers use the tropical zodiac, called *sayana*, and others use various *nirayana* or sidereal zodiacs; and because the knowledge of the original fiducial star has been lost, they try to determine the true *ayanamsha*, that is, the amount of difference between the tropical and sidereal zodiacs. This question would not arise if the proper reference-point were known. It will be mentioned again in the last chapter.

As happened in Greece and Rome, there was probably a period of several centuries when the effect of precession, and the consequent distinction between tropical and sidereal measurement, was not clear to astrologers, and perhaps not even to astronomers, since the two were not then distinguished. Hence the fact that the fiducial point was called *Asvini-adi* only meant that it fell somewhere in the asterism Asvini, which extended to about 12° west of Beta Arietis; and in fact the vernal equinox lay in that space between the years – 300 and +572. *Asvini-adi* will have meant 'the first point of Asvini' by analogy with the first point of Aries; and from this it may have been transferred to mean the fiducial point of the whole zodiac. And then it was later noticed, owing to precession, that the *yogatara* of the asterism Revati, Zeta Piscium, the tropical longitude of which was 359° 50′ in A.D. 560, was very close to the equinoctial point. And thus arose the idea that the zodiac should be measured from the small star Zeta Piscium—a notion which some Indian astrologers still accept.

A curious example of the transmission of knowledge in India was discovered in Pondicherry by a certain Lieutenant-Colonel John Warren, who published a collection of essays on Indian astronomy in

1825.[24] Warren met a calendar-maker who calculated for him the time of an expected eclipse of the moon by arranging shells on the ground. The man had no textbook, but worked by memory of various astronomical formulae which he carried in his head. His method of working revealed quite clearly that it came down to him from the works of Varaha Mihira in the sixth century, the Roman Empire in the third century, and ultimately from Babylonian texts of the Hellenistic period and the methods exemplified in Seleucid cuneiform tablets of the second and third centuries B.C.

Divination began very early in India, as it does all over the world. The constellations *gyeshthagni* and *vikritau* are mentioned as unlucky in the Atharva Veda,[25] and the Laws of Manu[26] lay down that astrology and fortune-telling are impure occupations and as such forbidden to ascetics. On the other hand it is astonishing how many types of divination are mentioned by Varaha Mihira in the Brihat Samhita, which is for the most part a textbook on the stars: they vary from knowing the signs of a person's face, and how to judge a sword or a jewel, to prognostications from the movements of tortoises, goats, elephants, or wagtails, from boils, torn garments, lamps, and umbrellas, to divination from the objects bepissed by dogs! Indeed, so many are the signs to be noted that, 'since the symptoms cannot be observed uninterruptedly by one man, an astrologer, if well paid, ought to keep in his service four other persons conversant with the science.' These four should be always on the look-out for meteors in all directions. For, 'as was said by the great seer Garga, the king who does not honour a scholar accomplished in horoscopy and astronomy, clever in all branches and accessories, comes to grief.'[27] Considering how few modern kings have done this, and how many have come to grief, the statement is without doubt statistically true!

Varaha Mihira has a long chapter on architecture, a short one on the culture of trees, and condemns those who speak evil of women; but his lists of objects ruled by the signs and asterisms, and of the character and destiny they produce, are very short. There are, however, extensive prognostications for the raising and lowering of prices: for instance, if there be an unusual appearance of the sun whilst in Virgo, one should buy up fly-whisks, donkeys, camels, and horses; for then one will be able to sell them for double six months later, though after any shorter or longer period one will only make a loss. The fly-whisks—chowries—are included among the animals because they are made from the tails of yaks.

As in China, the influence of a planet is good when it shines clear and bright; but when it is dim and 'wounded', then suffering will come to those ruled by it. This appears to be a pre-zodiacal form of divination, and thus it is not improbable that astral divination existed in India long before the zodiac was imported in Alexandrian times. And India was probably the origin of the system of 27 or 28 *nakshatras* which were later taken up and modified by the Chinese and Arabs. The Indian names for the asterisms, unlike the zodiac, are not those of animals.

TABLE 16   *The 28 Hindu Asterisms, or Nakshatras*

			long.	R.A.
1. Açvini	two horsemen	βγ Arietis	12°	11°
2. Bharani	bearer, yoni	35, 39, 41 Arietis	17°30'	16°50'
3. Krittika	(uncertain)	Pleiades	12°	12°
4. Rohini	ruddy	Hyades	13°30'	13°40'
5. Mrigaçiras	antelope's head	λφ Orionis	4°20'	4°40'
6. Ardra	moist	α Orionis (Betelgeuze)	25°40'	27°30'
7. Punarvasu	again brilliant	Castor & Pollux	13°	14°
8. Pushya	nourishing	θγδ Cancri	3°	3°20'
9. Açlesha	embracer	εHydrae	20°	20°40'
10. Mâghas	mighty	Regulus	15°	15°
11. Purva Phalguni	(?like a bed)	δθ Leonis	11°	10°40'
12. Uttara Phalguni	(same)	β Leonis	15°	13°50'
13. Hasta	hand	αβγδε Corvi	10°	9°20'
14. Chitra	brilliant	Spica Virginis	19°	17°40'
15. Svati	sword	α Boötis (Arcturus)	14°	13°10'
16. Viçakha	with spreading branches	αβγ Librae	11°	11°
17. Anuradha	success	ζδ Scorpii	5°	5°
18. Jyestha	oldest	Antares	12°	12°
19. Mula	root	ζηθικλ Scorpii	13°	14°
20. Purva Ashadha	unsubdued	δε Sagittarii	6°	6°30'
21. Uttara Ashadha	(same)	ζσ Sagittarii	6°40'	7°
22. Abhijit	conquering	Vega	13°20'	14°30'
23. Çravana	ear	βγ Aquilae	10°	10°40'

24. Çravishtha	αβγδ Delphini	most famous	30°	30°40'
25. Çatabhishaj	λ Aquarii	having 100 physicians	6°	6°
26. Purva Bhadrapada	αβ Pegasi	beautiful foot	11°	10°30'
27. Uttara Bhadrapada	γ Pegasi + α Andromedae	(same)	22°50'	21°10'
28. Revati	ζ Piscium	wealthy	8°10'	7°40'

The meanings are rarely very certain. The last two columns give the extent of the asterisms in longitude and in right ascension respectively.

11. *Babylonian Myths and Omens*[1]

THE Babylonians have the greatest reputation of any ancient people for astronomical study, and it is often said that the zodiac had its origin among them. However, the earliest Mesopotamian cities, such as Kish, Shuruppak, Ur, and Jamdet Nasr were founded before 5000 B.C., and the latest known cuneiform text is of the year A.D. 75.[2] In so long a time astronomy must have evolved.

The first great civilization of the Euphrates and Tigris valley was the work of the Sumerians, who were not Semites and worshipped a vast and complicated pantheon of gods. The Accadians, who invaded and took over the Sumerian civilization, perhaps about 3000 B.C., were Semites, speaking a wholly different language, coming from South Arabia, and worshipping, apparently, only three gods, namely the Moon, Venus, and the Sun. They were obliged, however, when they became civilized, to change the sex of the Sun and Venus, for among them the Sun had been a mother-goddess and Athtar, the planet Venus, was male. The Moon remained masculine, but lost its Semitic name of Shahar and was called by the Sumerian name of Sin. To suit the Sumerian liturgy Shamash, the Sun, became masculine, and Ishtar, the evening star, became the goddess of love and war. Thus she retained a double nature; in the morning she was goddess of war, and was called the Male Ishtar, but in the evening she became the goddess of love, and was called the Female Ishtar.

The Accadian period was brought to an end by another Semitic invasion such as the first, but often called Amorite. It was only then that Babylon rose to eminence. The First Dynasty of Babylon ruled from 1830 to 1531 B.C., and its most famous king is Hammurabi (1728–1686). This period is often regarded as the first flowering of both astronomy and astrology, because of the Enuma Anu Enlil (or Ellil) series of tablets which has come down to us.[3] This is a collection of over 7,000 celestial omens and observations.

After this came the Cassite period, and then, about 1000 B.C., the

Assyrians devised their great menologies giving rituals of the months founded on earlier Babylonian and Sumerian practice. King Asshurbanipal, the famous antiquarian (668–626), issued a definitive text in fifteen tablets, twelve for the standard lunar months, and three extra for intercalary months.[4]

The Assyrian empire copied Babylonian customs in almost every respect, and when it fell in 612 astronomy (or astrology) was still valued by the kings of the Neo-Babylonian empire. Then came in succession the Persians (538–330), Alexander the Great and his successors the Seleucids, and finally the Arsacids (about 250 B.C. to A.D. 230).

The original God of the Sumerians was An, meaning apparently 'That which is above'—just like Horus in Egyptian—and this word was written as a determinative before all names of gods, on the principle that 'all the gods are part of God'. The Semites, however, seem to have believed in a single male Creator who was father of the tribe; hence the monotheism of the Jews and Arabs is not peculiar to them, but can be paralleled in less extreme form among the Phoenicians and Canaanites, the early Aramaeans of North Syria, the Minaeans and Sabians of Arabia Felix, and the Aksomites of Abyssinia. In origin therefore Allahh, and the Hebrew gods Elohim and Yaw (IAO), were not so different from Bel or Baal, whose name means simply The Lord. The Earth-Mother, on the other hand, was not a native idea among the Southern Semites; yet once discovered she was called Allat (feminine of Allahh), and by the time of Alexander the Great had become, under many local names, the *Tychè* or Fortune of many a city, and also the goddess who ordained the future for men, with definitely astrological implications.

It was held as a matter of common observation that the gods, most obviously the Sun and Moon but possibly others, ordered the course of agriculture and human fertility, and there was an ancient belief in Mesopotamia that they held a congress at the beginning of each year in order to determine the fates of earth-dwellers. In Babylon this great assembly was dated to the eighth day of the spring festival in the month of Nisan, and the presiding god was Marduk, as later Asshur in Assyria; but earlier it was Enlil the earth-god who presided, and before that Ea the Sumerian fish-man.[5] Thus fate was determined not by the stars but by the earth-god, or by the god of

153

the subterranean fresh-water ocean, and in Syria by various mother-goddesses who were patronesses of cities.

Rather naturally, then, there are no astrological documents of the Sumerian period, and of the Old Babylonian era only one tablet of the usual 'omen' type has been recovered.[6] Yet omen-taking became a standard feature of Babylonian official life, though individual records can often not be dated because they survive only in Assyrian copies, and the Assyrians did not file them under date but under the nature of the phenomenon recorded.

Omens were taken at any time if anything notable appeared, but most of all on the first day of the month, that is, at the appearance of the new moon. Sometimes the sickle appears on the twenty-ninth day since the previous one, and sometimes on the thirtieth, so the month varied between 28 and 29 days. It was the Sumerian city of Nippur which first made observations accurate enough to predict the length of the month in advance, and hence the calendar of Nippur became the basis of the religious calendars of the Babylonians, Assyrians, Jews, Aramaeans, and Phoenicians.

Significance was allotted to the moon's colour and elevation, brightness or dimness, and the direction of its horns. Babylonian accuracy was much greater in regard to the moon than in any other direction, and when Kidinnu, about 380 B.C., defined the length of the lunar month as 29 days 12 hours 44 minutes $3\frac{1}{3}$ seconds he was profiting by two thousand years of continuous observation.[7] (Modern measurements give 2·9 seconds). But omens were also taken from all kinds of celestial phenomena, from the movement, colour, and stations of the planets, from mists and clouds and shooting stars, and very frequently from haloes. These things were located in heaven regardless of their distance from the earth, and by reference to the constellation in which they were seen.

Prognostication was thus common in Babylonia long before the zodiac was devised.

In the thirty-seventh year of Nebuchadnezzar king of Babylon [says tablet VAT 4956 (567 B.C.)], on the 1st of Nisan (the preceding month had 29 days) the new moon became visible behind the Hyades; duration of visibility 64 minutes. Saturn was over against the Southern Fish. On the morning of the 2nd a rainbow appeared in the west ... At the beginning of the night of the 8th the moon was one ell before the star at the hind foot of the Lion. On the 9th the sun in the west was surrounded by a halo. On the 12th Jupiter rose at dusk. On the 14th the god was visible with the god [that is, the sun and full moon were visible simultaneously]. 16 minutes passed between sunrise and moonset the next day. On the 15th it was overcast. On the 16th Venus appeared ... From the 8th of Second Adar till the 29th of Nisan the water rose 3 ells 8 fingers. This month a fox came into the city ... on the 9th Sivan summer solstice. On the 10th the moon passed $3\frac{1}{2}$ ells above Antares. This month's prices were: 1 *gur* would fetch 12 *ka* of barley or 60 *ka* of dates ... On the night of the 6th the moon was surrounded by a halo and within it were the Pleiades and Hyades and Beta and Zeta Tauri ... On the night of the 29th reddish clouds were seen in the west ... There was an earthquake on the 22nd, Mercury being $3\frac{1}{2}$ ells behind the fish-tail of Capricorn.[8]

Many similar documents are expressly addressed to the king. Here is one which reminds us of the parapegma quoted in Chapter III:

At the behest of my master and my mistress, an announcement in advance ... On Airu 30th, Saturn in Scorpio, Mars in Aries. On 2nd, heliacal setting of Sirius. On 6th, heliacal rising of Venus in Gemini in the west. Mercury appears in the east as Aldebaran, which has disappeared. 15th, full moon day. 20th, heliacal rising of Jupiter at the end of Taurus: Mercury's heliacal setting in the east as Aldebaran, which has disappeared. 26th, Venus reaches Cancer. 27th, last sickle of the moon.

The date of this is -239.[9]

Eclipses, however, could not always certainly be foretold, since at each occurrence of a given eclipse at a given place the shadow passes a little farther north (or south) than last time, and after five or six eclipses will miss entirely. Hence such a report as the following:

To the king my lord, thy servant Mar-Ishtar. Greeting to the king my lord. May Nabu and Marduk [that is, Mercury and Jupiter] be favourable to the king my lord. Length of days, comfort of body, and joy of heart may the great gods give to the king my lord. On the 27th day the moon was still visible. On the 28th, 29th, and 30th days we kept watch for an eclipse of the sun, but he went his way and did not have an eclipse. The moon was visible on the first day, which is the day expected for the month in question. Regarding Jupiter, about which I reported earlier to the king my lord: 'He is shining in the path of Anu in the region of Sibzianna; when the sickle disappeared he stood low on the horizon and could not be perceived, but we can say that he is in the path of Anu and such is his interpretation': now I report to the king my lord: 'He is retarded and therefore was not perceived, but he is in the path of Bel, below the constellation of the Chariot, he has really gone down as low as the Chariot. His interpretation was accordingly erroneous, but the interpretation of Jupiter in the path of Anu is as I earlier reported to the king my lord and would not be wrong. For the information of my lord the king.[10]

A great many ritual prohibitions were enforced on both king and people in connection with the observance of the calendar, and demons were always ready to take vengeance on any breach. There were days when the king must or must not wash his clothes, when he must recite a penitential psalm, when no one might go out in the street and no physician practise. This is the origin of the resentment at Jesus' healing on the Sabbath, for not only festivals but prohibitions and the intolerance of the Old Testament God seem to have been imitated from Babylon. Thus the Sabbath began as the four quarter-days of the moon, not as a festival or rest but as an ill-omened day on which it was unlucky to do business. In Assyria, and indeed since Hammurabi's time, all work was forbidden on the 7th, 14th, 19th, 21st, and 28th days, and in fact hardly any documents have ever been found dated on one of those days. On the other hand the Roman and Egyptian lucky and unlucky days are not derived from the Mesopotamian lunar system.[11]

The week and month began in the evening with the appearance of the sickle moon, and any days over the 28 were disregarded. The first day of the week was therefore Monday, not the Saturday of the Jews nor the Christian Sunday. 'The 26th and 27th were days of sorrow and penance,' says Langdon, 'preparatory to the 28th when the moon crossed the river of death and joined Nergal lord of the dead in the darkness of Arallu.' The 29th was unlucky for everything. 'The king shall not go out of the gate; he will meet with witchcraft in the wind of the street' on the 29th Tebit. If a man goes out on the 29th Nisan he will die, but if he goes out on the 29th Tammuz his wife will die. In the months of Nisan and Tebit it was illegal to take purgatives, and on the 13th Nisan we read: 'One may take a wife. One may not be merry. One should worship Sin.'[11]

Another feature of Babylonian life was a great fondness for consulting diviners, though that too, of course, was frequently forbidden on Mondays. There are extant lists of suitable signs of the zodiac for attempting various undertakings, for instance[12] to get a man's love for a woman the moon should be in Libra or Scorpio, and for the converse in Pisces or Gemini. For getting one's name favourably mentioned at court She (or rather He, Sin) should be in Pisces; to remove a spell, in Aquarius or Pisces; to bind or drown a ghost (a recognized way of getting rid of one), in Cancer; and to obtain a change of mind, in Leo. Many of these signs have nothing in common with modern astrological notions, but there is precedent for the traditional good influence of Jupiter, although in other documents, as in India and China, the goodness or badness of a planet depends on its luminosity: 'When Jupiter culminates, the gods will give peace, troubles will be cleared up and complications unravelled. Rain and floods will come' (so the crops will be good), 'the lands will dwell securely. Hostile kings will be at peace, the gods will receive prayers and hear supplications.'[13]

It is lucky for Mars to be dim, unlucky for him to be bright. 'When a planet stands at the left horn of the moon, the king will act mightily.' On the other hand, 'When Jupiter appears in the month Tammuz there will be corpses, and when Mars approaches Jupiter there will be great devastation in the land.'

Among these serious matters, written about 660 B.C., we come unexpectedly on a plaintive wail: 'The handmaiden of the king my lord has gone to Accad; I cannot wait, she has run away. Let the king my lord fetch her and give her to me. From Billi the son of Igibi the magician.'[14] One cannot help feeling that, had Billi been efficient as a magician he would not have needed police assistance.

It is highly significant that Hammurabi's laws, which mention every kind of profession then existing, make no mention of the *mašmašu* or diviners.[15] This implies that only since the seventeenth century B.C. did prediction spread down from being a purely official matter for king and city, and begin to be practised for individuals.

The most famous set of Babylonian astronomical tablets is called the mulAPIN series. The name means Plough Star, and refers to the constellation Triangulum, which lies between Aries and Andromeda but apparently included the Pleiades. These tablets, though only written about 700 B.C., give the results of observations going back to about 1300, and with their help an amazing number of Babylonian star-names have been placed in the sky. This was the great period of accurate observation in Babylonia, at any rate for the daily rising, setting, and culmination of stars, though more complicated phenomena such as computations in advance were done only approximately by simple arithmetical progression.[16]

In these tablets the ecliptic had not yet become the principal line of reference; the Babylonians spoke instead of the Three Ways of Enlil, Anu, and Ea. The Way of Anu was a band about 16° 40′ wide on either side of the equator, the Way of Enlil lay to the north of it and the Way of Ea to the south.[17] Thus the sun's path was divided into four sections, and it spent three months in the equatorial Way of Anu, three in the northerly Way of Enlil, the next three again in that of Anu, and the last three in the southerly Way of Ea. If these four zones were divided equally, the four points of passage would fall in the middles of the second, fifth, eighth, and eleventh signs of a tropical zodiac. Thus they are definitely older than the zodiac, and their equality determines the width of the Way of Anu.

Another important feature of Babylonian astronomy was the 'twelve times three', or 36 seasonal stars. The Egyptians also had a set of 36 seasonal stars, but theirs were of quite different origin, and not divided between the three Ways of Anu, Enlil, and Ea. In the fifth tablet of the Epic of Creation it is said of Marduk :[18]

He constructed stations for the great gods. The stars their likenesses he fixed, even the Lumaši. He fixed the year and designed the signs [of the zodiac]. For the twelve months he placed three stars each. After he had defined the days of the year by signs, he established the place of Nibiru to fix all of them, in order that none transgress or loiter. He appointed the places of Enlil and Ea with him [i.e. beside the Anu Way]. He opened gates on both sides, he made strong the lock-rails left and right. In her belly he placed the 'heights', and caused the new moon to shine forth, entrusting to him the night. He fixed him as a being of the night to determine the 'days'. Monthly without ceasing he magnified him with a crown: 'At the beginning of the month, the time of the shining forth over the land thou shalt shine with horns to determine six days, and on the seventh with a half crown. At the full moon verily thou art in opposition monthly, when the sun on the foundation of heaven has over-taken thee.'

Oddly enough, Nibiru is not taken by scholars to mean either the equinox or the fiducial star of the ecliptic, obvious though this might seem to the expectant reader. The word is translated 'place of crossing over', and refers in particular to the position of Jupiter in such a situation, especially on the meridian.

A good deal of puzzlement has been caused by the 36 stars, since they correspond to the twelve months, and one might expect that those in the Way of Enlil, being farthest north, should rise heliacally at the beginning of the month, those of Anu in the middle, and the stars of Ea at the end. However this does not work out, and further-more the constellations' names are accompanied by numbers, of which those in the middle ring are double those of the inner ring and half those of the outer ring. Probably this refers to the length of watches of the night, which varies with the seasons. But the list of twelve times three stars has a different origin, though this too is not entirely certain. These stars correspond very largely to the old lists of twelve stars each, which are attributed to Elam, Accad, and Amurru, and this is a regional division rather than an astronomical one. Originally, one would expect, the Elamites, Accadians, and Amor-ites would each have made a choice of twelve stars to mark the months by their heliacal rising, and some of these would be the same, but others not. When in Hammurabi's time the scribes tried to develop a single system for the whole Babylonian empire, they con-flated the local schemes, and whenever a gap was caused by two stars being the same in the local lists they filled it with a constellation that rose at the same time of year, or even with a planet. Thus in the first lists of stars of Enlil, Anu, and Ea, the star of Enlil was only the most northerly of the three, and did not, as in later times, actually have to be over 16° 40′ from the equator.[19]

Now since the ^{mul}APIN series dates from about 700 B.C. and makes no mention of the zodiac, presumably it was not yet known, for it was not required so long as the Babylonians were quite content with their Three Ways and their lunar calendar. But the names of months are often seasonal, so we ought to inquire whether the signs of the zodiac could be derived from seasonal phenomena. This leads us to one of the most curious blunders in the whole history of this curious subject.

Two astronomers, Mr and Mrs Maunder, writing in the *Monthly Notices of the Royal Astronomical Society* for March 1904, print the following list of meanings of the Accadian month-names, according to a certain Colonel Conder of the Royal Engineers:

> lambing, calving, bricks, harvest,
> very hot, dried up, thunder, irrigation,
> very cloudy, flood, very rainy, ploughing.

This list starts with the Lamb, a form of Aries, goes on with the Calf, of the nature of Taurus, gives 'very hot' in the fifth position, that of the Lion, and in place of the Goat-fish and Waterman says 'flood' and 'very rainy'. Mr and Mrs Maunder then comment:[20] 'It will be seen that this scheme has no zodiacal reference, but it is entirely climatic.' Yet why should the zodiac have no climatic reference?

If we draw up a table of Sumerian months, from which the Babylonian, Assyrian, and Hebrew month-names were derived, we find that a good number of them have seasonal references, such as 'brick-making', 'seed-corn', 'lighting braziers', 'wind and rain', and the rest are named from religious festivals. Indeed, according to Professor Langdon[21] 'a striking aspect of Sumero-Babylonian religion is the association of myths with each of the months and the attempt to find in the regnal constellations of the months figures which correspond to the ideas involved in the monthly myths'. Obviously therefore we must investigate the monthly myths in order to see whether by any chance they throw light on the origin of the zodiac.

These myths and festivals originated in the Sumerian period, between 3000 and 2000 B.C. The most famous is that of Tammuz, the beautiful shepherd loved by Ishtar. In the second month (Ayar) he celebrated with her the Sacred Marriage, but in the fourth, called after him, he died, the pasture being burnt up by the summer sun, and in the sixth, when the days become shorter than the nights, Ishtar descended into the lower world to bring him back. However, at Babylon Tammuz did not rise again until the 28th of Kislev, when the days begin to lengthen. Also in the fourth month, about June, the Sumerians celebrated the festival of the breaking of bread for Ninazu, another name for Tammuz, then the burning of torches in the fifth month was a festival of the dead, also for him, and 'purification', the name of the sixth month, refers to Ishtar's descent. Thus no less than four months are named from the Tammuz-Ishtar cycle. Indeed, Langdon suggested that the fire-festival may be the origin of the midsummer fire-festival on St John's Day both in North Africa and Europe, adding: 'And in Sardinia to this day the ritual of the Adonis gardens is incorporated in the festival for St John's Day.'[22]

Tammuz was identified with the constellation Orion, the name of which was Sib.zi.an.na, the Faithful Shepherd of Heaven. Orion's conjunction with the sun, when he is invisible and therefore might be said to have descended to the lower world, now takes place in June, but in 2000 B.C. it took place only about a month after the vernal equinox, hence the descent of Tammuz cannot have been in origin an astronomical myth, but only a seasonal one. Similar considerations preclude an astronomical origin for the festival of purification in the month of Elûl and the ox-procession at Nippur.

The first and seventh months were both marked by new-year festivals, since the early Semitic year began in the autumn and the Sumerian year in the spring. Hence the resemblance between the myths of the two months, both of which refer to the gods fixing the fates for the coming year. It seems, however, that the myth of the judgment of souls at the autumn equinox cannot be earlier than about 2000 B.C.

Both the eighth and ninth months are connected with the lighting of braziers, partly on account of the cold weather and partly also to symbolize the reascent of the sun from the shortest day. The tenth month, Tebit, was exceedingly unlucky, since ghosts were supposed

L

to return from under the earth, and demons were especially active. This, together with the season of storms, may be why Capricorn and Aquarius, both sacred to the water-god Ea, the one kindly god in the Mesopotamian pantheon, were also regarded as demons in the train of Tiamat. Finally the last month, Adar, means 'threshing-floor', and was the season of the barley harvest in all Sumerian cities. So it does not look as though the monthly myths were astronomical in themselves, though attempts were later made to fit them together with various constellations, some of which were adopted into the zodiac.

But although the zodiac seems not yet known in 700 B.C., 410 is the date of the earliest surviving personal horoscope. It was cast for a son of Shuma-usur, son of Shuma-iddina, and placed Jupiter in Pisces, Venus in Taurus, Saturn in Cancer, Mars in Gemini, and Mercury invisible, with the Moon beneath the 'horn' of Scorpio, that is to say in Libra. The Ascendant is not mentioned in this or any other Babylonian horoscope that has come down to us. The predictions are very brief, indeed in the oldest example seem to say only that the horoscope was a good one. In other cases 'he will be lacking in wealth', 'his days will be long', 'he will have children'. The customers for some of the third-century horoscopes bear Greek names such as Aristokrates and Nikanor.[23]

This raises the question, how early were the Babylonians able to locate the equinox, and where in Aries or Taurus did they place it? Kugler, writing in 1914, stated that before the eighth century B.C. eclipses were not observed accurately enough to predict their recurrence with certainty, and systematic intercalation of extra months was not possible before 528 B.C.; hence the finest flower of Babylonian astronomy occurred as late as the third and second centuries. By then, however, the Babylonians had ceased to observe the equinox, so their longitudes were $5\frac{1}{2}°$ out. Had the beginning of the year been accurately, and not just empirically, geared to the equinox, the fact of precession would have become evident from the gradual change of date in the heliacal risings of important stars. But the Babylonians did not discover precession.[24]

By the seventh century, the great period of astronomy in Assyria, the epact of eleven days had been discovered, which is necessary to bring the lunar year of 354 days up to the solar year of 365; but not so long before that the beginning of the year, though computed in advance, still needed to be checked by observation. A seventh-century text says: 'The place of the celestial equator seek and the days to be filled in thou shalt know; then fix thou the year and add the epact.'[25] The beginning of the year was thus fixed at the new moon nearest to the spring equinox.

(i) *The Eighteen Signs*

Theoretically, then, the vernal equinox fell a fortnight before this new moon, on the fifteenth day of the twelfth month about 1000 B.C., and later, about 700, on the fifteenth of the first month. (The Easter full moon still falls on the fifteenth day of the first lunar month after the equinox.) There were twelve schematical months of 30 days each, connected with the heliacal rising of certain stars, and the sun's path was divided into four parts, though not yet into twelve.[26] The twelve equal signs, as opposed to the figures of constellations, are first mentioned in extant literature in the Persian period, 419 B.C., in tablet VAT 4924. But there is evidence of an earlier stage at which there were not twelve but eighteen constellations of the zodiac. The list is as follows:

TABLE 17 *The Babylonian Zodiac of 18 Constellations*

Zappu	tuft of hair	Pleiades
Gud.an.na	bull of heaven	Hyades
Sib.zi.an.na	faithful shepherd of heaven	Orion
Šugi	charioteer	Perseus
gamlu	scimitar	Auriga
maš.tab.ba.gal.gal	great twins	Gemini
al.lul	(?crab)	Praesepe
ur.gu.la	lion or lioness	Leo
ab.sin	furrow	Virgo
zibanitu	horn, (later) scales	Libra
gir.tab	scorpion	Scorpio
PA.BIL.SAG	(uncertain)	Sagittarius
suḫur.maš	goat-fish	Capricorn
GŪ.LA	(?giant)	Aquarius
zibbati	tails	Pisces
šim.maḫ	great swallow	southern fish
anunitum	(a goddess)	northern fish
ḫunga (=agru)	hireling	Aries

Some scholars have thought this stage intermediate between an original set of 28 lunar mansions, as in eastern Asia, and the 12 equal signs, but there is no need to suppose so, for Babylonian interest in the moon was directed first of all to its light, depending on its relation to the sun, and so their mansions, had they existed, would have been the same as their days, and the first would have been the new sickle, regardless of the stars among which it appeared.

The eighteen are called 'constellations which stand in the path of the moon, and into the region of which the moons pass monthly, and which they touch'. One of the texts listing them is the first tablet of the mulAPIN series, compiled between 1400 and 900 B.C. and extant in a tablet dated 687, the other is British Museum tablet 86378.[27]

The conclusion seems to be unavoidable that about 1000 B.C. in Babylonia the zodiac had not taken form, but most of its constellations were known under the same names as we have today. A tablet of about 400 shows a later stage of the evolution, when the 'Charioteer' and the 'Scimitar' are missing, the two goddesses of Pisces have been replaced by the single constellation *Iku*, and the 'Square Field' (Pegasus, of course) and the 'Tails' have been exchanged for the 'Band of the Fishes'. Finally, the twelve usual signs are given in a late-Babylonian text of the Seleucid period.[28] A similar intermediate stage is found in an extant ritual for consecrating a new statue of a god.[29]

(ii) *The Eleven Signs*

The most striking thing about these Babylonian irregular zodiacs is the absence of the Ram: it suggests that the zodiac was not invented by the Babylonians alone, but perhaps their constellations were used for a syncretistic scheme in which Greece or Egypt may also have had a share. There is, however, no doubt of the Babylonian origin of most of the constellations, above all Capricorn. The Greek word for Capricorn, *aigokerōs*, does not mean 'goat' but 'creature with horns like a goat', and not till Claudius Ptolemy made Capricorn an earthy sign did anyone dream of forgetting that it had a fish's tail. As such it is of common occurrence on Babylonian monuments, especially boundary-stones (see Plate 10).

In Babylonia ownership of land was not protected, as in Egypt, by a set of markers along the boundaries, but a full-sized 'boundary-stone' was set up in the middle of the field, and a small copy or tally was kept at home. The stone was inscribed with the owner's name and necessary details, and at the top were pictured in relief the gods or demons invoked to protect the owner and punish infringement.

The oldest surviving boundary-stone belonged to King Entemena about 3500 B.C., but it was the Cassites (1746–1170) who made their use common for private citizens; being mountain people they were prepared to fetch stone a distance of a hundred miles, there being no stone in Babylonia.

One cannot pretend that all the gods represented on boundary-stones are astronomical—they vary too much; but among the most popular choices were Anu 'father of the gods, king of heaven', Anunit his wife, Ea the king of the subterranean fresh-water ocean and god of springs, Enlil 'the sublime lord who determines the fate of the gods', and the other greater gods such as Ishtar, Shamash, and Nabu (Venus, the Sun, and Mercury).

The commonest symbols are the crescent moon on its back for the god Sin, a star for Ishtar, and the winged disk or four-rayed wheel of Shamash, also seven stars or points for the Pleiades, and various dragons. There are frequently more or fewer than twelve gods represented, nor is the order in any way consistent, hence they cannot be zodiacal symbols, although a good number of them do have constellations associated with them. Also common are figures of Scorpio and Capricorn.

The general principle is that a deity can be represented by his shrine (all shrines look much alike), by his weapon or his animal, or by any combination of these. The lightning-fork of Ramman the weather-god may appear on a shrine or alone, with or without his symbol, the crouching ox; and the ram's head has nothing to do with Aries, but belongs to Ea, and often occurs on the back of the goat-fish which is his animal symbol. Ea is the only one of the Sumerian and Babylonian gods who was never angry, and always ready to help both gods and men out of difficulties. He is often represented as a man walking in a great fish-shaped cloak, the head over his head and pointing upwards like a mitre, the tail at his heels, and the forward leg showing his human form. He is said to have emerged four times at long intervals from the ocean to teach civilization to men, and each time he would retire into the water at night. Capricorn his symbolic creature symbolizes this dual life, and has as yet no association with the planet Saturn, which has never been reputed to help people out of scrapes. Saturn was represented by the lion-headed dragon and the god Nergal, who is the violent sun of summer and also the winter sun and god of the dead.

Among the titles of Ea[30] is 'antelope of the subterranean ocean', so there is no need to look further for the origin of Capricorn the fish-tailed goat. It is also called *kusarikku*, the fish-ram, and *suhurmashu*, skate-goat. The latter became the common name of the constellation Capricorn, and the former explains why a ram was also a symbol of Ea and sometimes appears on Capricorn's back. In late-Babylonian times the fish-ram and skate-goat were also used as monsters in the train of Tiâmat, but 'antelope of the Apsu' was a title of Ea as long ago as Sumerian times.

When Babylon rose to be chief of all cities, Marduk its local but hitherto minor deity had to be raised to the level of the great gods. A crisis was therefore engineered in heaven by the Babylonian scribes, and a monster appeared, Tiâmat, representing the salt and bitter sea (by contrast with the fresh waters of Ea). Tiâmat for merely grammatical reasons was feminine, and even Anu, the original creator, fled before her. Then Marduk undertook to do battle against Tiâmat on condition of being recognized as one of the great gods. He passed the preliminary test, which was to destroy and create again a garment provided by the examiners, and then successfully tore Tiâmat's body in two. Of the two halves heaven and earth were made. This was about three thousand years after the foundation of Ur and Kish.

Tiâmat had a train of eleven monsters, but this does not mean that she and they together comprised the zodiac, for she in herself comprised the whole of heaven, which did not exist so long as she lived. Marduk set the eleven demons in heaven as constellations, and they are not very zodiacal; they are the Viper, the Raging Serpent, the dragon Lakhamu, the Great Lion, the Gruesome Hound, the Scorpion-man, the destructive spirits of wrath, the Fish-man and Fish-ram.[31] To these were added Tiâmat and her husband Kingu, and the constellation Hydra, representing an unfortunate dragon called Mushkhusshu, which in Sumerian times had started life as a harmless vegetation-spirit but suffered, like other dragons, merely for being a dragon.

Very common on boundary-stones is the picture of a scorpion, and there sometimes occurs a scorpion-man drawing a bow (Plates 10 and 11). This looks like a combination of Scorpio and Sagittarius, and indeed Langdon says that the scorpion-man 'is universally identified with the archer Sagittarius'.[32] This explains why in some pictures the centaur has a scorpion's tail and a second scorpion beneath it. The two were not originally distinct, and only became so when the zodiac was schematized. This double nature may be the reason why Sagittarius was double-headed, with a human head facing forward and an animal head looking back. And this of course will have encouraged Ptolemy to make Sagittarius a double-bodied sign, although it seems now to be centuries since the two heads were mentioned in astrological literature.

There is no evidence that the scorpions on boundary-stones are astronomical; they might readily symbolize the curses with which these monuments are laden. Gilgamish, in the epic called after him, is terrified by a scorpion-man who guards the gates of sunrise, and such a figure would not be associated with one part of the zodiac more than another. Nor are the names of the two constellations any help: *gir.tab* means simply scorpion, and the name of Sagittarius, PA.BIL.SAG, cannot be interpreted because it never occurs in any other context. However, this sign was identified with Ninurta the god of war, and therefore, had the zodiac been a purely Mesopotamian invention, Sagittarius would surely have become the sign of war, whereas in fact it became something very different. But Scorpio as the sign of war may have its roots here.

Obviously, then, Scorpio, Sagittarius, and Capricorn are of Babylonian origin, since they occur in Mesopotamia well over a thousand years before they are carved in Egypt upon the zodiacs of Denderah and Esna. But this does not prove that they were already at that date constellations, much less signs of the zodiac or thirty degrees in extent.

Aquarius is a different matter. The god Hapi, watering from two jars, was an extremely ancient symbol of the Nile. But a similar figure would be natural anywhere. In Babylon there is a form of Ea which is sometimes called 'the god with streams', and sometimes he holds a pot, but more often the water flows spontaneously from his hands and arms,[33] as in Plate 12. He is not, however, particularly located in Aquarius. The Babylonian name of Aquarius is GU.LA, and this was at first taken for the name of a goddess patroness of childbirth and healing, whose wrath was celebrated by rest and mourning on the nineteenth day of the month. Later it was suggested that GU.LA might mean 'great star', which seemed unsuitable since no star of the first magnitude is found in this little constellation. The latest rendering is 'constellation of the great man', and its origin is supposed to be either the giant Enkidu watering an ox, or else the god of fresh water, Ea, also represented in Capricorn. These interpretations show how scholars have wanted to find a water-god here in order to explain Aquarius. The attempt has not been obviously successful, nor is it really necessary.

Enkidu was an extremely famous and interesting character, a friend of Gilgamish the Babylonian Hercules; and Gilgamish began his career as an historical personage, the fourth or fifth king of the First Dynasty of Erech, something before the year 3000 B.C. In myth, as probably in real life, Gilgamish became an appalling tyrant, and left 'not a son to his father nor a maiden to her mother,'[34] so to distract him from evil-doing the gods appealed to Aruru the earth-goddess, and she created Enkidu out of a piece of clay. He was naked and shaggy and behaved like a wild ox, in fact the euhemerists would say that he was a nomadic invasion. At any rate he was totally ignorant of civilized usages, so the people of Erech very wisely sent a harlot to seduce him; and she, having more brains than most, succeeded in educating him. He came to the city and wrestled with Gilgamish, and the two thenceforward became friends; so they left the city in peace while they went about the country wrestling with lions, bulls, and other public nuisances. Finally Enkidu died, and Gilgamish went to the nether world to fetch the plant of eternal life and restore his friend; but although he received the plant from the goddess of hell, he lost it on the way up! These two friends are very likely commemorated in the Great Twins, the constellation Gemini. Otherwise the most common twin-god is Nergal, as god both of the sun and of the lower world, and his emblem is two lions' heads back to back on a staff; but other gods also could be double-headed without any allusion to the constellation Gemini.

Besides the constellations already named, there is no reason to doubt the Babylonian origin of Taurus, Leo and Libra. UR.GU.LA (to be distinguished from GU.LA) does seem to mean a lion or lioness, although the Accadian version of the name means The Great Dog. Its position is known because it rises heliacally with Sirius and Hydra, Aquarius and Aquila set when it rises, and Libra rises when it culminates. Five of the individual stars are mentioned, of which our name Denebola is an Arabic version of KUN.UR.GU.LA, the Lion's Tail. In the same way Regulus (little king) is a translation of the Babylonian name of this star, LUGAL (=Sharru) meaning king.

Libra is often thought to be a late invention, somewhat unjustifiably suppressing the Scorpion's claws; indeed this is stated on a tablet in the British Museum, and also by Greek and Latin writers. The Accadian[35] name of Libra, *ziba.anna*, otherwise *zibanitu*, is of frequent occurrence, and means the 'horn' of the Scorpion, which must be its claws. The word *rin*, Scales, is found later, but Langdon remarks: 'About 2000 B.C. the constellation which governed this month [of Teshrit] was connected with the judgment of the living and the dead, the time when the gods fixed the fates, and consequently the Babylonians out of pure imagination saw the sign of the Scales, Libra, here ... Hence *zibanitu* also came to mean "Scales".' Then the exaltation of Saturn in this constellation caused him to be regarded as the planet of justice—though others have thought this was because his orbit is the least irregular of the planets. Also derived from this idea are the Mandaean angel of judgment, Abathur, the Islamic belief that in the ninth month Allahh will judge the souls of men, animals, birds, and spirits, and the Jewish day of Rosh ha-Shanah on the first of Teshrit, for which the 81st Psalm was composed.

Taurus the Bull seems to be a straightforward translation of the Babylonian *gud.anna*, bull of heaven, whose story is again connected with Gilgamish. When Gilgamish, with Enkidu's help, had demolished the terrible Humbaba, Ishtar, goddess of lechery, fell in love with him, but he repulsed her, pointing out quite justly that she was incapable of faithful affection: all her previous lovers she had herself brought to a bad end. Furious, Ishtar flew to heaven and demanded of Anu her father that he should create a Bull of Heaven to kill Gilgamish. Anu obliged, and this is the Bull that draws the Plough-star (the constellation Triangulum).[36]

A bull, however, is also the regular emblem of Adad, Hadad, or Ramman, the god of thunder and lightning, and this is the god signified by the bull on boundary-stones, not therefore the Bull of Heaven, and not zodiacal. But the Bull of Heaven, having been created at the desire of Ishtar, does naturally come to be ruled by Venus at the later date when planetary rulerships were invented. It was also represented by the white bull sacrificed at sunset on the fifth day of the Babylonian new-year festival, and is the origin of Virgil's 'white bull who with his golden horns opens the year'.[37] As will be later seen, this does go back to the time when the equinoctial new moon appeared in Taurus.

From the list of eighteen constellations six were later excluded, quite apart from those that were altered; and four of these six were in the region of Taurus and Gemini, namely the Pleiades, Orion, Perseus, and Auriga. In accordance with this we find a tablet of Nebuchadnezzar's time (604–561 B.C.) stating that the Moon's exaltation is in Perseus and the Pleiades.[38] Later it was said to be in 3° Taurus, and this is exactly the same spot, for the sidereal longitudes of the stars concerned are these:

Algol (Beta Persei)	1° Taurus
Alcyone, chief of the Pleiades	5° Taurus
Mirfak (Alpha Persei)	7° Taurus

So here is evidence that the Moon had an exaltation before the zodiac was reduced to twelve signs, and further that the exaltations are very much older than the rulership of signs by planets. The same tablet speaks of the exaltation of the Sun in the Square Field and the Hireling — the space which later became the Ram. Venus is given an exaltation in Leo as well as in Pisces, the others are the same as usual, Mercury in Virgo, Saturn in Libra, Mars in Capricorn, and Jupiter in Cancer.

Evidently, then, the famous ^{mul}APIN list is precisely what it claims to be, a list of constellations athwart the path of the moon. To provide a scale of reference for accurate measurement of the moon's position, Perseus and the Pleiades (or rather, the Charioteer and the Tuft of Hair) would not both be necessary, since they overlap, nor would both Auriga and Orion, which have much the same extent whether in longitude or right ascension. Thus although Mr Fagan[39] claims that the exaltations of the planets originated in 786 B.C., when the new temple of Nabu, who is Mercury, was opened in Calah by Adad-nirari III, king of Assyria, yet 200 years later, in the time of Nebuchadnezzar, the Moon's exaltation, though in the right place, is not spoken of as in Taurus, and hence the zodiac, though it had probably been imagined, had not yet superseded the earlier system.

The constellation Taurus is of particular importance for the history of the zodiac because of the question when and in what sense the vernal equinox fell in it. Mr Fagan has calculated that, on the basis of twelve equal divisions based on Spica in 29° Virgo, the vernal equinox passed out of Taurus into Aries about 1963 B.C. The Babylonians were not capable of any such calculation, and would have reckoned the Taurean Age to persist so long as the first new moon of the year was seen as a rule in Taurus; until it was usually seen in Aries the Ariean Age would for them not have begun. This is why we find Langdon writing: 'A date anywhere between 1100–500 B.C. can be assumed for the beginning of the Aries period.'[39] On this principle to speak of the Ariean and Taurean Ages is not a mere curiosity or abstraction, nor does it suppose any mysterious influence of the precession of the equinoxes; it arose as a matter of observation among peoples having a lunar calendar. At this rate, of course, the Piscean Age would not begin till A.D. 1000, nor the Aquarian Age before 3000.

In the Sumerian period writing was under the patronage of the grain-goddess Nidaba, doubtless because she kept account of the stores. In Semitic times it was taken over by Nabu, the messenger of Bel (The Lord). Nabu's city was Borsippa, and in the sky he was the sun at the winter solstice, the planet Mercury, and the star Aldebaràn. His function was to write on the tablets of fate the decisions taken at the vernal congress of the gods, and for this reason Aldebaràn was called the Star of the Tablet, which also became its name in China. This was because, as the brightest star in Taurus, it rose heliacally at the end of April and thus announced the beginning of the Babylonian year.[40] The meaning of the Arabic name Aldebaràn is often thought to be 'the follower' because it follows the Pleiades, but Dr Langdon suggested that it might mean 'the forecaster', as a reminiscence of Nabu the divine scribe writing the predictions for the year.

The grain-goddess Nidaba, or Shala, is shown in Plate 13, and seems the obvious origin for Virgo. The name of the constellation is *absin*, the furrow, and its western half, without Spica, represented the bunch of dates of the goddess Sarpanitum, described in tablet VAT 9428[41] as 'she has a star on her head and a whip in her right hand, the thong of which stretches out over the tail of Leo'. (This doubtless explains why on the zodiacs of Esna, Virgo appears to hold Leo by the tail.) The illustration is of the Persian period, but three earlier texts give Spica, the ear of corn, as the only ruler of the month Elul, and it appears that the Sumerians knew it as the corn-goddess so long ago as Gudea's time. Virgo thus has a Babylonian and in fact a Sumerian origin.

The 'winged bulls' so famous in Babylonian and Assyrian sculpture are sometimes said to represent the four 'fixed signs' of astrology, but, as we saw in Chapter IX, this was not the original belief. The four 'fixed signs' were first so called by Claudius Ptolemy in the second century A.D., or at earliest by some follower of Hipparchus not long before. Winged bulls, however, existed in the Sumerian period; they were called *alad* by the Sumerians and *šedu* by the Babylonians, and the Hebrews are accused of worshipping them in Deuteronomy xxxii 17 and Psalm cvi 37. Most of them were underworld demons which fed on blood, but a few were good, such as those set up at the doors to defend kings' palaces, and we are also told that the good *šedu* has the form of a goat. Thus they do not always comprise the four animals usually expected; sometimes there is simply a winged human-headed bull with no lion about it, sometimes there are four leonine feet and no trace of a bull.[42]

Of the twelve constellations nine have now been discussed, and seven of them had a convincing Babylonian origin. With Aquarius and Gemini the evidence was less conclusive, and of the remaining three at least one, the Ram, was absent from the Babylonian zodiac.

The Fishes are not perhaps absent, but divided up. By the end of the Seleucid Era they were called The Tails, and KUN, meaning Tail, is the oldest name of this constellation. It was also called The Band, a double string or leash, and the two fishes tied together upon it are the goddesses Anunitum and Šimmah. Anunitum, the northern one of the two, means 'female dweller in heaven', or words to that effect, and represents the River Tigris, while Šimmah, the southern, though it refers to the Euphrates, means 'the swallow', and apparently is the emblem of an ancient goddess called Nina who used to fly over the sea in the shape of a swallow—probably a tern. So the 'swallow-fish' is not so much the flying-fish *exocetus* of the Indian Ocean, as a typical Babylonian conflation of two separate ideas, bird and fish. Thus the Babylonians saw in this area a tail, a band, a tern, a goddess, and two rivers, but that they also saw two fishes here before the reign of Esar-haddon is not to be considered certain. For the tail is not inevitably that of a fish.

Cancer likewise is problematic. Its name *al.lul* according to Langdon means 'the wicked or rebellious one', which reminds us of Orion; and though he asserts that it was definitely known as *bulug* the Crab, more recently Goessmann denies this, and declares that no one has any right to call it a crab or crayfish; its later name NAN.GAR means a carpenter or indoor worker, by intentional contrast to *ḫunga* the Hireling, an outdoor worker. But if NAN.-GAR[43] should really be read *kušu*, it possibly means a water-creature of some kind; this would not be surprising, but we must beware of discovering signs of the zodiac in Babylonia merely because we think we ought!

Finally, to return to Aries, this was the region where the city of Babylon had its heavenly counterpart. Its constellation was *Iku*, meaning The Square Field, identified sometimes with our Aries plus Cetus, but more obviously with the Square of Pegasus; and this reminds one that Babylon was a more or less square city and its most conspicuous feature, the temple of Marduk called Esagila, was a square tower of seven diminishing storeys. These storeys were painted in the colours of the planets, and though the colours have now vanished, in the mid-nineteenth century Rawlinson identified them on the remains of Ezida, the temple-tower of Nabu at Borsippa, and recorded them as follows: the lowest storey was black for Saturn; then brown-red for Jupiter; rose-red for Mars; gold for the Sun; white-gold for Venus; dark blue for Mercury; and the topmost storey silver for the Moon.[44]

Next to the Square the Babylonians had no Ram; its place was taken by *ḫunga* the Hireling. And yet, by one of those unexpected turns for which scholars must always be prepared, the Ram, which does not exist in the Babylonian zodiac, tries to sneak in by the back door in a very curious manner.

Cuneiform is a tedious script to write, and after a time the scribes indulged more and more in abbreviations. Thus PA.BIL.SAG (Sagittarius) became first PA.BIL and then simply PA; *maš.tab.ba.-gal.gal*, was reduced to *maš*, and Leo, UR.GU.LA, became A. Thus from 272 B.C. onwards the first sign of the zodiac was *hun*, short for *hun.ga*, the man who works for wages. But the original form of the word was *lu.hun.ga*, and this was shortened to *lu*, which can also mean Ram! There is, however, no question of this being the original meaning.

This coincidence might enable one to maintain a wholly Babylonian origin for the zodiac if the word *lu* could be proved to occur before the reign of Esarhaddon, who conquered Egypt; but even then there is no proof that the Babylonians would have understood it as meaning Ram rather than as an abbreviation of the old Sumerian word for Hireling. Furthermore the older form of zodiac, with eighteen signs and no Ram, was still in use, together with the Enuma-Anu-Enlil system, two or three hundred years later than Esarhaddon. Hence it is not possible to maintain that the zodiac existed before Babylon and Assyria had felt the influence of Egypt.

12. *The Horoscope of Eternity*

When Julius Caesar decided to give the Romans a new calendar, the expert whom he chose to design it was an Egyptian—though probably of Greek descent—Sosigenes of Alexandria. This was because the Egyptians possessed the only wholly reliable calendar known to the ancient world. The Babylonians had a higher reputation as astronomers, and took more notice of celestial happenings; but their calendar was lunar and hopelessly erratic. Already in 488 B.C., when Darius I wanted to provide a better calendar for Persia, he had adopted the Egyptian system just as it stood.

The ancient Greeks, and after them the Romans, had great respect for the wisdom of the Egyptians; but modern professors have almost no idea in what that wisdom consisted. This is because learning is static and consists largely of information, while wisdom is dynamic and requires mastery of the art of life. Wisdom therefore is not the same as the ability to reason, and in any case the Greeks did not learn that from Egypt. Genuine wisdom cannot be written, nor congealed into asphorisms and avuncular advice. Being concerned with the problem of how to live, it is naturally apt to be religious, and the wisdom of the Egyptians was the ultimate driving-force behind the Mystery Religions; for they were all studies in the art of living. Man is always trying to get life under control, and among his methods of doing so are system, rule, legislation, dogma, and punishment. But the wise man does not try to get life under control; he adapts himself and swims with the stream instead of angrily trying to dam it.

Where wisdom and knowledge meet is in the solving of problems; and one problem for which the Egyptians alone of the ancient nations had found a reliable solution was the organization of the calendar. Modern scientists consider that the year should correspond as closely as possible to the period of the earth's revolution about the sun; and this is contrived in the Gregorian calendar by the insertion of a leap-year day once in four years, with an exception in centennial years and an exception against the exception in millennial years. But whether the year 10,000 will be a leap year nobody yet knows, and so by Egyptian standards the Gregorian calendar is irregular.

(i) *The Calendrical Basis*

In the ideal Egyptian calendar no irregularity was permitted. There were no leap years. Twelve months of thirty days each were followed, or preceded, by five days called 'epagomenal', and that was all.

The Egyptian year, therefore, was about a quarter of a day short, and in consequence its relationship to the seasons was not constant: it lost a day in four years, a month in about 120 years, and a whole year in fourteen and a half centuries. That is to say, 1,460 Gregorian years are equal to 1,461 Egyptian years, and after that time the Egyptian New Year's Day returns to its starting-point.

This return of their New Year's Day to its proper place was always important to the Egyptians, indeed it was the linch-pin of their whole astronomical system. Their agricultural year began with the rising of the Nile; but the inundation could be early or late, deep or shallow, depending on the melting of the snows in Abyssinia and Central Africa. Between A.D. 1873 and 1904 the interval between two successive risings varied from 336 to 415 days.[1] It must therefore have been a great convenience when the inundation could be predicted and anchored to a regular astronomical phenomenon. This phenomenon we know to have been the heliacal rising of Sirius.

The heliacal rising of a bright star such as Sirius, or of a planet, was a beautiful as well as an important occasion to those who first noticed these things. When a bright star can be seen in the west soon after sunset, each evening it shines lower and lower in the solar haze, until finally it can be seen no more. This is called its heliacal setting. Being now so close to the sun, it remains invisible for a period which the Egyptians averaged at seventy days, although it varies with the star's declination and the latitude of the place. At Babylon, for example, Sirius is absent sixty-nine days, but Spica, being farther north, only thirty-six.[2]

Then, when the sun has passed a little farther on in the zodiac, one morning when the sky towards dawn has lost its darkness and the

176

earth seems lit but empty, awaiting the sun, in the glow of the east appears a twinkling point between gold and silver which was not there the day before. This is the return of the star; and if it pre-signifies the rise of the Nile, the return of the flood and of all green things and crops, then it will be very important and well watched.

In a clear climate, with no street-lighting and no industrial smoke, and where dawn is the most comfortable and convenient hour to rise from bed, a survey of the half-lit sky is easily made, and the re-appearance of a star well known, but absent for the last month or two, is a practical guide.

This heliacal rising of Sirius is the origin of the legend of the phoenix; for the explanation which connects it with the 'anting' of birds, and their occasional love of playing with fire, is unconvincing because it bears no reference to Heliopolis.[3] The legend tells that there is only one phoenix, and that at the end of its life it returns to its birthplace, which is the 'Arabian Desert' between the Nile and the Red Sea. There it burns itself to death, and a new phoenix arises from the ashes of the old. Really the fire in which the phoenix dies is the glow of dawn. It is born in the 'Arabian Desert', because that is the eastern horizon of Egypt, and the length of its life is 1,460 years, which is 4 times 365. The event was known as 'the return of the phoenix to Heliopolis', and was commemorated by Antoninus Pius with a special issue of coins, which can be seen in Plate 4(c). This not only shows the respect in which the Romans held the Egyptian calendar, but also gives us a basic date for computing Egyptian eras.

Antoninus issued his coins, with the word *ΑΙΩΝ* meaning Era, about A.D. 139, and Censorinus, writing in A.D. 238, states that 99 years earlier the Egyptian New Year's Day had fallen on July 21st. This therefore will be the date of the Phoenix Era, and if we count back in periods of 1,460 years we shall find the Birth of the Phoenix occurring within four years of 1320 and 2780 B.C. In fact, of course, the length of the solar year is not exactly $365\frac{1}{4}$ days, but 365·2422; nor is the length of the Phoenix Period constant — according to Petrie[4] it decreased from 1,466 years about 600 B.C. to 1,448 about A.D. 2000, and should average 1,508. Nevertheless, the Egyptian calendar must certainly have been inaugurated on its New Year's Day, and since it existed long before 1320 the most probable date is about 2780.

M

The Phoenix Era which fell about 1320 is known as the Era of Menophres, and the name is generally thought to be that of the king in whose reign it happened, Menpehrê Ramesses I, who reigned only 16 months. Before that the cycle takes us back to the reign of Zoser at the end of the Third Dynasty; and this explains the amazing reputation of his chief minister, Imhotep, who was the architect of the first of the large pyramids, the Step Pyramid of Saqqarah, and later was deified as the healing god of Memphis. Imhotep is known to have been an astronomer as well as an architect and physician, and it seems at present not very likely that the Sothic calendar was devised 1,460 years earlier again. That would have been about 4240 B.C., 1,000 years before the First Dynasty; and the mention of the five epagomenal days in the Pyramid Texts does not actually prove this.

Because it rotated slowly through the seasons, the Egyptian calendar has been called The Wandering Calendar. Even so it was vastly superior to the lunar calendars of antiquity; for the prime purpose of a calendar is agricultural, and in order to keep those lunar calendars in time with the seasons an extra month was interpolated by proclamation whenever needed. In consequence the accurate computation of dates is impossible, whether backwards or forwards. The only exception is the Muslim calendar, in which no epagomenal months are allowed, and in consequence that calendar too rotates through the seasons, losing about 11 days each year, whereas the Egyptian lost only one day in four years.

The Egyptian too had its disadvantage: the festivals of the gods rotated through the seasons regardless of suitability. The change amounted to only about a fortnight in a lifetime, and the Egyptians had long accepted this when, in 238 B.C., Ptolemy III published the Decree of Canopus, by which in every fourth year a sixth epagomenal day was added. This spoilt the beauty of the system, and now one has to know that the extra day was used only between 238 and 57 B.C., after which it was very properly suppressed.

In 238 the 1st of the month of Thoth (New Year's Day) had been October 22nd, and Sirius rose on 1st Payni, but after 26–5 B.C. Augustus fixed 1st Thoth on August 29th, or 30th in leap years, with Sirius rising on 25th Epiphi.

Nowadays Sirius rises in Egypt in the middle of August, far too late to be of any use in agriculture; but throughout dynastic times it did conveniently precede the rising of the Nile.

In the present century, as Petrie remarked,[5] the Egyptians have had four calendars in use at the same time. These are the official Muslim lunar calendar; the Gregorian, imported from Europe; the Alexandrian, of the Coptic Church; and the agricultural festivals still attached to the names of the Coptic months.

In ancient times likewise the Egyptians had more than one calendar. Khnumhotep in his tomb at Beni Hasan says:[6] 'I decreed the offerings' (that is to say, I ordered the food) 'at every feast of the necropolis, at the feast of the beginning of the year, at the feast of the opening of the year, the feast of the long year, the feast of the short year, the feast of the last day, the great feast, the feast of great heat, the feast of little heat, the feast of the five days added to the year, at the feast of sand-throwing, at the twelve monthly feasts, at the twelve half-monthly feasts, at every feast of the living and of the blessed dead.' And when the priests of Senusret III at Kahun were paid on the 29th day of the month, this is cross-dated in the Wandering Calendar.[7]

In the XII Dynasty the 'opening of the year' was apparently the actual rising of Sirius, and the 'beginning of the year' was the next new moon,[8] but later the terminology became confused.

But though the ideal year retrogressed steadily through the seasons, Sirius did not rise on the same day in all parts of the country, and for this reason it was found more practical to date the official calendar from the first new month thereafter. And the Egyptians did not count their months from the appearance of the new crescent, as in most other countries, but from the invisibility of the moon. This is why we are told in the 'dramatic text' from the cenotaph of Sety I at Abydos: 'Horus provides himself with his two eyes on the second day of the month.'[9] The 'short year' and the 'long year' will then be alternative lunar years, according as the year had contained thirteen or fourteen new moons.

Now the zodiac, like the Egyptian agricultural year, is a calendar fastened to an astronomical reference-point called its fiducial. But the fiducial of the zodiac is not Sirius because Sirius lies too far to the south, outside the ecliptical belt. Is there, despite this difference, some connection?

(ii) *The Zodiacs of Denderah*

Several representations of the zodiac were discovered in Egypt when Napoleon invaded the country in 1798, and pictures of them were published in his enormous *Description de l'Égypte*.[10] At first, of course, they were taken to be amazingly ancient, and the most famous among them is the circular zodiac of Denderah, now in the Louvre, but originally a ceiling in the temple of Hat-Hor, goddess of heaven and also of love and joy. Photographs of this zodiac often look rather confused because it is only in low relief; it is therefore reproduced here in a line-drawing (Plate 14). To the unpractised eye the signs of the zodiac may not look strange, but to the Egyptologist they have a distinctly foreign air.

The Crab, the most northerly of the twelve, is a very round-bodied object not far from the diagram's centre, and immediately over the Lion's head. A goddess holds the Lion by the tail, and behind her stands Isis with her ear of corn; this of course is Virgo with the star Spica. Harpocrates in the disk of the sun is represented on top of the Scales, but the lion below him has nothing to do with Leo of the zodiac. Scorpio, Sagittarius, and Capricorn, being farther south, lie near the outer circle of figures, which represent the decans.

This outer circle is not, oddly enough, intended to be aligned with the zodiac and constellations, and therefore the disk with eight decapitated figures, to be found beneath the Water-bearer, does not signify the moon eight days old. A little farther on in this outer series four rams' heads rise from a single stem, and the third figure behind them is a child on a lotus flower. Both of these are calendrical indications, and so is the hawk on top of a papyrus column, which marks the summer solstice. Beyond it is Sirius, represented as a cow lying in a boat; and the royal figure on the other side of it, under the Bull's hoofs, is Orion.

In the centre are the circumpolar constellations. The Wain or Dipper had always been thought of as a bull's foreleg, which was a common sight on the altar of sacrifice, and it is sometimes drawn with a bull's head at the broader end. It is held in leash by a hippopotamus-goddess, who often has a crocodile on her back, but her hand rests on Menat, the Mooring-Peg, and this is the straight line from Arcturus to Spica, the original measuring-point of the zodiac.

The other northerly constellations include a lion and also Selket the scorpion-goddess, who is not, however, in the place of our Scorpio. And it is odd that on the oblong zodiac of Denderah the Foreleg and the Hippo-goddess are figured between the southerly constellations Sagittarius and Capricorn, whereas at Edfu they appear just to the right of Sirius and Orion, apparently on the opposite side of the sky. This shows how Egyptian diagrams cannot be taken literally and applied to the sky like transfers.

The oblong zodiac of Denderah was carved on the ceiling of the portico. It is over sixty feet long, and each half is twelve feet wide. There are two registers, running one above the other along the body of Nût the sky-goddess, who is dressed in a design of ripples. The lower register shows the decans as human and animal-headed figures in boats (since the Egyptian gods always used boats to cross the sky), and beside them are written their names and a rough design of two or three stars to help recognition. The upper register gives the signs of the zodiac and various other constellations, the planets, and the hours of the day, each drawn as a woman with a star over her head.

When it became possible to read the inscriptions on the walls of the temple of Denderah, it turned out to have been built in the reign of the Roman emperor Tiberius. The actual date has been computed by Mr Fagan to be the evening of April 16th Julian, A.D. 17, and the oblong zodiac contains, according to him, four different New Year's Days. The new moon of April 17th is shown on the back of the Bull, and this is the Babylonian 1st Nisan. The Sothic New Year occurred on July 19th, the year of the Wandering Calendar began on August 19th, and finally the 'New Year's Day of the Ancients' with the heliacal rising of Spica on October 5th. The vernal equinox is shown by the baboon of Thoth following the Ram. The planets on the circular zodiac are rather small and in the signs of their exaltations, which gives no clue to the date, but in the oblong diagram they are in their zodiacal positions.

The two zodiacs of Esna have been dated by Professor Parker to A.D. 175–6, but this is unsuitable because they are for New Year's Day and show the heliacal rising of the constellation Virgo, just as the Denderah zodiacs show that of Leo. The Egyptians considered the first sign of the zodiac to be that which rose heliacally on New

Year's Day, hence the 'first' sign changed about every 112 years, and in a retrograde direction. The 'first' sign actually changed from Virgo to Leo in the first century B.C., and the Esna zodiacs must be within 117 years previous to that change. Mr Fagan has given their exact date as September 26th, 137 B.C.[11]

Thus by Egyptian standards none of these four zodiacs is at all old. And the same applies to the two horoscopes found on the ceiling of a tomb at Athribis, and shown in Plate 15. They were dated originally by Knobel to May 20th, A.D. 52 and January 25th, 59, on the assumption that the horned hawk was Mars.[12] But the horns must surely be those with which the name of Jupiter is written, and Mars should be the hawk with the head of the beast of Setekh; and in that case the dates will be April 26th, A.D. 141 and February 14th, 177.[13]

Another Egyptian astronomical picture which is often quoted comes from the coffin of Heter;[14] but the date of that is A.D. 93. In fact not one of the zodiacal diagrams found in Egypt is as old as the Thirtieth Dynasty, which ended with Cleopatra. And this makes it extremely unlikely that the zodiac was known to the Egyptians of dynastic times; for no culture has left more abundant monuments in record of its beliefs.

The zodiac may have a connection with Egyptian astronomy none the less.

(iii) *The Decans*

There is a tradition, both in India and the West, that each sign of the zodiac may be divided into three segments of 10° each called decanates or decans. To astrologers, this subdivision was useless unless the decans could be distinguished in character, and there were devised several methods of doing this. One was to allot the first decanate of a sign to the pure influence of that sign, and the other two to the two other signs of the same element, earth, air, fire, or water. This system was used by Varaha Mihira, but cannot be older than Claudius Ptolemy because he first regularized the allocation of the elements to the signs. It never became very popular, indeed Hindu astrologers were so little impressed by it that they invented subdivisions of signs by 9 and 12, called *navamsas* and *dwadashamshas*.

Manilius allotted the decans to the signs in straightforward order, so that the three decans of Aries were ruled by Aries, Taurus, and

Gemini, those of Taurus by Cancer, Leo, and Virgo, and so forth. Another attempt to control the decanates gave them ruling planets, beginning with Mars for the first decanate of Aries and continuing in the 'Chaldean' order, which is not that preferred by the Babylonians, but is the order of speed of movement—Saturn Jupiter Mars Sun Venus Mercury Moon—until Mars again ruled the last decanate of Pisces. This arrangement was traditionally called (for instance by Lilly in the seventeenth century) the 'Egyptian' system, and indeed it is found in Teucros; but the name only shows a last faint realization that there ought to be an Egyptian system; for the decans are of Egyptian origin.

The arrangement whereby the first and last of them are ruled by Mars is obviously factitious, but Wilhelm Gundel put forward an ingenious explanation for it.[15] The third part of a sign is also called its 'face', and these faces were originally actual portraits of the ruling gods, as can be seen for instance on the marble tablet of Bianchini.[16] After Ptolemy III had inserted the sixth epagomenal day, the cycle of the year consisted of 36 decans plus 6 extra days, a total of 42 phases—in leap-years only, however. Since 42 is divisible by 7, this leap-year count could be allotted to the 7 planets; but the notion of starting it with Mars and Aries, which is the ruling sign of Rome, was probably invented by Sosigenes once he had moved to Rome, where the year began in March. For the Egyptians the beginning and end of the cycle was the first decan of Cancer, because this was the meridian longitude of Sirius. Originally, however, the decans were not divisions of the zodiac at all. That is what they later became, and as such they can be seen arranged round the edge of the circular zodiac of Denderah. But they go back to the third millennium.

It is not possible to draw up a single authentic list of the 36 decans, for the Egyptian lists vary, and over thirty are known, from the Tenth Dynasty to Roman times. Some of the older asterisms either went out of use or were renamed, which was natural enough; not all the lists were copied accurately; and since the celestial equator is not constant it is even possible for decans to change their order of rising over a long enough period.[17] They were evidently selected from constellations already formulated all over the sky, and it was likely that in different parts of the country different stars would be chosen. This explains why so many decans are named as the beginning, middle, or end of various larger constellations. The list of them printed on Table 21, facing page 200, gives a conflated order of their sequence on the monuments, and runs to a total of over forty. It could be extended considerably by taking account of all the variants found in and out of Egypt; for as Gundel showed, the lore of the decans survived into far more recent times than we should expect and in doing so developed all kinds of fantasies and divagations.

One of the least fantastic of these is probably the catalogue of barbarous names found in Harleian MS. 3731, where the presiding genii of the three decans of Aries are named Aulathamas, Sabaoth and Disornafais. The occurrence of Sabaoth, a Hebrew word, shows that we are in the Gnostic world of Alexandria in the early centuries A.D., the melting-pot of religions and mythologies; but most of the other names are Greek attempts to spell Egyptian words: Zathor, for instance, is the son, man, or some part of Hat-hor; Seneptois may be similarly related to Ptah, Psineus to Neith, and Rempsois suggests Reʿ in some situation or other.

The Byzantine list of Johannes Kamaterôs (eleventh century) is that of Hephaistion (fourth century) in a corrupted form; an even more altered version occurs in one of the books attributed to Hermes Trismegistos.[18] Rationalization, bad handwriting, and sheer guess-work had already done a good deal by the time Cosmas Indico-pleustes came to write in the sixth century. He was an India merchant from Alexandria who later turned monk and wrote an account of his travels. He attributes each decan to some Greek divinity, beginning with Hades, Persephone, and Eros for the Ram, and ending with Ocean, Wile, and Hope for the Fishes. One or two of his attributions seem to have some shadow of reason, in that Libra, the sign of justice, is divided between the Pursuing Fury (Erinys), Opportunity, and Nemesis; and Hestia comes at the end of Virgo, which is tolerable, though Plato put her in Capricorn. But it is not so clear why the Nymphs should rule the first decan of Scorpio, nor why Aquarius should be divided between Justice, Terror, and Osiris, with evident reference to the Last Judgment.[19]

Yet so late as the seventeenth century Athanasius Kircher[20] was still summing up the tradition, and allows himself more freedom even than Cosmas, for he includes not only Greek and Egyptian deities, but also the Persian Arimanius, the Cyclops, Typhon, and a few possibly Semitic names such as Nephan and Sourut. But these later developments appear frequently capricious and not always genuinely connected with the zodiac.

Firmicus quotes an interesting passage from the famous textbook of Nechepso and Petosiris:

> In each sign there are three decans which occupy certain degrees and leave others void. The degrees in which decans were found are called 'full' degrees (*plenae*), and 'void' (*vacuae*) those which have never borne the number of a decan. So whoever has in his horoscope the sun and moon and five planets in full degrees will be like a god and raised to the height of majesty. But this can never happen. Those who have one planet as well as the sun and moon in full degrees will be moderately well off, those who have two will attain to every kind of happiness, those who have three will receive extraordinarily numerous blessings of fortune, and those who have four will attain to the power of royal felicity.

Naturally those who have no planets in full degrees will be always poor and destitute, and Firmicus gives the alleged names and longitudes of the decans, with the extent of the void spaces between them. The names Senator and Romanae look highly suspicious, but at least Sothis appears in the right place; the other names should be compared to the decan-lists on Table 21.

TABLE 18 *Full and Empty Degrees*

	void	full	void	full	void	full	void	TOTALS void	full
Aries	3	senator 5	9	senacher 4	5	sentacher 4	0	17	13
Taurus	3	suo 7	2	aryo 8	5	romanae 5	0	10	20
Gemini	0	thesogar 7	2	ver 5	3	tepis 6	7	12	18
Cancer	7	Sothis 6	2	sith 4	2	thiumis 9	1	11	19=31
Leo	0	craumonis 7	4	sic 3	6	futile 10	0	10	20
Virgo	5	thumis 4	2	tophicus 6	6	afut 6	3	16	14
Libra	0	seuichut 5	6	sepisent 8	3	senta 6	3	12	19=31
Scorpio	3	sentacher 5	6	tepisen 6	2	sentineu 5	3	14	16
Sagitt.	0	eregbuo 9	3	sagon 7	4	chenene 7	0	7	23
Capri.	7	themeso 3	5	epiemu 4	5	omot 6	0	17	13
Aquarius	4	oro 5	4	cratero 6	3	tepis 8	0	11	19
Pisces	6	acha 6	3	tepibui 5	6	uiu 2	2	17	13

If now we turn back to the original Egyptian list, as written in hieroglyphs, we notice three water-pots in a rack, a pair of fishes, and a sheep. They occur in that order, and roughly the same distance apart. Can they have anything to do with the Urn, the Fishes, and the Ram, three successive signs of the Hellenistic zodiac? It is usually thought not. In that zodiac, where the decans were 10 segments of the ecliptic, the apparent water-pots (which may be simply a phonetic sign for spelling the syllable *khent*) fall in Libra, the two fish in Scorpio, and the sheep in Capricorn — but we have no reason to suppose that the Egyptians, like the Chinese, failed to distinguish sheep from goats.

Not only were the decans in late times 10°-segments of the ecliptic; so early as the Eleventh Dynasty, about 2000 B.C., on the coffins of Tefabi and Khiti,[21] we find the first decan, Kenmut, following the last, which is Sirius, so that they appear to form a complete circle. But it does not follow that they were already at that date arranged along the ecliptic, nor that they represented equal divisions of space. Before jumping to conclusions we have to explain the standard form of Egyptian celestial diagram, which occurs at all periods from the Eleventh Dynasty to Roman times, and of which nearly twenty examples are now known.[22]

There is also a key diagram in the cenotaph at Abydos of the king usually called Sety I, but sometimes Sethos or Setekhy (Plate 18). Now we have to remember constantly that Egyptian celestial diagrams are neither scientific observation nor literal-minded representational art. Comparisons make it plain that the figures were often arranged to suit the artist, and not in the style of a map; discrepancies must be regarded as normal, nor is there any difficulty in finding definite mistakes. It is therefore essential to realize what the Egyptians were about in making these diagrams. They were never intended for use on earth in any case: they were designed to help the deceased in finding his way to the sky after death, when he would join the Sun in His boat as He crosses heaven and the underworld. The standard diagram has therefore quite justly been called 'The Horoscope of Eternity'. Sety's example of it is shown in Plate 16.

(ii) *The Standard Diagram* (given in part in Plate 16)

In the middle of this diagram Sirius appears in a boat, sometimes in the form of a resting cow, but more often as Isis standing. To her right Orion may appear in another boat, in the form of a king running; but since he is always included among the decans his boat may be omitted. Sometimes he lies in it,[23] face up or face down, because that was the attitude in which he rose, and for that matter still rises. His name in Egyptian is Sahh, apparently meaning The Toe, and the name of Sirius is Sopdet, which the Greeks pronounced as Sôthis, and it means something like Sharp One, Arrow-head, or Pointer. From here to the right the picture lists the names of the decans, sometimes with a rough diagram of their appearance.

More importantly, we find to the left of Sirius two or three of the planets, which will always be Saturn, Jupiter, and Mars, next Two Turtles, then about five names of obscure meaning called Meta-decans, then Mercury, and finally a large heron, which is 'Venus the bennu-bird of Osiris'.

One must not imagine that because Sirius is enthroned in the middle of the diagram she is on the midheaven; quite the contrary, she is on the eastern horizon. And the decans to her right, as well as the planets and meta-decans on her left, are not a chart so much as simply a catalogue.

Why then did the diagram take this form? Why is Venus always represented so large, and on the extreme left? What are the meta-decans? And why are the directions of Mars, Saturn, and Jupiter usually but not always stated? For the answer to the first of these questions we are indebted to Mr Fagan; some of the others will be answered here for the first time.

The importance of Sirius is well known: its rising marked the New Year. Hence the original of all these diagrams must have represented the sky at dawn on New Year's Day, and therefore most probably at the inauguration of the Sothic calendar. Having realized this, Mr Fagan calculated that the only possible date was 2767 B.C.[24] As can be seen from Plate 23, the appearance of the sky at that moment was extraordinary. It showed a close conjunction of no less than four planets all within 7° of each other, rising on the eastern horizon at the same moment as Sirius, while the Moon, just past the full, was declining in the south-west. Such a close quadruple conjunction on the Ascendant on the day of Sirius' rising may never have occurred since. And furthermore the date was that of the summer solstice.

This very striking combination of phenomena cannot have failed to impress the Egyptians of the time of Zoser. Not only was it memorable in itself, falling on the one day of perfect harmony in the Wandering Calendar; dawn is also the natural opportunity for the deceased to catch the Sun's boat and sail to heaven. So it is not surprising that the event should have been perpetuated, both as the fixed point of the calendar and also as the beginning of life in the world to come.

This explains why the planets are all grouped together at the left of Sirius; indeed the repeated mention in the Pyramid texts[25] of 'those four youths who sit on the eastern side of the sky' may be a reminiscence of this event. The Pyramid texts make Horus the ferry-man of the sky, and that is why the planets, sometimes including Venus, are identified with him. There is also the oft-repeated statement: 'He ascends to heaven among the imperishable stars, his sister is Sothis, his guide is the Morning Star.'

The Morning Star is feminine in the Pyramid texts, except when identified with Horus, and Professor Mercer thinks that it was whichever asterism rose just before the sun — there is no mention of the decans. This, however, does not agree too well with the enormous importance attached to Venus in these diagrams. She is always drawn very large, and on the extreme left, probably because on that morning in Heliopolis she rose last, at the same moment as Sirius. She takes the form of a heron because that is the bird of the inundation; when the Nile begins to flood, the herons leave the restricted bed and fly all over the country fishing in the canals and fields.

Accepting this, we can explain the meta-decans. They are so called because they come after the decans, in the left upper corner of the diagram. Various suggestions have been made to account for them. Dr Chatley, for instance, thought they might be the constellations visible on winter nights to the south of the equatorial zone; and this would be possible, since the Egyptian artist placed his data where it suited him, and not where they belonged.[26] The thirty-six decans are usually crowded into about twenty-seven columns; the pictures of constellations resemble each other about as much as do medieval pictures of the Lion or Crab; and the rising-times of star-groups are inserted on Plate 18 wherever space allows, those on the goddess's arms belonging next to those on the ground.

Mr Fagan took the meta-decans to be the stars in the Sickle of Leo, which rose in the north-east about the same time as Sirius in the south-east, and this is not far off the mark. In fact, however, Sirius and Venus in 2767 were on the horizon simultaneously, and their distance apart in azimuth, that is to say along the horizon, was no less than 55°. The planets Mars, Saturn, and Jupiter were, as we already know, included in this space, so the meta-decans also would most naturally belong to it.

The first of them is the Two Turtles. The Turtle was a symbol of drought and an enemy of the Sun-god; it is sometimes shown being speared by one of the gods in the solar barque. The two must therefore represent some pair of stars which rise when the Nile is at its lowest, in the last month before the rising of Sirius. They might be Castor and Pollux, which in −2800 rose respectively forty and thirty-four days before Sirius; but Castor and Pollux are quite likely to be the Twin Stars of the Ramesside hour-tables. The Two Turtles are always represented exactly the same size, so it seems less suitable that they should be Procyon and its companion; Procyon in −2800 rose thirteen days before Sirius. The third possibility is the two Aselli, which lie very close together in the constellation of the Crab, and in those times rose nineteen and fifteen days before Sirius. These Turtles are then probably the first hard-shelled creatures to be associated with what later became the constellation of the Crab.

After the Two Turtles the second meta-decan is called *nesru*. It is hard to give the meaning of Egyptian star-names because the determinative is almost always omitted; in the commonest form of Egyptian spelling the vowels are not given, only a framework of consonants, and then an unpronounced ideogram which determines the range of meaning. Thus SH S P followed by the sun means 'light', but if followed by a picture of a house it means a room or courtyard. If it be followed by neither, one is left in some doubt; a rectangle is not uncommon in the sky, but so is light. *Nesru* is said to be an island where the sun is born, but its standard determinative is a picture of a fire. As a meta-decan, therefore, it most probably means 'the glow of dawn', and in that case it is not an asterism.

The third meta-decan is called *shesep* or *shespet*, and this can mean either a rectangle or light, more probably the latter, for we shall meet this word again in a mysterious text from Abydos.

The fourth is variously spelt as *'Abesh, 'Abshes, Ipsedj* or *Ipdjes*, and is followed by a fifth called *Sobshosen*. Both of them appear in the Greek decan lists as *Aposot* and *Sobkhos*, but there they occupy the last decanate of Virgo and the first of Libra; so what are they doing here on the eastern horizon? We shall see later.

The last meta-decan is called *wash-neter*, which ought to mean 'divine power and glory'; and perhaps this is just what it does mean, alluding to the approach of the sun. In Greek times the word meant a palanquin, which has somewhat the same suggestion: 'Here comes the king.'

(v) *The Hour-Stars*

On Plate 17 may be seen an amusing picture of a priest sitting cross-legged on a temple roof in order to help a colleague to observe the stars. His ears are drawn double-sized because they are supposed to mark the midpoint between shoulder and eye. Over his head are drawn seven vertical lines, to show how the stars were supposed to be observed descending in the south-west over his eye, ear, or shoulder, and over his 'heart', meaning his middle line; the thirteen horizontal lines indicate an hour of twilight, and the twelve seasonal 'hours' of the night. To exemplify this supposed observation here is a translation of the table for the first day of the month of Paophi:

> Second month of the season of inundation, beginning of
>   night, neck of the Giant exactly central.
> 1st hour, his dagger exactly over the left eye.
> 2nd hour, his thigh exactly central.
> 3rd hour, his knee exactly central.
> 4th hour, 'Aryt exactly central.
> 5th hour, the Goose's Head over the left eye, obliquely.
> 6th hour, its Tail exactly central.
> 7th hour, Thousands exactly central.
> 8th hour, Sa'r over the right eye, obliquely.
> 9th hour, the beginning of Orion over the right eye.
> 10th hour, the star of Orion over the right eye, obliquely.
> 11th hour, the star of Sothis over the left eye.
> 12th hour, beginning of the Two Stars exactly central.

The instrument tucked into the priest's girdle is an astronomer's staff (called in Egyptian *merkhet*), consisting of two small sticks or a small split palm-branch, with a plummet hung in the middle. The Star of Sothis is of course Sirius, the star of Orion is Betelgeuze, and Thousands are the Pleiades. To identify the other stars, though it might seem difficult, is not impossible, because they are not mentioned in a haphazard way, but in twenty-four dated catalogues similar to the three shown in Plate 17; and thus we can say with reasonable assurance that 'the start of Orion' is Betelgeuze and not Bellatrix or Rigel; and also make various other identifications.

But it also turns out that the practice so picturesquely illustrated can never have taken place exactly as one might suppose, for the simple reason that, if so southerly a star as Sirius was marked by a man's right shoulder, as we are told that it was, than a more northerly star such as Spica, which also appears on the list, would not have been marked by his left shoulder; it would never have come near him at all.

This makes it plain that these lists of hour-stars have not come down to us in their original form. Like most Egyptian monuments, these twenty-four lists of apparent hour-stars have been 'traditionalized'. Almost half the circle of the heavens is taken up by two enormous constellations, The Hippopotamus and The Giant. In the other half various identifications are possible, once one has realized that these stars were not originally chosen as hour-stars at all but, like the Indian *yogataras*, were markers along the path of the moon. Here then is a list of the Egyptian hour-stars in their original form as Moon-markers:

TABLE 19 *Egyptian Moon-markers*

The Goose's Head	Sharatain (β Arietis)
Its Tail	Menkar (α Ceti)
Thousands	Pleiades
Jawbone ('Aryt)	PrimaHyadum (θ Tauri)
Sa'r	Aldebaran (α Tauri)
Beginning of Orion	Bellatrix (γ Orionis)
Orion	Betelgeuze (α Orionis)
Beginning of The Twins	Alhena (γ Geminorum)
The Two Stars	Castor and Pollux

Stars of the Water	Praesepe, Aselli, Cancer
Lion's Head	Regulus (a Leonis)
His Tail	Zosma (δ Leonis)
Numerous	Coma Berenices
Beautiful Boy	Vindemiatrix (ϵ Virginis)
Mooring-Peg	Spica

It will be noticed from this, which is a direct translation of the ancient document shown in Plate 17, that the Egyptians had a constellation of the Lion somewhere between Sirius (Sothis) and Spica, and also another not far away, between Sirius and the Pleiades, called the Two Stars, which therefore might possibly be our Gemini—Gemini at this date consisted of a group in which the two principal stars were of much the same brightness—and also between the Lion and the Two Stars a constellation called Stars of the Water, which might be the origin of our constellation Cancer, more especially as there exist various Egyptian pictures of this constellation in the form of the Two Turtles; and a river-turtle, which does occur in the Nile and also in Asia Minor, is a hard-shelled water-creature just as a crab is.

Apart from these three constellations, and the Ram (illustrated in Plate 19), there are two other signs of the zodiac which may have an Egyptian origin, as we shall see later on. But it is also worth mentioning that there do exist various inscriptions which state the directions of the planets. Naturally there is no reference to the zodiac, but we do get a notion of how the Egyptians thought about the stars. In all these inscriptions we are always told that Mars is retrograde, which is ridiculous, since of the five planets which the Egyptians knew, Mars is the one which is least often retrograde. Mercury was obviously never observed, since his direction is never given. The inscriptions tell us whether Saturn, Jupiter, and Mars, were in the south, east, or west, leaving us to infer that a planet mentioned without any direction stated had been seen but had now set and was therefore in the north, whereas a planet not mentioned at all was in conjunction with the sun and therefore invisible. Since the directions of the planets are simply given by stating 'east', 'south', or 'west', the notion of classifying a planet as being 'in' a constellation had obviously not yet become common practice.

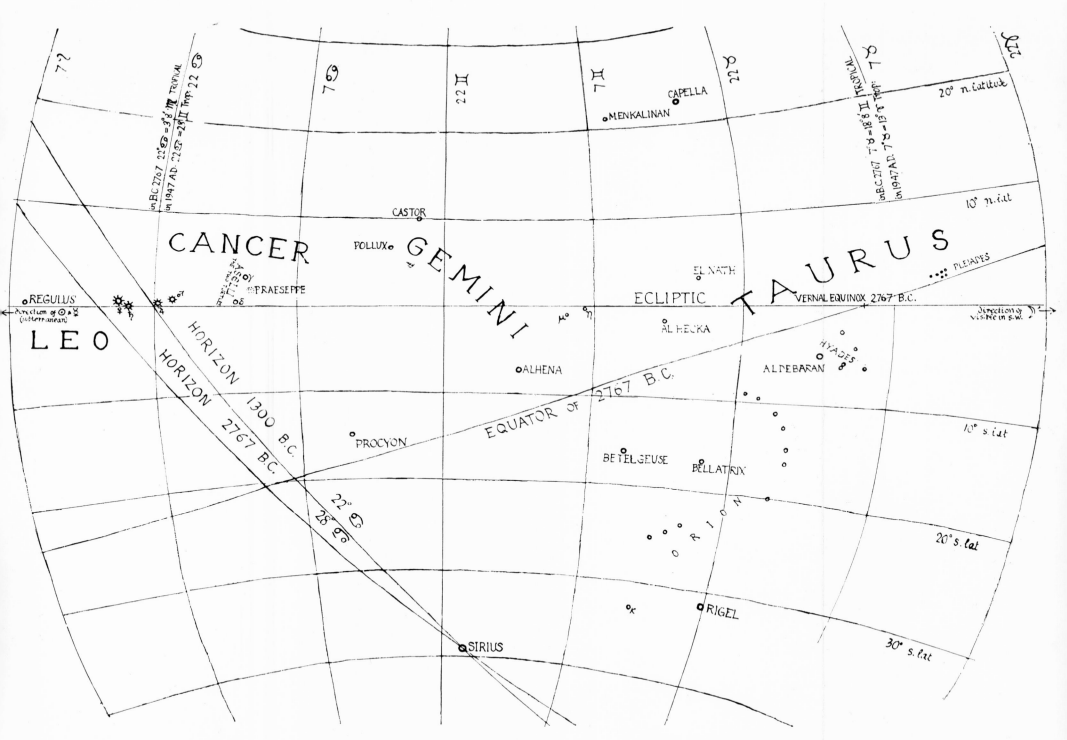

23. THE ORIGINAL 'HOROSCOPE OF ETERNITY', 2767 B.C.

The Nût Diagram

In none of these diagrams is the moon so much as mentioned, although they were all diagrams, or horoscopes, for the rising of Sirius, and in three of the six she was visible. The reason is that the diagrams were all for New Year's Day, and the Egyptian year effectively began not on the date of Sirius' heliacal rising, which would have given slightly different dates for different parts of the country, but at the following new moon. Actually there is an inconspicuous moon on the haunch of Nût in the key diagram from Abydos, shown in Plate 18. No inscription is attached to it, but close by is the brief notice: ☺ ✳ 'eastern horizon', and not far away is the decan of Orion's foot. The moon therefore should be rising. In shape she looks like a new ☽, but this is impossible, since a new moon does not cross the eastern horizon until the sun is already up. Besides, if the moon by Orion's foot were new, Sirius would be invisible.

No planets are shown in the diagram, which therefore does not apply to any particular year. As usual, Nût the sky-goddess is seen bending over the earth. She is upheld by Shu, the god of space, and near his toes is written the word 'sand'. The columns of writing on either side of Shu are computations to the effect that if a star culminates at dusk on a certain day (and the dates given are all at intervals of ten days), then it will set at dusk 90 days later, and its heliacal rising will occur 70 days later again. These computations are not for different stars, as might be expected; the intervals being the same in every case, in theory all should apply to Sirius, and constitute a key whereby its rising, southing, and setting could be roughly computed throughout the cycle of the Wandering Calendar. But as it happens, they are astronomically impossible, or at any rate highly schematic.

The sun in Plate 18 is represented four times. Touching Nût's lips he folds his wings to set, for she eats the stars as they set, and they are born from her in the east. We are even told in one of the accompanying texts that Shu quarrelled with Nût and told her that she ought not to eat her children in this manner, but she replied that it was quite all right, they would be born again in due course. The two hieroglyphs on Nût's cheek read 'western horizon', corresponding to the eastern horizon on her groin.

Down on her foot the sun is shown again, and the inscription beside him declares: 'The majesty of this god comes forth from her hinder parts.' Another on her thigh announces that he 'opens the thighs of his mother Nût'. Beside her thigh he is shown in the form of a scarab with wings outspread flying up towards the eastern horizon. The fourth sun is quietly reposing in the underworld.

Since the sun appears three or four times, this must be a composite diagram, like the circular zodiac of Denderah. To which sun, then, is the moon to be related? If to the setting sun, which seems most important from its enormous wing, then it becomes a full moon, as Lange and Neugebauer propose; but the full moon is not of outstanding importance in Egyptian astronomy, not more so than the new. And the inscription over Shu's head reads: 'This happens in the 1st month of Akhet at the time of the rising of Sirius.' The sun therefore is at the beginning of the constellation Leo, near Regulus, and the full moon will fall in Aquarius; it cannot therefore be near Orion's foot.

This interpretation is, however, usually accepted. It is thought that the decans are each 10° long and extend all round the sky, hence the fact that all 36 are represented on Nût's body cannot mean that all of them were visible simultaneously. And this appears to be sound, since a sun setting in Leo cannot be opposite to Orion, although his foot is drawn near the eastern horizon. If sunset is the hour of the chart, we are using the temple calendar in which the day began in the evening, and neither Sirius nor Orion is visible. But in view of the inscription over Shu's head for Sirius to be invisible would be distinctly odd.

If, on the other hand, we relate the moon to the unrisen sun in the form of the scarab flying up Nût's thigh, then this is also partly (being composite) a dawn chart for New Year's Day, and in that case the decans of Orion and Sirius were indeed seen above the eastern horizon where they are drawn. The decans next to the setting sun are unimportant, being invisible.

In the horoscopes dawn was the operative hour, and the date was the day of the moon's invisibility. But the old moon is never seen in the evening, hence the day for this purpose must have begun at dawn, and the last day of the old year was the last day on which the old crescent was seen before sunrise. The day on which it failed to appear was New Year's Day. Hence the importance of observing the crescent moon in the east, and hence the crescent ☽ on Nût's haunch. In drawing it as a new ☽ the artist has strictly perpetrated something impossible; but had he drawn it as an old ☾ the diagram would have represented the last day of the old year and not the first of the new. This explains why he turned it round and drew the impossible; and after all the invisible moon is a 'new moon' and used as such, so there was some reason for drawing it that way round. Possibly the importance of the setting sun is because the day in the temple calendar, as opposed to the civil calendar, began at sunset.

If this be the true explanation of the Abydos diagram, and it contains elements of both dawn and sunset, then it cannot quite so well be used as evidence that the decans were only five degrees in extent, although all thirty-six of them appear between the two horizons.

(vi) *Planetary Dates computed from the Heliacal Rising of Sirius*

Various ancient Egyptian monuments give a version of what has here been called the Horoscope of Eternity, but with indications of the directions in which the soul of the deceased should expect to find the planets. Rather naturally, these have not been taken seriously by Egyptologists. There can, however, be little doubt that they were seriously meant, so it has seemed worth while to calculate the dates to which they refer. But in order not to bore the reader with a long and learned disquisition, and at the same time not to waste a good many hours of study, it has been decided to include here (without further explanation, which would only interest the few experts) a table summarizing the results. It should be borne in mind that, if these computed dates are for any reason rejected, there is no saying whether others could be found or not; it might so happen that another date which would fit the planetary positions stated could be found in the very next year, but it might also happen that no other suitable date could be found within a hundred years.

TABLE 20 *Egyptian Planetary Dates Computed from the Heliacal Rising of Sirius*

monument	date expected	date computed	New Year's Day	SATURN		JUPITER		MARS		VENUS	
				stated	found	stated	found	stated	found	stated	found
tomb of Senmut	1503–1481	1501	Aug. 13th	east	east	south	south	omitted	combust	rising	rising
Karnak clepsydra	1415–1380	1407	July 25th	not given	north	south	south	omitted	combust	rising	rising
tomb of Seti I	1310–1290	1306	July 18th	west	west	omitted	combust	east	east	rising	rising
Ramesseum	about 1281	1295	Aug. 15th	east	east	not stated	combust	west	west	rising	rising
right-hand diagram in tomb of Ramesses VI	1158–1143	1236	July 24th	east	east	omitted	combust	east	east	OMITTED!	combust
left-hand diagram in tomb of Ramesses VI	1158–1143	1156	Aug. 12th	west	west	uncertain	west	east	east	rising	rising

(combust = invisible under the sun's rays)
Computed with Schoch's tables (margin of error 1° bzw. 1 day)
The formula for computing meridian longitudes is: cot long. (tropical) = cos obliquity cot R.A.

(vii) *Decans or Pentads?*

In late times the thirty-six decans were a complete circle of asterisms, each 10° long; Sirius headed the list in the first decanate of Cancer, the forefeet of Sagittarius were placed 'in the middle of the boat', and the last decan, at the end of Gemini, was called '*phuhor*', meaning 'end of the sky'. Even so early as the Eleventh Dynasty the 'diagonal calendars' on coffins show the decans making a complete circle of 360°. On the coffins of Khiti and Tefabi the columns are headed 'first ten days', 'middle ten days', and 'last ten days', and after Sirius, normally at that period the last decan, the circle continues directly with Kenmut, which is the usual beginning.

Now we have already seen that three constellations of the zodiac may have had an Egyptian origin, namely Gemini, Leo, and Cancer; the Egyptian names of these constellations were the Two Stars, the Lion, and Stars of the Water, also known as the two Turtles; but their Babylonian names were the Great Twins, the Great Dog, and Allul (an unidentified water-creature). The question now arises, may any other constellations of the zodiac have had an Egyptian origin? Among the Egyptian constellations are three names which make one wonder, but the problem remains, do they occur in the right positions? These names are the Fish, the Sheep, and the Water-pots or Jar-stand. If we accept the placing of these constellations according to the Greco-Roman scheme whereby the decans are all 10° long, agreeing with the opinion of most modern astronomers and Indian astrologers, then these constellations cannot have anything to do with the zodiac, for the Fish fall in Scorpio, the Sheep in Capricorn, and the Water-pots in Libra (*see* Table 21). But if we take it that the so-called decans were originally divisions of the ecliptic 5° long, then the sheep falls on Aries the Ram, the Fish on our modern Fishes, and the Water-pots or Jar-stand on what the Greeks called the Urn, and we call Aquarius.

We ought therefore to consider whether the decans should be regarded as 10° spaces, as the Greeks and Romans took them to be, or simply 5° spaces. For this latter possibility, revolutionary though it may sound, nine arguments have been advanced by Mr Cyril Fagan, and to these nine, three more can now be added. The arguments are as follows:

1. On the Nût diagram (Plate 18) the whole of the 36 decans

are represented on the body of the sky-goddess, as if they were all above the horizon at the same time. The first decan. 'beginning of Kenmut', is at the base of her neck, quite close to the inscription 'Western horizon', and near the last an inscription expressly states 'Eastern horizon'. We know that the Egyptians always had 36 decans; any semi-circle measures 180°, and 36 divided into 180° gives 5°.

2. This list of decans is divided in the middle by the inscription over the head of Shu, which ought to indicate the south point. Seventeen decans are shown east of his head and twenty to the west, and allowing 5° per decan this accurately corresponds to the obliquity of the arc of the zodiac visible when Sirius rose.

3. The Pleiades and Hyades are placed 9 and 11 decans distant from Sirius, making respectively 90° and 110°, but their actual distances in meridian longitude in 2767 were 47° and 59°, almost exactly half as much.

4. Orion is not infrequently allotted four decans, or 40° of space, and yet the maximum extent of this constellation is little over 20°.

5. In the Ramesseum the whole of the 36 decans are allotted to the last $5\frac{1}{2}$ months of the Sothic year, making 6 to each month instead of 3. (Part of this allocation can be seen in Plate 19.)

6. On the Denderah zodiac (Plate 14), under the constellation Pisces is found a disk with a human figure holding a pig by its hind foot. The same picture has been found on a Mesopotamian clay tablet of the third century, where it falls between the Pleiades and the Bull.* It does not therefore refer to the region of Pisces, but to the decan Akhui, the Two Spirits, which is seen below it and corresponds, as a pentad, to some part of Taurus.

7. The disk containing eight captives, which is so conspicuous in the Denderah circle, has no explanation if it falls at the end of Capricorn, but by the pentad arrangement belongs to Aries and marks the eighth degree, which was the equinox of the Hellenistic zodiac.

8. Still on the same zodiac, the decan 'Heads of the Two Souls', marking one of the cardinal points, is placed underneath Pisces, where it has no particular significance; but in 2767 B.C. this pentad marked the Spring Point.

* Illustrated in Langdon, *Semitic Mythology*, Fig. 92 on p. 305.

9. The Egyptian word for 'five' was drawn with a picture of a five-pointed star, which was also the ideogram for 'star'.

To these nine arguments, of which the first four are fairly solid and the fifth very difficult to ignore, three more can be added.

10. The conspicuous absence from the decan-list of the Lion's head and tail, the Beautiful Boy, Spica, the Hippopotamus, and the Giant is easily explained by supposing that the Egyptians used different stars, or the same stars under different names. But that is a mere guess, and an equally good guess would be that the half of the sky which the decans cover did not include those constellations—in fact that were under the earth when Sirius rose.

11. The Nût diagram gives the dates in the Egyptian calendar for the evening southing and setting, and the heliacal rising, of several decans. Since these dates are astronomically impossible, it does not much matter that they fill a whole circle instead of a half, but the one point where they may touch reality is at their beginning. The first of the list of decans in point of time is not Sobshosen, whose name is written on Nût's breast, nor yet Ipsedj and the Pregnant One, which appear on her forearms, but 'Under the Foreleg of Kenmut', which is placed behind the heels of Shu. Its culmination at dusk is given for the 6th day of the fourth month of inundation, which then fell about October 11th Gregorian, so the sidereal longitude of Kenmut would be near the beginning of Aquarius. Its evening setting, 90 days later, falls at the same sidereal time as the rising of Sirius, which puts it close to the end of Capricorn. Its heliacal rising, of course, does not fit, but none the less we have two further pieces of evidence that Kenmut sets when Sirius rises, and hence the decans only occupy 180°. Kenmut, in fact, takes the place of our constellation of the Eagle, and may mean Vulture or, since it has a foreleg, the Ape.

12. The Egyptians paid considerable attention to the constellations of the Ram and the Boat, both of which are made especially conspicuous in several of the diagrams. In Greek times the Ram fell in Capricorn, and the Boat under the forefeet of Sagittarius; but when Sirius rises Sagittarius is under the earth, so it seems odd to draw an especially handsome picture of it!

The Ram is several times drawn with five stars along its back and four on its belly, and this does partly agree with Capricorn, whose back has a straight line of stars. But Senmut makes the Pleiades egg-shaped and gives the Hyades twice too many stars, and both of them can be seen at the right of Plate 18, in the shape of a lop-sided V and a cow's ear. The Ramesseum schematizes Gemini and the upper half of Orion as two stars, then many, then two, then three; also it turns the Boat into something only a firework display could equal (Plate 19). I never expected, therefore, to identify the Boat, when suddenly I saw it staring up at me from the precessional globe in the Science Museum (Plate 20).

The boat in which a god crossed the sky or processed through a town would have a high straight prow and an equally high but bent stern, with a rectangular cabin or shrine amidships. And a very conspicuous rectangular constellation for which the Egyptians must surely have had a name was the Square of Pegasus. The resemblance is so striking that it is hard to doubt.

But if the Boat is the Square of Pegasus, then the Egyptian Two Fishes, just underneath it, fall on our Pisces; the Egyptian Sheep on Aries the Ram, which in any case, as we know, was not a Babylonian constellation; and the Egyptian Water-pots coincide with Aquarius, which the Greeks and Romans simply called the Urn. The Babylonian names of the constellations Pisces, Aquarius, and Aries were not by any means those to which we are accustomed, but were GU.LA (name of a goddess); Kun (the tail) and Anunitum (female dweller in heaven); and The Hireling.

(viii) *The Mysterious Text from Abydos*

A final point on the Nût diagram is the two inscriptions running from the sun's wing towards the wrists of the goddess. The upper one reads in Dr Frankfort's translation: 'The majesty of this god enters into her mouth in the Netherworld. The Netherworld is opened when he sails in it. The stars enter after him and they come forth after him and they hasten to their places.' But when the cenotaph was first published by the Egypt Exploration Society no attempt was made to translate the lower inscription, which seemed very obscure. I suggest translating it as follows:

'The majesty of this god enters at the hour [which is called] 'her time of twilight', he shines and is beautiful for the waters within, which Osiris gave him and in which he washed him. The majesty of

TABLE 21 *The 36 Egyptian Decans*

Name	Meaning	Location as Pentad	XI	Tf	Sn	St	R3	30	Dend.	Brugsch Thes.I.137	Hephaestion	Cosmas	Late
tpy-ʿ Knmwt	beginning of Kenmut				1	1	1	6		(seta)	σίτ	Aidoneus	♋2
knmwt	(?ape)	Aquila	1	1	4	2		1	2	knum	χνουμίς	Persephone	♋3
sꜣwy knmwt	2 sons of K.				2	2		2					
hr ḥpd knmwt	under rump of kenmut		3	3	3	3	3	2	3	χαρ-knum	χαρχνουμίς	Eros	♌1
hꜣt ḫꜣw	beginning of Thousands	Milky Way near Delphinus	4										
pḥwy ḫꜣw	end of Thousands				5								
ḫ,t dꜣt	beginning of ferry (?or crane)				5	4		3	4	ha-tet	ἠτήτ	Charis	♌2
pḥwy dꜣt	end of same				6	5		4	5	phu-tet	φουτήτ	Horai	♌3
tmꜣt ḥrt	top of box or throne or wing		6	6	7	6	7	5	6	tom	τώμ	Litai	♍1
tmꜣt ḥrt	bottom of it		7	7	8	6	8	5	7				
wšꜣt	bird		8	8	9	7		6	8}	uste-bikot	οὐεστεβκώτ	Thetys	♍2
bkꜣt	pregnant				10	8	10	7	9}				
sbꜣw mhw	full of stars		9			9		8					
ipds	?								10	aposot	ἀφοσό	Kybele	♍3
sbšsn	? clear patch			9					11	sobχos	σουχωέ	Praxidike	♎1
tpy-ʿ ḫnt	beginning of jar-stand				12		11	9	12	tpa-χont	ττηχοντ	Nike	♎2
ḫntt ḥrt	top of jar-stand	Aquarius	11	10	13	11	12	10					
ḫntt ḥrt	base of same		12	11	14	12	13	11		χont-har	χονταρί	Herakles	♎3
ḫntt n tns	(part of same)		13	12	15		14	12					
isty	cabin (or crew)	square of Pegasus			13								
spt ḥnwy	lips (of the fishes)							13	14	spt-χηр	σττηχνηξ	Hekate	♏1
ḥnwy	two fishes	Pisces			14								
ḥry-ib wiꜣ	in the middle of the Boat	square of Pegasus			15	17	15	16	14	13	hre-ua	ῤηουα	Sarapis	♐1
snsn	to fraternize				16								
ššmw	the press					17	15	15	sesme	σεσμέ	Hephaistos	♏2
											σεισμέ	Themis	♐2
										si-sesme	σιστεμέ	Isis	♏3
knmw	? dark place		18	17	19		18	16	17	konime	κονιμέ	Moirai	♐3
tpy-ʿ smd	beginning of Divider				20	17		17	18				
smd	The Divider	meridian when Sothis rises	19		21		20	18	20	smat	σμάτ	Hestia	♑1
smd srt	Divider of The Sheep			18									
pa-siou-oua	the lonely star	? Menkar							19				
srt	The Sheep	Aries	20	19		18	21	19	21	srat	σρώ	Erinys	♑2
sꜣwy srt	2 sons of Sheep		21	20		19	22	20		si-srat	ἰσρώ	Kairos	♑3
hr ḥpd srt	under rump of sheep		22	21	24	20	23	21					
tpy-ʿ ꜣḫwy	beginning of 2 spirits		23	22	25		24	22	22	tpa-χu	ττηχύ	Nemesis	♒1
ꜣḫwy	2 spirits		25	24	26		25	23	23	χu	χύ	Nymphai	♒2
imy-ḫt ꜣḫwy	after them				23								
tpy-ʿ bꜣw	beginning of Souls								24	tpa-biu	ττηβιῦ	Leto	♒3
bꜣwy	2 souls				27		26	24	25	biu	βιου	Kairos	♓1
sꜣwy bꜣwy	2 sons of 2 souls					23	27						
ḫnty ḥry	top of —?				28	24		25	26	χont-har	χονταρεττηβιου	Tolmos	♓2
ḫnty ḥry	base of same				29	25		26–7	27–8	χont-χar	χονταχρε		♈2
										tpibiu	πτιβιου		♓3
										χont-har (again)	χονταρε		♈1
qd	pot or building (?)		26	25	30		29	28	29				
sꜣwy qd	2 sons of same				30		30	29	30	siket	σικέτ	Hygieia	♈3
ḫꜣw	Thousands	Pleiades	27	26	31			30	31	χau	χώου	Tolma	♉1
ʿrt	jawbone	Hyades	28	27	35		31	31	32	arat	ἔρω	Dike	♉2
ḥry ʿrt	under same				28								
rmn ḥry	higher arm	Orion		29	36				33	remen-hare	ῤομβρόμαρε	Phobos	♉3
ts ʿrḳ	girdle	Orion's belt							34	θosalk	θοσολκ	Osiris	♊1
rmn ḥry	lower arm	Orion	30		32	32	32	34	35				
wʿrt	leg	Orion diagram of Gemini	32	31				33	36	uaret	οὔαρε	Oceanos	♊2
					34		33						
Sꜣḫ	Orion	Orion				31	35					Dolos	
tpy-ʿ Spdt	beginning of Sothis			32									
Spdt	Sothis	Sirius	34	33		36	36	35	39	Sopdet	σωθίς	Elpis	♋1
pḥwy ḥry	end of sky								37	phu-hor	φούορι		♊3
									38	seta	σίτ		♋2
										(as above)			

This table gives the order in which the decans appear in various lists. (*See also* W. Gundel, *Dekane und Dekansternbilder*.) The lists have a good deal of incompleteness and inconsistency.

Sources:

XI = *Tomb of Msahiti* (XI Dyn.), 'in so far as it agrees with later lists' (E. Zinner in *Isis* XVI [1931], pp. 97–8).

Tf = *Coffin of Tefabi* (XI Dyn.), pubd. A. Pogo in *Isis* XVII, Plates D and E.

Sn = *Tomb of Senmut*, A. Pogo in *Isis* XIV, 301–25.

St = *Seti I*, pubd. H. Frankfort, Eg. Expl. Soc., London 1933, cp. *Isis* VII and Lepsius, *Denkmäler* III.137.

R2 = *Ramesses* II, *Ramesseum*, in Lepsius, *Denkmäler*, III, 171.

30 = 30th Dyn. list from E. Zinner, ibid.

Denderah, oblong zodiac, F. J. Lauth, *Les Zodiaques de Dendérah*, Munich 1865.

H. Brugsch, *Thesaurus*, I.137.

Hephaestion, ed. Engelbrecht.

Cosmas Indicopleustes, in Migne, P.G.88.

this god sets in life at her 2nd hour as 'The Pregnant One'. Then the majesty of this god gives prosperous words to the westerners and issues orders in the Netherworld. The majesty of this god comes forth upon the lower earth, becoming a ... [break in text] ... his might like the Goose's head on the horizons. Then he becomes a great god in Edfu ... [break in text] ... to the iron limits of heaven, she causes him to enter, she makes it night at the hour of dusk when he sleeps in the waters within.'

This translation may not be entirely certain, but it mentions the Goose's Head, which to us is the Head of Aries, and tells us that the second hour of night is called the Pregnant One.

But if the decans are only 5° each, the problem remains, what happens in the other half of the sky? The Ramesseum implies that it merely had no decans. Mr Fagan suggests that those six months were omitted in order to avoid bad weather in the afterlife. This is conceivable, but not very likely, since it would mean a year with no harvest time. There remains another possibility.

The mysterious text from Abydos contains the expression, literally translated: 'As the time Head-of-Goose its two horizons.' And once again we must realize that in a non-materialist culture the apparent effects of forces receive far more attention than the shape of objects, just as the impact of an actor or speaker is far more important than the shape of his face. The magical influence of the hour called the Goose's Head would not lie on one horizon to the exclusion of the other, but would be characteristic of that moment, at which when a certain star rises another certain star necessarily sets. From the magical point of view, therefore, the hour of the Goose's Head could well control both horizons at once.

But at that rate the hour of Kenmut would always follow the hour of Sirius, and we need not feel puzzled because half of the circle has been omitted. Or we might choose to suppose instead—though this is far less likely—that the decans had pairs of opposing stars of similar declination, chosen because each rose as the other set, like Scorpio and Orion.

Further, the Pregnant One is sometimes spelt in the dual, as the Two Pregnant Ones; why does it not matter whether she is one or two? And whenever the 'sons' of any asterism are mentioned, they are always put in the dual as 'the two sons'. It is easy enough to fancy that this may simply refer to two small stars near a bigger one, but it is not likely that the smaller stars would always be two, and never one or three. Why do we find 'The Two Spirits', 'The Two Souls', 'The Two Sons of the Sheep', 'The Two Sons of Kenmut', and the two pairs of two men fraternizing?

This argument will seem far-fetched in a culture where material objects are thought more important than the living powers which use them. But there is another reason why no more decans were needed to fill out the other half of the sky, and that is that in Dynastic times the Egyptians already knew what happened under the earth; there was a subterranean landscape through which the sun passed and which was described in the Book of Gates. Hence the stars passed through it too, and the presence of stars beneath the earth never became a living idea to the Egyptians until the Alexandrian period, when the function of the decans had been forgotten and they were inflated to cover 360° and allotted to the zodiac at the rate of 10° each. Since all Egyptian charts were drawn for the rising of Sothis, the lower half of the celestial circle was never shown and there was no call to devise decans for it.

The Goose's Head, however, is of particular importance because throughout Dynastic times it culminated when Sirius rose. Hence *Smed-sert*, the Divider of the Sheep, which occurs among the decans, must originally have occupied the meridan, the halfway point, just as the similar word *Smedet* means the halfway point of the moon, Full Moon Day.

Not infrequently the decans have the names of presiding gods attached to them. It is not clear on what principle these rulerships were allotted, but certainly this is the root of Plato's doctrine that each sign had its ruling god, and thus, of the later astrological doctrine, that each sign has its ruling planet. It also explains the alternation of the Ram and Goose in the constellation Aries, and reveals the fallacy of supposing that the only origin of the names of the constellations was a fancied resemblance to a physical object.[27] The Egyptians did not believe that kickable objects were the only reality; indeed they would have called that notion not just a fallacy, but a demonstrable untruth. For to them, as to all peoples for whom the reality of experience has not been killed by argument, both gods and men were powers which act in a characteristic way, and the purpose of understanding either was to cope with whatever kind of force each one of them could bring to bear. For in every one of us still dwells, under the conscious surface, the savagery of Mars, the justice of Ma'et, and the elemental terrors and joys of Hat-hor.

If the decans had ever in dynastic times covered the whole circle, it would have been a constant sight for the Egyptians to see only half of them at any one time, and at least one monument might have survived showing only half the decans. But this has not happened, and before Roman times no such possibility is even hinted at. At Abydos (Plate 18) the decans stretch from Nût's head to her hind-quarters, and all thirty-six of them are shown as if comprised in this space. Since the rising of Sothis seems to have been to the Egyptians the only important astronomical moment, this will doubtless have been the origin of the astrological notion that certain celestial moments are more important than others, and also that the decans represent the condition of the sky at the particular moment of the 'horoscope of eternity', that is to say, of taking up residence in eternity.

It must not be supposed that each decan comprised two opposite spaces of 5° each; that would be to attribute to the Egyptians modern notions of accuracy and literal-mindedness. In dynastic times the invisible stars would not be important. Just as Horus, and later Mars, was called 'Horus of the Two Horizons', and as is shown by the constant use of the dual in such phrases as 'the two sons of the Sheep', so each asterism would have its two moments when it was 'lord of the horizon' and therefore lord of the hour, and this would make it unnecessary to have 36 more asterisms to fill up the other half of the sky. For with 180° allotted to pentads there would always be some known asterism on one horizon or the other, just as, in a horoscope, if one knows the Ascendant, one does not need to be told the Descendant as well.

As shapes, a ram and a goose are not alike, but Goose and Ram were the two sacred animals of the god Amun of Thebes, hence they represented to the Egyptians the same divine Power; and so, if the Egyptians had invented the zodiac, the ruling Power of Aries would not have been Mars, but Amun, the Hidden One, the Unknown God to whom St Paul found an altar in Athens and whom the Egyptians had known two thousand years before Moses.

Since all Egyptian horoscope-charts are diagrams of the heliacal rising of Sirius, it seems that the large heron drawn on them is not just traditional decoration, but represents an actual observation of Venus rising. Thus Sirius represents Isis, and Venus, which is always represented as a *bennu*-bird or heron, represents Osiris, who incidentally is also represented by the constellation Orion. So these astronomical diagrams with planets may justly be called horoscopes because they are observed celestial moments, which is what a horoscope is. Nothing was predicted from them either in this world or the next, but each one was the moment of a Sacred Marriage of Isis and Osiris; and this, in the simultaneous rising every eight years of Sirius and Venus, was the moment when the ideal touched the real.

Much more could be said, of course, about Egyptian astronomy. Three hundred and sixty-three years before the invention of the Sothic calendar there may have been a Horakhti calendar, and the date of its inauguration would be September 15th, 3130 B.C.[28] At that period the traditional ideogram of a cow in a boat, with a star between its horns, would have meant the heliacal rising of Spica, not of Sirius, and drawings of it have been found from the reign of King Djer early in the First Dynasty.[29] Again, the remarkable orientation of various pyramids would not have been possible without accurate observation of the transits of the stars, and this probably began with another king of the First Dynasty, Semerkhet, whose name apparently means 'the man with the astronomer's staff'.

But in the zodiac it seems certain that Aries was originally an Egyptian constellation, possibly Gemini, and probably also Aquarius, Pisces, and Leo. Egyptian bottles and jars were frequently made with a pointed base suitable for thrusting into the sand, hence any house built on solid ground needed a jar-stand to hold them upright; and this, rather than the Nile-god or the 'god with streams', will be the origin of what the Greeks and Romans called The Urn.

It only remains to confront the Egyptian evidence with the Babylonian.

TABLE 22 *Planetary Positions at the Inauguration of the Sothic Calendar*

Sirius (magnitude −1·58°) rose at Heliopolis (30° 08′ north, 31° 18′ east) on July 16th (Julian) 2767 B.C. (=−2766) at 4·01 a.m. L.M.T., which gives the following positions (Spica=29° 0′ Virgo):

	Latitude	Longitude	R.A.	Declination
Midheaven	—	10° 43′ Aries	331° 41′	—
Hamal (αϒ)	+9° 55′	13° 24′ Aries	330° 39′	− 1° 42′
Mars	+0° 53′	19° 07′ Cancer	65° 50′	+23°01′
Jupiter	+0°18′	21° 41′ Cancer	68° 42′	+22° 50′
Saturn	nil	25° 04′ Cancer	72° 23′	+23° 00′
Venus	+0° 29′	25° 48′ Cancer	73° 07′	+23° 35′
Sirius	−38° 30′	20° 10′ Gemini	49° 05′	−21° 42′
Zodiacal				
Ascendant	nil	28° 58′ Cancer	—	—
Sun	nil	10° 40′ Leo	89° 22′	+24° 00′
Mercury	+0° 50′	29° 00′ Leo	109° 27′	+23° 38′
Moon	+3° 25′	19° 08′ Aquarius	278° 24′	−20° 22′

Obliquity of the ecliptic 24° 00′. It was the day of the summer solstice. (From C. Fagan, *The Symbolism of the Constellations*, London, 1962, pp. 52–3.)

Gregorian date: June 23rd.

Distance from Sirius to Venus in azimuth (round the horizon) 55°.

13. *The Naming of the Constellations*

THE origin of an idea is naturally hard to trace; it appears to spring full-grown like Athena from the head of Zeus. But when Athena was called on to create she produced an olive-tree out of the earth; and the study of human intuition shows that there is normally some soil in which the idea has grown. Its genesis, like that of anything else, is by conflation: the meeting and mating of two old and known ideas produces one which is new.

The zodiac grew up, and must have grown up, as a device for measuring time. Only later did it come to be used for divination, and later still for the analysis of character. But divination is not and never has been based on cause and effect. The principle, which has been best explained by Jung and Pauli,[1] is synchronicity, or the interpretation of signs occurring simultaneously. Divination is a matter of signs, not causes, and the ancients did not suppose there to be any mysterious causative influence of the stars. It is therefore a waste of time for either astrologers or their enemies to try to establish or disprove the existence of such an influence.

The Babylonians were deeply addicted to taking omens, and in particular to observing them in the sky. This is one half of astrological practice. But their method was basically empirical; they expected a similar sign in heaven to be followed by a similar event on earth in virtue of correspondence between heaven and earth, not in consequence of any cause. And, most important, they did not time their omens closely. The occurrence of a halo round the moon and enclosing Venus would have two different significations according as it appeared in the west or east, and possibly according to the width of the conjunction; but it was only expected to foretell one event in the near but not precise future, and it was not taken as a significant moment from which the future should be counted. This, which is the other half of astrological practice, was unknown to the Babylonians in the second millennium.

The Egyptians, on the other hand, were not given to celestial divination. Next to telling the time at night and the seasons of the year, their chief interest in the stars was in learning how the soul could ascend to heaven and join the Sun in His boat. They did, however, believe in lucky and unlucky days, and each hour of the day or night had its tutelary spirit, whose name was known. It was inevitable that eventually some hours, and later some ruling spirits or some groups of stars, should be regarded as more favourable than others. The same idea could have arisen equally well in Babylon.

In addition, the Egyptians possessed two calendars which were far superior to anything known to the Babylonians; and because one of them rotated through the seasons there occurred once in fifteen centuries an epochal beginning-point when the first day of the Wandering Calendar returned to its ideal position in the Sothic Calendar. Thus the recurrence of epochal dates was part of Egyptian culture in a way that it could not be in Babylon. Furthermore, the Egyptians had a traditional celestial diagram which they copied from century to century, and although it was more traditional than contemporary it did represent a particular moment from which time was counted. Thus it is not unfair to say that the first horoscope ever drawn was, so far as we know, that of the Phoenix Era of 2767 B.C.

The Egyptians will not have made any predictions from this horoscope, nor was it drawn in terms of the zodiac; but when the Assyrians conquered Egypt in 671 B.C., or even through cultural contact in the previous century, there was likely to occur a conflation of influences from which both the zodiac and the notion of astrological prediction could arise. The evidence for this is in the timing.

Of the Babylonian zodiac, with 18 irregular signs, various copies have been found dating from the sixth to the third centuries. This does not prove, however, that the zodiac of 12 signs was still uninvented; the Babylonians and Assyrians, like the Egyptians, were great copiers of traditional documents, and in the less organized world of those days the regular zodiac will not have superseded the older systems in a week or even a century. We should expect to find texts from the transition period, when the zodiac was not yet used as it later came to be used. And such texts exist.

As late as the first century A.D. the technique of prediction was still undecided. A Coptic horoscope published by Griffith[2] divides the life of man into periods ruled by different planets. Two of the few complete sentences in it read as follows: 'The third period, which is that of Jupiter, is from 28 years 2 months 15 days to 34 years 5 months 24 days ... Jupiter became a hostile star on the day of his birth, perhaps he will desert his wife or be hostile to her or towards his children.'

This system of prediction, though normal in India, has never had a vogue in Europe. Ptolemy, writing about A.D. 135, makes no mention of it, but gives the totally different method usual in the West. And the fragments of Nechepso and Petosiris, which ought to enshrine the ancient teaching if anything does, reflect the political conditions of Egypt and Syria in the third century B.C., while their techniques differ again. They speak of 'full' and 'empty' degrees, the lore of the Part of Fortune, and the 'progression' of the Ascendant, but lay the chief emphasis on the actual condition of the sky, including the direction of the wind (quite in the Babylonian manner) at the rising of Sothis on the Egyptian New Year's Day.

Other transitional documents are the moon-staircases of the second century B.C.[3] They represent the moon's progress from new up to full, when the Eye of Horus is enthroned under the guardianship of Thoth. In one of these the Ram appears on the 4th day, the Bull on the 7th, Hapi the Nile-god (the later Aquarius) on the 11th, and the Bow, which suggests Sagittarius, on the 13th. Another list shows Aries 1st, Taurus 4th, and a scorpion 6th. Yet another puts Aries 2nd, Taurus 5th, and Hapi-Aquarius 9th. At first sight it looks as though the zodiac had been at this date still unorganized. But the constant interval of 3 days between Aries and Taurus implies that these two are signs of the zodiac, though the rest are not. Hapi is followed by Sothis, which puts him at the end of Gemini and enables him to introduce the inundation by his heliacal rising. The Bow then falls in the middle of Cancer, not Sagittarius, and the Scorpion is the Egyptian constellation and not zodiacal.

Then again, early horoscopes do not always mark the meridian and ascendant. The two horoscopes from a tomb at Athribis, shown in Plate 15, show only which signs were above the horizon and which below. No aspects between the planets can be measured since only the sign-position is given.

Finally, there are the two different circles of animals, the annual circle which became the zodiac with its ruling planets, and the hour-circle, which has a completely different set of animals and no ruling planets.

All these uncertainties do suggest that as late as the beginning of the Christian era the zodiac was not yet an old and tried tradition, nor were the techniques of astrology generally agreed upon, any more than they are now.

After all, when Babylonian priests were brought to Egypt in the train of Esarhaddon, and after some years discovered the unchanging Sothic calendar and the Horoscope of Eternity, their first question would naturally have been: 'And what did you predict from that celestial event?' The Egyptian priest would have blinked before answering: 'We did not predict anything.' At which the Assyrian priest's jaw would have dropped. Fancy missing such a wonderful opportunity! I do not suggest that this little romance at Heliopolis actually occurred; but it could have done: place, time, and climate of thought converged.

That was in the seventh century B.C. No direct evidence has survived for the use of the zodiac in prediction before the fifth century, and in Egypt before the third.[4] But Proclus, writing of the philosopher Theophrastus, Aristotle's immediate successor who died about 288 B.C., says that 'the most extraordinary thing of his age was the lore of the Chaldeans, who foretold not only events of public interest but even the lives and deaths of individuals.'[5] So astrology as an effective technique invaded Greece in the latter half of the fourth century. To have reached such a stage of development there must already have been behind it a hundred years of practice. This suggests that the first notion of astrology as we know it was begotten on Babylon by Egypt between the seventh and fifth centuries, and the zodiac itself, as a calendrical device, was of similar origin but may be a little older.

Plato, writing about 365 B.C., still has the signs of the zodiac ruled by gods and goddesses, and doubtless two or three centuries were required to establish the transition from divine powers to mechanical planets. The earliest known personal horoscope has a date of 410 B.C.,[6] in Plato's youth, so the well-known passage in the Timaeus[7] may be the first reference to horoscopy in literature; but little or no interpretation is found attached to early horoscopes. An equinox in 15° of the constellation Aries was used by some Hellenistic astrologers,[8] but this was sheer guesswork, for it was only correct in the ninth century, long before their time; but an equinox in 10° Aries was quite correctly established about 500.[9]

Thus the zodiac certainly existed before 500 B.C. But the conflation of Egyptian and Babylonian astronomy need not have waited until the Persian occupation of Egypt, which lasted from 525, under Cambyses, to 405. Nor is it likely to be the result of the brief occupation by Nebuchadnezzar II of Babylon in 567. The Assyrian conquest and occupation lasted from 671 till 610, and the astronomical library of Nabu was transferred from Calah to Nineveh by Asshurbanipal, who reigned from 668 to 626. Astronomy was a great interest at the Assyrian court, and at the same time the fashion ran strongly towards Egyptian art, which was imitated and sold in great quantity to the Assyrians by Phoenician artists.[10]

This takes us back as far as the seventh century B.C. To carry the argument further we shall have to look to the exaltations of the planets. Traditionally each planet is 'exalted' in a certain degree of the zodiac, and has its fall in the opposite degree. Astrologers have naturally assumed that each was especially strong or weak in those degrees or in the signs containing them. Their origin, however, remained a mystery, since they cannot be explained by juggling with the planets' nodes, aphelions, or epicycles, or their proximity to the zenith.

The word translated 'exaltations' means in fact 'hiding-places', and the hiding-places of a planet are obviously those parts of the zodiac in which it is invisible, and especially the degree in which it disappears from view into the sun's rays at heliacal setting and the degree of its reappearance at heliacal rising. The same is true of the moon, and is proved by the distance of the moon's 'hiding-place' from the sun's, 14°, which is a typical elongation for a new crescent. Since these phenomena change their positions every time they occur, we are evidently faced by an historical date, and there can be no doubt whatever that this date is 786–785 B.C. As for the sun having a hiding-place, it emerges from darkness at dawn on New Year's Day.

Until the zodiac drew attention to the position of planets in constellations, the chief focus of interest in them was their heliacal disappearances and reappearances, and in 786 all the planets had heliacal phenomena in or very near the degrees of their exaltations — an event so improbable that it cannot plausibly be ascribed to chance. The list of these phenomena and the exaltations which they fit is as follows:

TABLE 23   *Exaltations of the Planets*

Exaltation

1 Nisan=April 4th, 786= New Year's Day.

May 10th	Venus	heliacally set in the east in			9° Cancer.	
June 22nd	Jupiter	,,	,,		15° Cancer.	15° Cancer.
July 24th	Venus	,,	rose in the west in 18° Virgo.			
July 30th	Jupiter	,,	,,	,, ,,	21° Cancer.	
August 25th	Mars	,,	set	,,	11° Pisces.	
September 14th	Mercury	,,	,, in the east	,,	16° Virgo.	15° Virgo.
September 23rd	Saturn	,,	,,	west	21° Libra.	19° Libra.
October 27th	Saturn	,,	rose	east	26° Libra.	
February 4th, 785	Mars	,,	,,	,, ,,	1° Aquari.	27° Capri.

The positions of Sun, Moon, and Venus are for New Year's day : Sun 19° Aries. 19° Aries.

Moon 29° Aries. 3° Taurus.

Venus 26° Pisces, 27° Pisces

(Mercury's 13 other phenomena omitted)

The year 786 B.C. saw the opening in Calah of the new temple of Nabu (Nebo), the god of writing associated with the planet Mercury. This is the origin of Mercury's connection with writing, wisdom, commerce, and all similar subjects. The Egyptian god of writing and wisdom, Thoth-Tahuti or Hermes Trismegistos, was not associated with the planet Mercury until astrology was in full sail across the Hellenistic world; for Thoth as god of time-measurement was a moon-god. He readily became director-general of celestial happenings, as he was of the weighing of the soul before Osiris, but there was no Egyptian reason to associate him with Mercury.

There are two slight weaknesses in this argument. The heliacal risings and settings are not as close together as they might have been; and also some are risings and others settings. This apparently haphazard selection may leave us unconvinced that the coincidence is not an accident.

But the exaltations are not and cannot be the horoscope for the foundation or opening of the temple of Nabu, for Mercury cannot be in Virgo while the Sun is in Aries. They are simply heliacal phenomena recorded in that year; and since they are not those closest to a given date, and since they include an arbitrary mixture of settings and risings, it becomes probable that they were not observed and catalogued at the time, but were looked up in the temple records when the priesthood conceived the notion that they might be especially important. But what could have given them that idea?

It is a curious thing about Egyptian astronomy that we often find the year treated as of 360 days, the 5 epagomenae being ignored. If we could believe that by 'days' the Egyptians meant 'degrees' they would be using our system. And there is an extant text which says: 'A temple day is $\frac{1}{360}$ of a temple year.'[11] This is not an astronomical text at all; on the contrary, by 'a day' it means a day's rations. But it exemplifies once more the Egyptian habit of dividing the circle of the year into 360 parts.

When Assyrian priests came to Egypt and compared notes with their Egyptian colleagues, as they would naturally do, not being monotheists, they might easily think, if the esoteric lore were not full explained to them, that the Egyptians divided the circle into 360 equal parts. Thus the ideal circle of days invented by the Egyptians for use in the afterlife would have become a real circle of new and convenient degrees. This is possible even if a year of 360 days was used in the mulAPIN tablets.

And similarly when the Assyrians met the Horoscope of Eternity and realized that it was drawn for the beginning of an era, they would be likely to return home and look up the records to see what they could do in the same line. They could not choose a more significant epoch than the foundation of the temple of their own god of astronomy. And because the Egyptians mentioned planets in the west and south as well as the east, they would think it natural to make a mixture of heliacal settings and risings. If this hypothesis be correct, then the exaltations were an Assyrian imitation of the Horoscope of Eternity, not observed at the time but looked up in the records, and thus perhaps a century or more later than 786 B.C. For almost a century scholars have said that the zodiac was of Babylonian origin and left it at that; it now seems more probable that it was the product of interaction between Babylon, Egypt, and Assyria.

For the Ram, to begin with, is definitely not a Babylonian constellation. It was also thought not to be Egyptian because on the later system of decans it fell in Capricorn. But the Ram and Boat were both extremely important in Egypt, and this cannot be explained if both were invisible at the rising of Sothis. It has of course nothing to do with the later position of Aries as the first sign of the 12. The Ram was important because it culminated when Sirius rose, and the Boat as a particularly obvious sacred emblem which stood on the same occasion conspicuously high in the sky. If we accept the identity of the Boat with our own Pegasus (Plates 19 and 20), then the Ram was an Egyptian and not a Babylonian constellation.

The Bull on the other hand is not Egyptian. Had it been so, then its ruler, when ruling planets were allotted, should have been Saturn and not Venus, just as Mars would have been the ruler of Leo. The Egyptians called Saturn 'Horus the Bull of Heaven', and bulls are not uncommon in Egyptian astronomy, but they are not attached, like the Babylonian Gud.anna, to this part of the sky.

The Twins are the Babylonian Great Twins, Maštabba.galgal. It is not quite so certain, but very likely, that they were the Two Stars of Egypt. This is one of the few constellations which is named from its shape, the others being the Boat, the Lion or Dog, and the Scorpion, or at least its tail.

As a Crab, Cancer is Babylonian, but it derives nevertheless from both countries, since the Egyptian Two Turtles were also hard-shelled aquatic creatures, the origin of the Tortoise which was put here by both the Greeks and the Chinese. And Hermes ruled this constellation because his Egyptian correspondence was Thoth, who as god of astronomy ruled the time of Sirius' rising, in his name of Tekhi the Accurate.

The Lion again is Egyptian, and goes back to the third millennium, like the Ram; its Babylonian name was the Great Dog.

The next five signs are all Babylonian, and a possible reason is that in this part of the sky the Egyptians had their enormous constellations of the Hippopotamus and the Giant, which could not be cut down to fit. In Gemini, Cancer, and Leo, the Assyrian priests who standardized the zodiac had had no difficulty in combining Babylonian and Egyptian ideas, but from Virgo to Capricorn they used the constellations of Mesopotamia.

Virgo originally was the Great Mother as corn-goddess, hence the title of Spica, the Ear of Corn, and hence also Demeter, corn-goddess of Eleusis, placed by Plato to rule this constellation. From a corn-mother to a pretty maid is not a contradiction but simply a different stage of evolution: at Eleusis the harvest-goddess Demeter was always associated with her daughter Korè, The Maid, who is the seed-corn and springing wheat. And the Virgin Mother, of course, is still worshipped.

The position of Virgo has obviously nothing to do with shapes imagined among the stars. The corn-goddess belongs to her proper season, and the full moon in Virgo, which happens nowadays in April, occurred two thousand years ago at the beginning of March, and earlier still in February. This does not fit the Babylonian harvest, which began in May, nor the Assyrian, which happened in June, but it fits the first appearance of the spring corn, for the fields become green in February, and that is why we have the Virgin rather than the Earth-Mother. The Babylonian title is the Furrow, which clearly does not refer to harvest; but in Egypt the harvest began at the evening rising of Spica, when the moon was full in Virgo, and this fits in with the Ear of Corn even if not the Virgin. The goddess who holds the Ear was original to Babylon, and can be found centuries earlier than our Plate 13.[12]

Zibanitu, the Scales, is a well-known Babylonian constellation and corresponds to the myth of the Last Judgment in the autumn and the weighing of souls. It happens also to be seasonally suitable to Egypt, for the harvest would be weighed, and taxes assessed, when the moon was full in Libra.

Selket the scorpion-goddess does appear in the Egyptian heavens, but in the northern sky, far from the constellation Scorpio. She is drawn sometimes as a scorpion and sometimes as a woman, so there is no question there of fanciful resemblances. Mr Fagan makes this constellation seasonal in Egypt on account of the Khamsin wind, when scorpions are common, but its real origin doubtless is the scorpion-man of the Babylonian boundary-stones.

The Centaur with his bow has no precedent in Egypt, and the Goat-fish is a well-known Babylonian monster. Since the goat does not require lush pasture, the obvious implication of this hybrid symbol is 'end of the dry season'. This, however, does not suit the climate of Babylonia, where the Tigris is in flood from early March until the middle of June (Gregorian), and the Euphrates from mid-March until September; but the first rain, putting an end to the dry season, falls in the month of Tishri, which was October–November. The full moon of Capricorn, however, occurs now between July 27th and August 16th Gregorian, but about 700 B.C. it occurred between June 27th and July 18th Julian. Although these dates do not fit the Babylonian seasons, July 18th Julian is the day after the rising of Sirius in dynastic Egypt, so that the dry season ended when the moon was full in conjunction with the star Denéb Algédi, or Delta Capricorni, the Goat's Tail. This close piece of timing, coupled with the seasonal suitability to Egypt of the full moon in Aquarius and Pisces during the inundation, suggests that the traditional Babylonian Goat-fish was employed by Assyrian astronomers resident in Egypt in the train of Esarhaddon and Asshurbanipal to indicate the Egyptian end of the dry season.

This may seem slightly improbable. But the Assyrians were a parvenu people, always imitating the Babylonians because they had little creative ability of their own. They must have been amazed by the Egyptians, who boasted readily of their superior knowledge and justified their boast by having a better calendar than the Babylonians. Indeed, as we saw, the Assyrians were so impressed that they went home and invented the exaltations of the planets in imitation of the Horoscope of Eternity. Can it have been they who put the Goat-fish into the sky, about 650 B.C.?

There is no question of this emblem having been invented in Assyrian times or for this purpose; it is far older. But its occurrence on monuments does not prove that it had any reference to the sky, the more so since it belonged to the god of the waters under the earth. It is quite simply 'The Antelope of the Subterranean Ocean', a symbol of the god Ea. It occurs in the zodiac of 18 signs, and is not absent from the mulAPIN tablets of about 700 B.C. But these tablets may represent a tradition as old as the ninth century, when the equinox really was about 15° of Aries, where Eudoxus was taught to put it before he came to visit Plato. So it seems rather more probable that the Assyrian astronomers, who marked the season of ploughing by the full moon in Taurus (Gud.anna, the Bull of Heaven), and the springing of the green corn by the moon's repletion in Virgo (Ab.sin, the Furrow), were much struck by the fact that she was, by pure chance, full in the tail of Sukhur-mashu the Goat-fish when the Nile began to rise. Hence when they wanted to regularize the last two signs of the zodiac they abandoned their goddess GU.LA in favour of their 'god with streams', who could carry the Egyptian urns, and adopted the Egyptian Two Fishes in the place of The Tails and the Great Swallow.

It is legitimate to wonder whether anyone in Egypt still knew that this was the longitude of the Two Fishes, since the late system of decans omitted them, apparently from the region of Scorpio. But, against this, whence did the Babylonians and Assyrians obtain their Ram, if not from Egypt, where the Ram was of special importance? It is hard to believe, when one studies Plates 19 and 20 and the sky itself, that the Egyptians can ever have forgotten the constellation of the Boat, which we can still see so plainly. And in that case both Ram and Fishes will still have been known because they were next to the Boat.

This first zodiac, of course, cannot have been tropical. It was not supposed to be either tropical or sidereal, but was simply assumed to be both at once. When this turned out to be untrue, no one could claim to have been using the moving equinox without knowing that it moved; for astrologers had been using the fixed stars without realizing that the equinox was no longer where it used to be. That the first zodiac can only have been measured from the stars was not only inevitable but also a fact[13] — although, of course, it was no sooner invented than it was thought to be tropical and used as such.

The animals of the hour-circles found from Egypt to China are certainly less ancient than the signs of the zodiac, for they do not go back to Babylonian and Egyptian constellations. When it was found that the twelve regular signs take roughly the same time to cross the meridian (but not the horizon), it must have seemed convenient to use their names for the twelve double-hours of day and night. This, however, would not work because their positions change once a month. Hence a different circle was devised to name the hours, regardless of the stars, and the animals of this circle, not being traditional, vary from country to country, and were also used for numbering years, months, and days. This fits in with the twelve-year cycle of predictions for the prospects of harvests, found in various lands.[14]

This second circle of animals did not originally run in the opposite direction to the zodiac, but, as we learn from a text published by Gundel, its animals were selected from paranatellonta of the zodiac, that is, from small asterisms rising with particular degrees at a particular latitude[15] — in this case, of course, Alexandria. These asterisms, together with various versions of the hour-circle or dodecaoros, are given in a table at the end of this chapter, and the Cat which figures under Aries is the same Cat as, according to Teucros, 'makes designing cowards'.

If the far eastern cycle is compared with the lists given by Teucros and in the Papyrus of Paris, more than half the animals are seen to be the same, but the order seems confused. There is, in fact, only one way in which they will fit together. For if we equate the Chinese sheep with Teucros' goat, or the dog with the dog, the ox with the bull, or the dragon with the crocodile, we get no other suitable correspondence; and if we equate the ape with the ape we get only one other, the hawk with the cock. But if we equate Nos. 3, 4, 5, and 6 in each cycle, we get tiger corresponding to lion, hare for ass (and both have long ears), dragon (or the Kirghiz crab) for scarab, and snake for snake, besides cock for ibis, and dog for dog-faced baboon (which is the kind of ape intended).

Hence the Twelve Branches of the far eastern hour-circle are derived from the Greco-Egyptian animal circle given by Teucros, but naturally in reverse order because they were needed to measure time instead of space. The twenty-eight animals of the Chinese show nothing more in common with Teucros' list than do the Twelve Branches, but they do pair off in couples, with four added to make up the number of lunar days, so we can say that we have here the origin of both Chinese circles of animals, and the origin is the same, although they run in opposed directions.

It would be useful, perhaps, to end with a brief history of the twelve glyphs or sigla commonly used as abbreviations for the signs. This is only partly possible because not enough work on the subject has been done. In medieval manuscripts the sun is represented by ♂, so our modern ⊙ cannot claim to be derived directly from the ancient Egyptian ⊙. In Greek manuscripts the constellations are frequently spelt out in full or referred to by numbers. On demotic Egyptian ostraca and papyri of the early centuries A.D. the abbreviation is either the first letter of the name, as in Berlin Papyrus P.8279, or the determinative which follows it, as in the Stobart Tablets. Thus there is in most cases a traceable derivation from hieroglyphic.

The last table (Plate 22) is derived from three publications of Professor Neugebauer.[16] The hieroglyph for Aries is an animal's pelt and tail, and for Taurus a phallus. In neither case is the modern glyph derived from it. There is a hieroglyph resembling ♈, but it has nothing to do with the case, and the Egyptian ⚐ is the origin of the letter A but not so far as we know of ♉ . ♋ is suggested by the abbreviated scarab in column S, but Leo is drawn in demotic as a knife, and Pisces likewise has no great resemblance. Of the rest, Scorpio, Sagittarius and Aquarius, are clear, and Virgo may be seen in the glyph of the seated woman if it be turned on one side. Capricorn comes from the symbol for 'face' because it was drawn either as 'goat' or 'face' to represent 'goat-face'. (The word for 'goat' was spelt with the same consonants as the word for 'life', hence the appearance of the well-known 'ankh', which was pronounced something like *onekh* or *anehh*.) Libra came to be written with the hieroglyph for 'horizon' some time after 250 B.C., when it began to rise heliacally on New Year's Day and thus became for the time being the first of the signs.

Finally perhaps one might suggest that the meaning of the zodiac for the human race is not to be found merely outside ourselves, with radio telescopes and statistics, but by looking into the source of all meaning, which is referred to as 'God' in the following quotation from Plotinus:[17]

Now the Supreme, because within it are no differences, is eternally present; but we achieve such presence only when our differences are lost … We have at all times our centre There, though we do not at all times look Thither. We are like a company of singing dancers, who may turn their gaze outward and away, notwithstanding they have the choirmaster for centre; but when they are turned towards him, then they sing true and are truly centred upon him. Even so we encircle the Supreme always, and when we break the circle, it shall be to our utter dissolution and cessation of being; but our eyes are not at all times fixed upon the Centre. Yet in the vision thereof is our attainment and our repose and the end of all discord, God in his dancers and God the true Centre of the dance.

TABLE 24   *The Hour-circle or Dodecaoros*

original asterism	Teucros and Plate 22	Egyptian god	Country	Bianchini tablet	Pagoda at Trichinopoly	Magic Papyrus of Paris	Mimaut Papyrus	Kirghiz cycle	Far Eastern cycle	Numbers in the Chinese 12 Branches	28 asterisms
26–27° Aries	Cat	Bast	Persia	Cat	Lion	Cat	Ape	Sheep	Goat	8	23
14° Taurus	Dog	Anubis	Babylon	Dog	Tiger	Dog	Unicorn	Horse	Horse	7	25
6–7° / 19–20° / 22–27° Gemini	Snake	Uto	Cappadocia	Snake		Snake	Cat	Snake	Snake	6	27–28
24–26° Cancer	Scarab	Khepra	Armenia	Crab	Boar	Scarab	Bull	Crab	Dragon	5	1–2
? Leo	Ass	Setekh	Asia	Ass	Ass	Ass	Lion	Hare	Hare	4	4
? Virgo	Lion	Re	Ionia	Lion	Elephant	Lion	Ass	Panther	Tiger	3	6–7
20–30° Libra	He-goat	Goat of Mendes	Libya	Goat	Bull	Goat	Camel	Cow	Ox	2	9
12–18° Scorpio	Bull	Apis	Italy	Ox	Cock or Hen Hawk	Bull	—	Mouse	Rat	1	11
27–30° Sagitt.	Hawk	Horus	Crete	Hawk	Dog	Hawk	Ibis(?)	Pig	Pig	12	13
2–4(?) Capri.	Ape	Thoth	Syria	—	Snake	Baboon	—	Dog	Dog	11	15–16
4–30° Aquar.	Ibis	Thoth	Egypt	—		Ibis	—	Cock	Bird	10	17–19
4–30° Pisces	Crocodile	Sobek	India	—	Rat	Crocodile	—	Rat	Ape	9	20–21
	W. Gundel, F. Boll, *Sphaera*, Footnote 15 above, p. 296.	Paulus Alexandrinus ch. 7.		See Chap. XII, *Sphaera*, Note 16.	F. Boll, *Sphaera*, p. 344.	C. Wessely, *Denkschr. Akad.* Wien, 1888.	R. Reitzenstein, *Poimandres*, Leipzig, 1904.	F. Roeck, *Kalender der Tolteken*, Wien, 1922 (in reversed order).			

Notes and References

THE references, numbered serially by chapter and collected here for convenience, have been deliberately kept as few as possible: to the general reader a superfluous display of learning is not attractive. This explains the absence of references to a number of well-known books which, though good in themselves, are not or are no longer directly useful. Examples of these are T. L. Heath's work on Greek mathematics, Duhem's *Système du Monde*, the *Phainomena* of Aratos, Daressy's *L'Égypte Céleste*, the *Mandaean Book of the Zodiac*, the works of Kepler, Bouché-Leclerc, Sir Norman Lockyer, Emmeline Plunkett, and numerous Arab astronomers and astrologers, besides a large number of outdated Sitzungsberichte. Finally, I am not convinced of the zodiacal reference of the well-known Gezer Tablet published by Macalister in *Palestine Exploration Fund*, Oct. 1902, p. 262.

CHAPTER 4: MEDIEVAL MAGIC AND PSYCHOLOGY

1 See for example Franz Cumont, *L'Égypte des Astrologues* (1937), and the picture of Sicilian society in the fourth century given by Firmicus Maternus.
2 Cardan's *Aphorisms*, etc. trans. Lilly (London, 1676).
3 When not otherwise stated, authority for statements in this chapter can usually be found in Lynn Thorndike, *History of Magic and Experimental Science* (Macmillan, 1923).
4 *Confessions* VII, cap. 6 (Loeb edition p. 356, but not the Loeb translation!).
5 xxv, 5.
6 Luke xxi 25.
7 H. de La Ville de Mirmont, *L'Astrologie chez les Gallo-romains* (Montpellier, 1904).
8 *Mineralium*, II, iii, 3.
9 P. E. M. Berthelot, *Collection des alchimistes grecs*, I, 88–92.
10 Cp. also Hugh Ross Williamson, *The Arrow and the Sword* (Faber, 1947).
11 Latin in Migne, P.L. 171, 1446. Juno is the planet Venus.
12 This tradition goes back to Berossos, a priest of Bel who settled in Cos about 290 B.C. (Seneca, *Nat. Quaest.* iii, 29).
13 *Autobiography of a Yogi*, by Yogananda (Rider, London, 1950).
14 *Opera Omnia* (Basel, 1550), cols. 2037–42.
15 *Opera* 27, 249, ed. J. de Vercellis.

16 *Secretum Secretorum*, ed. R. Steele (Oxford, 1920), p. 15.
    For a good collection of medieval zodiacal illustrations see Henri
    Stern, *Le Calendrier de 345* (Paris, 1953).

CHAPTER 5: THE TWELVE GODS: PLATO AND AUGUSTUS

1   *De Caelo* II, xii, 292a.
2   41–2.
3   *Journ. Near Eastern Studies*, IV (1) (Jan. 1945), pp. 21–2.
4   II. 34 Kroll.
5   *Vita Augusti*, c. 94, transl. Rolfe. On Augustus's coins, cp. Deonna in
    Journ. Warburg, XVII 47–86.
6   *Suet. Tib.* lxix. Cp. F. H. Cramer, *Astrology in Roman Law and Politics*
    (Amer. Philos. Soc., 1954).
7   *Nat. Quaest.* vii, 30.
8   id. ii, 32.
9   *De Natura Deorum* ii, 21; *De Div.* ii, 88–99.
10 IV, 773 and Housman *ad loc.* Laurentius Lydus p. 8, l.8 Teubner.
    Ginzel in *Sitzb. Berlin Akad. 1887*, 1122 ff.
11 Longitudes of the planets, April 6th, 753 B.C., about noon L.M.T.
12 *Starlore* vol. III, no. 23 (Sept. 1899), p. 43, where the date is errone-
    ously given as July 15th, 481. The Greek in *CCAG (Catalogus Codicum
    Astrologorum Graecorum)* vol. I, pp. 103–4.
13 *CCAG* I, 107. Cp. O. Neugebauer and Van Hoesen, *Greek Horo-
    scopes*, p. 147 *Trans. Amer. Philos. Soc., 1959)*. Other fragments of
    Palchus in *CCAG* I. 80–107, VI, 63, etc.
14 *Fragment* 2, col. A.
15 ii, 77–82.
16 III *ad fin.*
17 ix, 14.
18 Pliny, *Nat. Hist.* xviii, 59; Achilles Tatius, *Isagogue* 23.
19 *Works and Days*, 385.
20 *Georgic* IV, 231–5.
21 A. Rehm, *Parapegmastudien (Abh. Bayr. Akad. d. Wiss., phil.-hist. Kl.,*
    neue Folge, vol. 19, 1941). The illustration is from H. Diels and A.
    Rehm in *Sitzber. Berlin Akad. 1904*, pp. 92 ff., 752 ff. Another
    pegged calendar, found at Coligny near the Franco-Swiss border, is
    illustrated in T. D. Kendrick, *The Druids* (London, 1927), p. 116.
22 *De Div.* II, 87.
23 *Phaedrus*, 246e *ad fin.* All the quotations from Plato are given in
    Jowett's translation, which seems the best at present.
24 *Timaeus*, 38.
25 252c.
26 *Phaedrus*, 246 c 6; *Timaeus*, 40 a 3, 41 a 3.
27 II 439 foll. Variant lists in W. H. Roscher, *Ausf. Lexikon d.gr.u.röm.
    Mythologie*, VI, 786.

28 H. Stuart Jones, *Catalogue of the Sculptures in the Museo Capitolino*, Pl. 29;
Roscher's *Lexikon*, VI, 798.
29 *Laws* V 745, VIII 848.
30 *Laws* VIII, 828.
31 *Laws* VIII, 767 c.
32 246 e.
33 *Od.* xiii, 96–112.
34 Symposium, 188.

CHAPTER 6: THE ZODIAC IN CHINA

1 L. de Saussure, *Origines de l'astronomie chinoise* (Paris, 1926–31), p. 523;
but see also Needham (note 13 below) vol. III, 260.
2 id. p. 185.
3 *Uranographie chinoise* (The Hague & Leyden, 1875) esp. pp. 583, 585.
4 *Ostasiatische Zeitschrift* (Berlin, 1919–20), vol. 8, pp. 42–48.
5 J. Edkins in *China Review* (Hongkong), vol. 14 (1885), p. 345 ff.
6 E. Chavannes, *T'oung Pao* (Leyden, 1906), p. 71.
7 Id. p. 87.
8 Saussure, op. cit., p. 134.
9 id. pp. 124, 127.
10 This is explained in Li-ki xi, 1, 3 (Legge), see following note.
11 Translated by James Legge in *Sacred Books of the East*, vol. 3 (Oxford,
1879).
12 P. V. Neugebauer, *Hilfstafeln zur astronomischen Chronologie* (Berlin and
Leipzig, 1912–25).
13 The standard work on this subject is now J. Needham, *Science and
Civilisation in China*, esp. vol. II, pp. 346–95 (divination), and vol. III,
pp. 210–82 and 390–408. There is an illustration of a Chinese horoscope in vol. II, Plate XVII (p. 352).
14 Spring and Autumn, viii, 1; Li-ki, second month of autumn; id.
iv, 12.
15 Derk Bodde, *Statesman, Patriot and General in Ancient China* (New Haven
1940). Richard Wilhelm, *Frühling u. Herbst des Lü-Bu-We* (Jena,
1928).
16 Needham, op. cit., III, 259–61; also III, 182–282, 436, esp. pp. 218,
402.
17 *De Die Natali* 18.
18 W. Eberhard, *Beiträge zur kosmologischen Spekulation Chinas* (Bässler
Archiv, Heft 16), esp. pp. 58, 63, 67.
19 Giles, *Chinese Dictionary*, vol. I; W. Eberhard, in *Sitzber. Preuss. Akad.*
1933, ii, 937.
20 M. Cantor, *Vorlesungen über Geschichte der Mathematik*, I, 27–8;
Ideler, *Mémoire sur la chronologie chinoise*, Abh. Berlin Akad. Feb. 16th,
1837.

21 Ebenezer Burgess, translation of Surya Siddhanta, ed. Sengupta, Calcutta, 1935. (Beware of misprints in this edition.)
22 See above; notes 13 and 18.
23 *Asiatic Review*, Jan. 1938 (with bibliography); other articles by this author in *Journal of Royal Asiatic Society*, Oct. 1938, *Occasional Notes of Roy. Astron. Soc.*, June 1939, no. 5.
24 xix, 58. I am grateful to Mr E. D. Grinstead of the British Museum for this reference.
25 Boll, *Sphaera*, p. 320 gives these equations for other far-eastern countries.

CHAPTER 7: FROM MEXICO TO TIBET
 1 Vol. II (1816), p. 3.
 2 C. P. Bowditch, *Maya Numeration* (Cambridge, Mass., 1910), pp. 287–289.
 3 Berard Haile, *Starlore Among the Navaho* (Sante Fé, 1947).
 4 Fritz Roeck, *Kalender der Tolteken* (Vienna, 1922).
 5 F. K. Ginzel, *Handbuch d. math. u. techn. Chronologie* (Leipzig 1906), I, 434.
 6 For a desperate effort to maintain the contrary, E. J. Webb, *The Names of the Stars* (Nisbet, London, 1952).

CHAPTER 8: PERSIA AND THE FOUR ELEMENTS
 1 *The Sacred Books of the East*, ed. Max Müller (Oxford, 1880 onwards), vol. 5, *The Bundahish*, transl. E. W. West, Chap. 2. Vol. 23, *The Sirozahs and Yashts*, transl. Darmesteter. Vol. 31, *The Avesta*, transl. L. H. Mills.
 2 Tishtrya is the Persian name of Mercury in Budge, *History of Alexander* (1889), p. 9.
 3 The ninth asterism, towards the end of Cancer.
 4 West, op. cit., pp. 397–400.
 5 F. Cumont, *Textes et Monuments figures relatifs aux Mystères de Mithra* (Brussels, 1896), Vol. II, 244–5, fig. 77.
 6 id. Vol. II, p. 389, fig. 304, and p. 395, fig. 315. Cp. Vol. I, p. 300.
 7 On Mithraism in general see S. Dill, *Roman Society from Nero to Marcus Aurelius* (1904); W. J. Phythian-Adams, *Mithraism* (1915).

CHAPTER 9: THE BIBLE AND BIRTHSTONES
 1 Kalt, *Biblisches Reallexikon* (Paderborn, 1931).
 2 Sigmund Mowinckel, *Die Sternnamen im alten Testament* (Oslo, 1928).
 3 J. J. Hess, 'Die Sternnamen in Hiob 9^9 und 38^{31} (Festschrift Jacob).

4   D. Feuchtwang, 'Der Tierkreis in der Tradition und im Synago-
    genritus' (Breslau, *Monatsschrift f. Geschichte u. Wissenschaft d.
    Judentums*, Nov.–Dec. 1915).
5   G. A. Cooke, 'The Book of Ezekiel' (*Internat. Crit. Comm.*, Edinburgh
    1936), p. 14.
6   Schrader, *Die Keilinschriften u. das alte Testament*, ed. Zimmern &
    Winckler, pp. 631 ff. (1903).
7   F. J. Boll, 'Aus der Offenbarung Johannis', Stoicheia I (1914); cp.
    J. Freundorfer, 'Die Apokalypse d. Apostel Johannes' (*Bibl. Studien*
    Vol. 23, 1930).
8   Josephus, Bell, Jud. v. 5.5; Philo, *Quis rer. div. haer.*, ed. Cohn, 221 ff.
9   Gunkel, *Schöpfung und Chaos* (Göttingen, 1885), pp. 302–8; but see
    Charles, *infra* note 11.
10 ii. 31.
11 R. H. Charles, *The Book of Revelation* (Edinburgh 1920), I, 130–2.
12 Daniel vii, 7 and 24.
13 Bundahish iii, 11.
14 Dieterich, *Abraxas*, p. 120, n. 4.
15 As note 6 above, Vol. 3, p. 360, n. 3.
16 *De Nupt. Philol. et Merc.* i. 75 (Teubner, p. 34).
17 Genesis xxxvii 9.
18 Jubilees II 9 and VI 36–8. Ed. R. H. Charles (S.P.C.K., 1917).
19 Enoch VIII 3.
20 Enoch XXXIII 3, cp. XXXVI 3.
21 *Oedipus Aegyptiacus* (1653) II, ii, 177; Charles, op. cit. I, 315.
22 Cooke, op. cit., pp. 26 near top, 317, 323.
23 Charles, op. cit., II, 166.
24 *Ant.* iii, 7, 7, transl. W. Whiston (1928). Cp. id. iii, 6, 7; Bell. Jud. v,
    5, 5, and 7.
25 G. F. Kunz, *The Curious Lore of Precious Stones* (Philadelphia, 1913),
    p. 299.
26 Kunz, pp. 124, 316–17, 342.
27 Nothing much can be learnt from the magical properties attributed
    to gems, see for instance *Mani Mala*, by S. M. Tagore (Calcutta,
    1879).
28 Jerome, Epist. ad Fabiolam=Migne PL XXII 616; agrees with
    Revised Verson except for exchange of Nos. 3 and 4, jasper instead
    of diamond, and chrysolite before beryl and onyx.

CHAPTER 10: INDIA AND THE ASTERISMS

1   Brihat Samhita, Chapter 2, transl. H. Kern (1913), in his collected
    works, Vol. I, 173.
2   Transl. Ebenezer Burgess, introduction by P. C. Sengupta (Calcutta,
    1935), p. viii.

3   Muhammad ibn Ahmad Al-Biruni's *India*, English transl. by Edw. C. Sachau (London, 1910).

4   Ujjain lies 23° 13′ N, 75° 52′ E; Alexandria 31° 10′ N, 30° 0′ E. Models of the astronomical buildings at Ujjain may be seen in the Science Museum, London.

5   By for instance Das and B. G. Tilak; see Needham, *Science and Civilisation in China*, III, 86, and G. R. Kaye, *Hindu Astronomy* (Calcutta, 1924).

6   Sengupta, op. cit., p. xxxi.

7   Adi, Chap. 3, cp. Sengupta, ibid.

8   Bangalore, 1919, chap. XXVII.

9   *Surya Siddh.*, Chap. III, 12.

10   id. II, 1–2.

11   Kaye, op. cit., pp. 30 ff.

12   Sengupta, op. cit., p. xxx.

13   G. Thibaut in *Grundriss d. indo-arischen Philologie* (Strasbourg, 1899), Vol. III, Part 9, p. 7.

14   Sengupta, notes. 12 and 2, *Supra*.

15   *The Poona Orientalist*, Jan., Apr., and July 1941; *Hindu Heritage*, Feb. 1942; see also the astronomical section in Vedic Bibliography by R. N. Dandekar (Bombay, 1946).

16   Šalya 34, 3.

17   Atharva Veda XIX, 7, and 8 ad init.

18   Kaye, op. cit., p. 98.

19   Thibaut, op. cit., p. 14 ff.

20   Needham, op. cit., III, 82.

21   A. Weber in *Abh. Akad., Berlin, 1862*.

22   'Mémoire présentée à l'Acad. des Inscriptions et Belles-Lettres.'

23   cit. Kaye, op. cit., pp. 61–2.

24   O. Neugebauer, 'Tamil Astronomy', in *Osiris X* (1952), 252–76.

25   Atharva Veda VI, 110.

26   Laws of Manu IX, 258, and VI, 50. Cp. *Baudhayana II*, 1, 2, 16 and *Vasishtha* X, 21 (in same volume of *Sacred Books of the East*, ed. Max Müller).

27   As Note 1 above, but p. 178 and Chap. II, 17.
     B. L. Van der Waerden finds that Pap. Rylands 27 (Kgl. Dansk Vidensk. Selskab, hist.-vil. Meddeler xxxii) bridges the gap between the last cuneiform texts and Varaha Mihira.

CHAPTER II: BABYLONIAN MYTHS AND OMENS

1   'The reader who is unable to control the ancient Mesopotamian and Egyptian sources is hereby warned against using R. Eisler, *The Royal Art of Astrology* (London, 1946). The author writes with an air of authority, but virtually everything he says about Mesopotamian

astrology is either hopelessly muddled or incorrect.' (Prof. A. Sachs in *Journal of Cuneiform Studies*, Vol. VI, No. 2, 1952).

2 Otto Neugebauer, *The Exact Sciences in Antiquity* (First edition, Copenhagen, 1951), p. 132.

3 Cornelius' dates, in B. L. van der Waerden, *Jaarboek Ex Oriente Lux* (Leyden, 1952), Vol. III, pp. 414, 419.

4 S. Langdon, *Babylonian Menologies* (London, 1935), p. 1.

5 id. 68, 107; *The Epic of Creation* (Oxford, 1923), p. 27; *Semitic Mythology* (Boston, 1931), p. 307.

6 O. Neugebauer in *Journal of Near Eastern Studies*, IV (1945), p. 15, §11.

7 *Menologies*, p. 11.

8 P. V. Neugebauer and E. F. Weidner in *Sitzber. Sächs. Akad. Leipzig, 1915*, pp. 82–5.

9 F. X. Kugler, *Sternkunde und Sterndienst in Babel*, II, 474.

10 id. II, 71.

11 *Menologies*, pp. 48, 54, 73, 77, 84–9.

12 A. Ungnad in *Archiv für Orientforschung*, XIV, 278.

13 R. Campbell Thompson, *Reports of the Magicians and Astrologers* (London, 1900), No. 186.

14 id. No. 183.

15 Carl Bezold in *Sitzber. Heidelberg Akad., phil-hist. Kl., 1911*, pp. 22–3. Cp. Ungnad, op. cit.

16 van der Waerden in J.N.E.S. (as Note 6 above), VIII (1949), p. 21, cp. X (1951), p. 20 ff.

17 Schaumberger in Kugler, op. cit., *Ergänz.* III, 322.

18 Langdon, *Epic*, 149 ff.

19 id. 152; E. F. Weidner, *Handbuch der bab. Astron.* (Leipzig, 1915), 41, 62; van der Waerden, J.N.E.S., 1949 § VIII, and pp. 22 to end.

20 p. 495.

21 *Menologies*, p. 10.

22 id. p. 20.

23 A. Sachs, 'Babylonian Horoscopes', in *Journal of Cuneiform Studies* VI, No. 2, 54–7.

24 Kugler, op. cit., Erg. I, 130–5.

25 *Menologies*, pp. 107, 64.

26 B. L. van der Waerden's 'History of the Zodiac' in *Archiv für Orientforschung* XVI (1952–3), 216–30 and references there.

27 ibid. 218–19; *Amer. Journ. Sem. Lang.* XL (1923), 192; Kugler, op. cit., Erg. I, 70; S. Weinstock in *Journ. Hellenic Studies* LXIX (1949), p. 54.

28 van der Waerden, ibid., note 13; Thureau-Dangin, *Tablettes d'Uruk* (Paris, 1922), No. 14; E.F.Weidner, *Handbuch der Bab. Astron.*, p. 121.

29 *Journ. Roy. Asiat. Soc.*, 1925, pp. 37–60.

30 Langdon, *Sem. Myth.*, pp. 105–6; *Epic.*, p. 10.

31 id. *Epic*, Tablet I, 140–2.

32 *Epic*, p. 88, footnote 4; Wm. J. Hinke, *A New Boundary-Stone* (Philadelphia, 1907), pp. 98–103 and 231; *Arch. f. Or.* (see Note 26 above), XVI, 227.

33 E. D. Van Buren, *The Flowing Vase and The God With Streams* (Berlin, 1933), Plates VIII 30, XIII 43, et passim. M. Joachim Menant, *Recherches sur la Glyptique Orientale* (Paris, 1883), I, 111–12, figs. 60–65.

34 *Sem. Myth.*, p. 236.

35 P. F. Goessmann, *Planetarium Babylonicum* (Vatican, 1950), p. 176; BM. 86378, II, 19; *Menologies*, p. 99.

36 The full story is in *Sem. Myth.* 29 and illustration there.

37 *Georgics* I, 217.

38 *Arch. für Orientf.*, I, 69–78; *Menologies*, p. 12.

39 *Zodiacs Old and New* (Anscombe, London, 1951), p. 21, cp. *Menologies*, p. 2.

40 *Sem. Myth.*, pp. 158–60; *Menologies*, ibid.

41 Goessmann, op. cit., No. 126 (VAT 9428; cp. Thureau-Dangin, op. cit., No. 12).

42 *Sem. Myth.* Figs. 96, 97.

43 Goessmann, op. cit., No. 14; contrast van der Waerden, *Journ. Near Eastern Studies*, 1949, p. 13, Note 17 and 31; *Arch. f. Or.* (above), p. 226.

44 *Sem. Myth.*, p. 159.

CHAPTER 12: THE HOROSCOPE OF ETERNITY

1 Richard A. Parker, *The Calendars of Ancient Egypt* (Chicago, 1950) p. 32, and R. Weill, *Revue d'Egyptologie* V (1946), 255–6 and VI (1951), 224–5; Parker and Neugebauer, *Egyptian Astronomical Texts* (1964).

2 Karl Schoch, 'Planetentafeln für Jedermann', *Spalte* XLIV, Tafeln A and A (Berlin, 1927).

3 Maurice Burton, *Phoenix Reborn* (London, 1959); R. T. Rundle Clark in *University of Birmingham Historical Journal* II (1949–50), 1–29 and 105–40.

4 *Wisdom of the Egyptians* (London, 1940), pp. 4 ff.

5 id. p. 5.

6 P. E. Newberry, *Beni Hasan I* (Egypt Explor. Soc., 1893), p. 61.

7 L. Borchardt in *Zeitschrift für Aeg. Sprache* 37 (1899), 89–103.

8 H. E. Winlock, 'Origin of the Anc. Eg. Calendar' (*Proc. Amer. Philos. Soc., 1940*), p. 463; Parker, op. cit., p. 151.

9 H. Frankfort, *The Cenotaph of Seti I at Abydos* (Egypt Explor. Soc., London, 1933), p. 84.

10 *Ant.* i, Plates, 79, 80, 87; iv, 18–22.

11 *The Astrological Magazine* (Bangalore, January 1954), p. 82.

12 W. M. Flinders Petrie, *Athribis* (British School of Arch. in Egypt), pp. 23–4.
13 First given in Duncan Macnaughten's not generally accepted *Scheme of Egyptian Chronology* (1932), pp. 327–8.
14 H. Brugsch, *Recueil*, I, 30–35 and Pl. XVII; O. Neugebauer in *Journ. Amer. Or. Soc. 1943*, p. 115.
15 W. Gundel, *Dekane u. Dekansternbilder* (Warburg Studies, Vol. 19, Hamburg, 1936), p. 252.
16 Illustrated in Gundel, op. cit., Plates 16, 17; Henri Stern, *Le Calendrier de 354* (Paris, 1953), Pl. XXXIII.
17 cp. L. de Saussure, *Origines de l'Astronomie Chinoise* (Paris, n.d.), pp. 144–5.
18 Gundel, op. cit., pp. 77–81.
19 id. p. 81 =*CCAG* viii (3) 120–1.
20 *Oedipus Aegyptiacus* (Rome, 1653), II (2), 182–6, quoting Abenragel (eleventh cent.).
21 A. Pogo in *Isis*, xvii (Bruges), pp. 6–34, also *Osiris*, i (1936), 500–9; P. Lacau, *Sarcophages antérieurs*, ii, 107.
22 H. Chatley in *The Observatory*, Vol. 63 (March 1940), No. 790; O. Neugebauer in *Journ. Near Eastern Studies* IV, 1 (1945), p. 5, n. 11.
23 e.g. at Edfu (*Descr. Eg.* i. 58).
24 As Note 11 above, pp. 81–90.
25 Nos. 1104, 1708, 360, and cp. 1123. Ed. K. Sethe (Leipzig, 1908 foll.); S. B. Mercer (New York, 1952).
26 *Journ. Egyp. Archaeol.* 26 (1940), pp. 120–6.
27 e.g. E. J. Webb, *The Names of the Stars* (London, 1952).
28 Note 11 above, pp. 81–2.
29 Petrie, *Royal Tombs*, II, Plates V, 1 and VIa, 2.

CHAPTER 13: THE NAMING OF THE CONSTELLATIONS

1 C. G. Jung, *The I Ching or Book of Changes* (English translation, 1951), introduction; Jung and Pauli, *The Interpretation of Nature and the Psyche* (London, 1955).
2 *Zeitschr. f. aeg. Sprache* (1900), pp. 71 ff.
3 J. Duemichen, *Kalenderinschriften* (Leipzig, 1866), Plates cxvii, cvii, xcviii–xcix.
4 O. Neugebauer, *Journ. Amer. Or. Soc.* I (1943), 122.
5 *In Timaeum*, 285 F.
6 Above, Chap. X, n. 23.
7 40 C–D.
8 C. Fagan, *Zodiacs Old and New* (Anscombe, London, 1951), pp. 17–25 and references there.
9 Ibid.
10 *Illustrated London News*, January 17th, 1959, Plates II–IV and pp. 99–100.

11   F. L. Griffith, *Siut* (Lindon, 1889), Plates 7, 11.285, 300; S. Schott, in *Abh. Akad. Mainz* (Wiesbaden, 1952), ad init.

12   E. D. Van Buren in *Analecta Orientalia* XII (1935), 327–35.

13   Kugler, *SSB* II, 582; *Erg.* I, 130–35; id. *SSB* I 163; Fagan, op. cit.; v.d. Waerden in *Archiv für Orientforschung*, XVI 222, para. 5.

14   e.g. *Geoponica* I, 12 (Jupiter in the 12 signs); Censorinus, *De Die Natali*, 18; and the *Chi Ni Tzu* (Needham, op. cit., III, 123 n.).

15   *Neue Texte des Hermes Trismegistos* (Munich, 1936), p. 229 ff.; F. Boll, *Sphaera*, pp. 296–346.

16   *Trans. Amer. Philos. Soc.*, 1942, p. 246, and 1959, p. 1; *Journ. Amer. Or. Soc.*, 1943, p. 124, n. 38.

17   *Enneads* VI, ix, 8, tr. Dodds; cit. E. Wind, *Pagan Mysteries in the Renaissance*, p. 171 (Faber, 1958).

Index

'day for a year' method, 37
day-names, Mexican, 113
decan(ate)s, 181–8, 199, 202–3, 216
decimal point, 138
declination, 17
decumbiture, 50
Demeter, 83, 213
Democritos, 77
demons, 156, 162, 165, 172
Denderah, zodiac of, 167, 180–81, 198
Denéb algèdi, 215
Denebola, 169
determinism, 45
Deuteronomy XVIII, 124
Deuteronomy XXXIII, 123–4
'diagonal calendars', 197
Diodorus Siculus, 127
dipper, the big, 180
diviners, divination, 21, 25, 84, 148–9,
    157–8, 206–7
dodecaoros, 217–19
Dodeka Theoi, 80
double-bodied signs, 70
Dragon's Head (Rahu), 40, 56
druids, 48
dwadashamshas, 182

EA, 153, 160, 162, 166, 168
Eagle, constellation of, 199
Ear of Corn, constellation of, 213
eclipses, 155, 162
ecliptic, 17, 88–9, 101, 139, 158
Egypt, 164, 174, Chapter 12
Egyptian lucky days, 156
eighteen signs, 165–6
eight 'houses', 38
'elections', 71–2
elements, the four, 41, 119
Elohim, 153
Enkidu, 168–9
Enlil, or Ellil, earth-god, 153, 160
Enoch, Book of, 129
Enuma Anu Enlil series, 152, 174
epact, 162–3
epagomenae, 176, 178, 183, 212
Epic of Creation, 158
epicycles, 142

Epinomis of Plato, 85
equal signs of zodiac, 163–4
equator, 17, 18, 89, 101, 139, 163
equinox, 18, 27, 51, 73, 142, 147, 162,
    181
Esarhaddon, 173–4, 209, 215
Esna, zodiac of, 167, 172
Eudoxus, 74, 78, 215
Euphrates, River, 152, 172
Evangelists, 112, 126
exaltations of the planets, 169, 170–71,
    210–12
Exodus, Book of, 130, 135
Ezekiel, Book of, 126, 130

FABULOUS ANIMAL, 107, cp. 166, 214
'face', 50
Fagan, Mr, 27, 55, 170–71, 182, 187,
    189, 197, 201
faith, 48
Farnesina Palace, 59
ferryman of the sky, 188
fiducial of the zodiac, 179
Firmicus Maternus, 52, 111, 185
First Point of Aries, 19
Fishes, constellation of the Two, 172,
    216
'fixed' signs in astrology, 41, 125–6, 172
flowers of the signs, 85–6
'forgeries', Chinese, 94
Forlì, 49, 50
Fortune of a city, 153
'fortune-telling', 21–2
four calendars at same time, 179
Four Holy Creatures, 112, 126
freemasonry, 120
free will, 45
full moon not important in Egypt, 194

GALATEA, SALA DI, 59
Gates, Book of, 202
Gauricus, 48
Gemini, constellation of, 20, 197
'general prognostication', 63
Genesis, Book of, 123, 130